In Black and White

In
BLACK
and

Race and Sports in America

Kenneth L. Shropshire
Foreword by Kellen Winslow

NEW YORK UNIVERSITY PRESS
New York and London

NEW YORK UNIVERSITY PRESS
New York and London
Copyright © 1996 by New York University
All rights reserved

Library of Congress Cataloging-in-Publication Data

Shropshire, Kenneth L.
In black and white : race and sports in America / Kenneth L.
Shropshire.
p.   cm.
Includes bibliographical references and index.
ISBN 0-8147-8016-4 (cl. : alk. pap.) ✓
1. Discrimination in sports—United States. 2. Racism—United
States. 3. Afro-Americans—Sports. I. Title.
GV706.32.S48
305.8'00973—dc20   95-50200
                          CIP

New York University Press books are printed on acid-free paper,
and their binding materials are chosen for strength and
durability.

Manufactured in the United States of America

10 9 8 7 6 5 4 3 2 1

For Theresa and Sam

The only change is that baseball has turned Paige from a second-class citizen into a second-class immortal.
  —Leroy "Satchel" Paige, following his induction into
         a wing in Baseball's Hall of Fame dedicated
                       to Negro League baseball players

Contents

■ ❏ ■

Foreword

Kellen Winslow

I must admit to you how much I have struggled in writing the foreword for this book. When first asked, I quickly accepted, feeling honored to be selected by a person I respect and admire a great deal. My first attempt was adequate but not what he was looking for. He wanted me to bare my soul, to talk about issues that most people do not wish to think about when it comes to the sacred world of sports. That's when my task became difficult. To do the job requested of me, I had to revisit my experiences and emotions. I had to share with others those things that I and no doubt many others similarly situated had buried and hidden from myself.

The truth of the matter was and is simply this: I am an African-American male who had a special talent to play sports, in my case football. As long as I was on the field of play I was treated and viewed differently than most African-American men in this country. Because of my physical abilities, society accepted and even catered to me. Race was not an issue.

Then reality came calling. After a nine-year career in the National Football League filled with honors and praises, I stepped into the real world and realized, in the words of Muhammad Ali, that I was "just another nigger."

Now that my special talent to catch a football and run over, around, and away from would-be tacklers was gone, the images and stereotypes that applied to African-American men in this country attached themselves to me. Maybe they always applied to me, but I was too deeply entrenched in the artificial environment of collegiate and professional sports to see the light. In other words, as I believe many African-Americans who enjoy some level of success in society do, I had begun to read and believe my own press clippings. I was a collegiate All-American, a first-round draft pick, the 13th player selected in 1979 by the San Diego Chargers. I became a Pro Bowl performer, an All-Pro selection, and was named to the All-Decade team of the 80s and the All-Quarter Century team. I appeared on television and radio, hosted my own golf tournament for local charities, and ran a flag football league for boys and girls as an alternative to tackle football. A prominent citizen of the San Diego community, I was at one time a member of seven different charitable and community boards, an active member in my church, and if I do say so myself, maybe not the most intelligent and articulate athlete ever, but certainly not the least.

Given this background, I believe, again as many other African-American men similarly situated, that my opportunities in the sports industries and society after my playing days were over have not been as lucrative as those of my white counterparts. Many individuals have moved from the playing field to the front office or from the playing field to the broadcast booth. The overwhelming majority of those individuals were not African-Americans. Why is that when a majority of players on the field of play are African-American? I will not bore you with numbers to validate this statement. Simply turn on your television and see for yourself.

When I retired from the San Diego Chargers in 1988, I had one year remaining on a five-year guaranteed contract. I had planned on playing out the final year of my contract and then retiring but was not physically able to due to a knee injury. During the negotiation process over the final year, I raised the possibility of joining the organization in some official capacity. I didn't suggest the coaching staff for several reasons. First, at the time I did not want to coach. Secondly, the Chargers already had an African-American on the coaching staff, my dear friend and former roommate Charlie Joiner. It had been my experience in college and in the pros that there is rarely more than one, perhaps two African-American coaches on a staff.

I had delusions of starting off with some small title—perhaps assistant general manager—that would allow me to learn the business and go to law school at night. After finishing law school, I might take over as general manager spending the majority of my career in professional football with this organization. Why not? I was a star on the field, an asset to the community, and an intelligent, educated, articulate individual. Besides, I had seen others—granted most were not African-American—do the same thing on other teams and in other sports. Yet, when I asked, that opportunity was not made available to me. It was time to go. Unceremoniously cast to the street.

Was race a factor in that decision? Maybe there were other factors to be considered and weighed to some lesser or greater extent, but one would be hard pressed to convince me that race was not a major factor in that decision. Maybe I cut my own throat when asked by a reporter a few weeks before my early retirement whether or not I would like to join the coaching staff when I did retire. I couldn't help but wonder, when asked that question, about the white reporter's limited view of my abilities and desires. Why not ask me if I wanted to join the front office? Maybe because he had never seen such a transition before. His question recalls the white high school counselors who advise black students to go to trade school so they can get a job rather than go to college where they could get an education. Expectations were limited based on the color of my skin.

My response to the reporter's question was frank and surprised even me. I told him that I did not want to coach and besides, even if I did, there was already one African-American on the staff and I did not want Charlie to have to leave so that I could have a job. Then I told him that I would really like to work in the front office, but I felt those chances were nil because when I walked down that hall of power I did not see anyone who looked like me. Reality was setting in. In hindsight, I should not have been surprised when the Chargers were not interested in my joining the front office staff, because by example, they had told me so many times before. I just had not heard them.

In 1993, while doing color-commentary for my alma mater, the position of athletic director opened up. I was, of course, flattered when asked by the search committee if I would be interested in submitting an application and I did so with one understanding. That understanding was that I be considered as a serious candidate and not be used as the black candidate so often needed to fulfill, in this case, state requirements of affirmative action and equal opportunity.

With this understanding in place, I proceeded to rally my support and prepare myself for the interview process. I solicited and received letters of recommendation from members of the athletic, corporate, legal, and political community stating my abilities to do the job despite my lack of actual experience in an athletic department. My initial interview with the selection committee went well. I was placed on a short list of three for final interviews with the Chancellor, the outgoing Athletic Director, the Director of Admissions, and the Intercollegiate Athletics Committee.

My final interviews went fine and the feedback was very positive. I was told that the Chancellor would have the final say and would be settling on a final choice soon.

His decision to name the then-Associate Athletic Director as the new athletic director came to my attention the day before the press conference when I received a call from a member of the press attempting to confirm a rumor he had gotten wind of. That rumor was that the Chancellor was holding a press conference the next day to announce his selection of the Associate Athletic Director and wanted to know if I had a comment. I chose not to comment on a rumor because I had heard nothing from the Chancellor himself. I hoped it was only a rumor.

To my dismay, it was not idle gossip. Early the next morning, twenty minutes before the press conference, I received a call from the Chancellor informing me of his decision.

I admit my disappointment in not getting the position, mostly because I am a competitive person and hate to lose. But, my greatest disappointment was over the timing and manner in which I was informed of the final decision. Up to that point, I had considered myself a serious candidate. Now I began to wonder if I was just that high-profile African-American needed to make everything look proper. In hindsight I should have seen the writing on the wall, but I was blinded by the possibility that the University of Missouri was considering hiring me, an African-American, as their Athletic Director. The tell-tale sign should have been when the school hired a new football coach before hiring a new athletic director. The logical progression would have been to hire an athletic director, who would then be responsible for hiring his or her own football coach. I knew this at the time, but the allure of being the first African-American athletic director in the Big Eight Conference prevented me from acting. I even went against the sound advice of individuals I respected greatly to withdraw, holding out hope that their instincts were wrong. Not so. They were right and I was wrong.

Was race a factor in the final decision? Again, I believe so, but how much of a factor I will never know. I do know however, that everyone involved in the final decision process was a white male over the age of fifty-five with a background a great deal different from my own. Certainly it is possible that the other individual was much more qualified for the position than I. I have no problem accepting that possibility. However, I cannot shake the feeling that with all I brought to the table—a law degree; practical business experience; my status as a former student athlete, a collegiate All-American, and an alumnus; my stellar professional career; leadership skills; a bit of charisma; a command of the English language—that, if I were white, the job would have been mine to turn down.

What my experiences have taught me time and time again is that race is still, and will be for some time to come, a major factor in the decision-making process for off-the-field positions in professional and college sports. In the world of sports there exist two sets of rules: those for the field of play and those for off the field. On the field of play the rules are clearly defined, fair, and unambiguous. What has to be achieved in order to be the victor is set in concrete. It is here, on the field of play, where your race, with a few exceptions, does not matter. Winning is the name of the game.

Off the field, the rules for success become racially abstract. In his book, *In Black and White: Race and Sports in America*, Kenneth Shropshire literally paints in black and white a realistic picture of the racial climate in sports for all to see. The impressions left upon the reader are precise and stark. Race still matters in the decision-making process and change will only occur when the decision-making body, on all levels, becomes more diverse. *In Black and White* is a must read for anyone seeking to understand the obstacles that have impeded the natural progression of African-Americans as head coaches, administrators, agents, and owners.

■ ❑ ■

Preface: Sports, Race, and Scholarship

Sports

It was the first Baseball Network meeting.[1] One by one, the African-American baseball heroes of my youth stepped up to microphones and told each other how they had been treated by the teams that formerly employed them as players. Some went on to talk about what they had wanted but, due to their color, baseball had not allowed them to receive.

Willie Stargell prodded those he knew had been hurt to step up and speak to the group. This was a room filled with true believers in the existence of racism and in the idea that opportunities had been denied to them because of their race. Many heroes cried. Some could not find the words to explain how they had suffered. The meeting was private, but this was validation to me that black men, no matter how powerful, famous, or intelligent, were defenseless against racism.

My motivations for writing this book are many. The main goal is to respond to those who ask, "What can we do about the underrepresentation of African-Americans in the top-level positions in sports management?" The first time I truly recognized the difficulty in responding to this was while serving as an attorney for the Baseball Network. On the heels of Al Campanis's 1987 statement that blacks lacked the "necessities" to manage in baseball, the Network's initial meeting, where Stargell urged the ballplayers to speak, was organized by an ad hoc group of active and retired Major League Baseball players.[2] The ultimate goal of this group was to pull together these athletes and to push those minorities who had the "necessities" into the old boys' network of which they had never been a part.

The first meeting included a stunning array of over two hundred active and former ballplayers. Those who attended that first meeting and subsequent gatherings featured a list of baseball legends, including Frank Robinson, Willie Stargell, Donn Clendennon, Don Baylor, Dusty Baker, Dave Winfield, Bob Watson, and Vada Pinson. Although not all chose to speak, those who did detailed their desires to coach, manage, scout, or work otherwise for the game they loved and to which they had given much of their lives. Often individuals mentioned that they had not received opportunities that their white teammates had.

Over a two-year period, the Baseball Network met with Commissioners Peter Ueberroth and Bart Giamatti and the management of Major League Baseball on several occasions. The meetings also included league consultants and the longtime civil rights leaders Clifford Alexander and Harry Edwards. Together the parties were able to "network" and to cross-reference information regarding management opportunities and minority candidates. It is impossible to measure the continuing impact of this organization. The group was able to convey—quietly—the availability of baseball jobs for many of those who gave their lives to the sport. The group also was therapeutic, enabling many to share—some for the first time—the frustration of seeking employment in baseball.

In 1987, I was in a room with the then commissioner and his advisers, and some Network board members, discussing the minority hiring problem, when the Commissioner asked, open-endedly, "What should we do?" Several suggestions were thrown out and comments were made. One was "Why don't you use your power to act in the 'best interests of baseball'[3] and mandate that each team in the league hire at least one minority at a top-level position by X date?" The response was that African-Americans had been through that before. In the late 1960s, we were told, when there was some success in getting universities to increase their minority hiring, the negative outcome was that the school administrators snatched up anyone in sight. A janitor might be made an assistant coach simply because he was black.

There was not much dissent to this response. This book seeks to respond to the query by the commissioner and to others seeking change in sports.

I have been involved in sports at other levels as well. I earned a scholarship to play football at Stanford University in 1973. I did not play much, but the experience is one of which I am mindful. This was at a time when there were fewer than a half-dozen African-Americans on full scholarship on Stanford's team. Almost all of the African-Americans on the team had been high school quarterbacks, but they were "converted" to other positions at the college level. The quarter-back converts included future Pro Bowl wide receivers Tony Hill of the Dallas Cowboys and James Lofton of the Buffalo Bills. This was a classic problem of a previous era that today has almost ceased completely.

I was an offensive lineman. Often I was the only black player on my end of the practice field with fellow linemen. Further, the black players voluntarily sat at separate tables for meals during training. (This still frequently occurs, at all levels of sport.) During my freshman year, there was not one African-American on the coaching staff. There also were no African-Americans in administrative positions in the athletic department.

These are all memories of an experience of which I am very fond, because of the camaraderie with both African-American and white players. But certainly the influence the experience had on me is differ-ent from that it had on the white offensive guards who lined up next to me.

I have also worked in sports management. At the 1984 Los Angeles Olympic Organizing Committee, I had the second longest tenure for an African-American male. I reached the level of assistant vice presi-dent prior to the completion of the committee's work. The African-American male with the longest tenure was John Carlos, one of the greatest sprinters of all time, of 1968 Mexico City Olympics black-gloved fist-salute fame. He certainly influenced my views on these issues through years of conversation as well.

Race

A letter my father received as he sought to begin his professional career reflects an earlier time and the types of issues I became aware of early on. Although the setting in my father's case was not sports, the issue still was race in America:

December 6th, 1952

Dear Dr. Shropshire:

Thank you for your recent application for an assistant residency in surgery in Peoples Hospital beginning July 1, 1953.

Peoples Hospital has never had a Negro as a member of our house staff, even though we recognize the importance of making facilities available to your race. At present, we are working on a plan to integrate Negroes into our house staff and have discussed this with various community leaders.

We are extremely anxious that this program succeed and in view of the fact that we prefer to make promotions for our resident staff from within the organization, it was agreed by all interested parties that it would be better to start the first Negro at Peoples Hospital as an intern and promote him as merited.

We realize that this does not meet your needs for residency training at the present time, but felt that you might be interested in knowing that more and more hospitals are recognizing their obligations to members of minority groups.

We do appreciate your interest in Peoples Hospital and regret that we cannot offer you the training you desire.

Very truly yours,
Peoples Hospital

There are times when I reflect on how much race relations have improved in this country since 1952. That letter would not be sent today. But as I completed the first draft of the manuscript for this book, my wife jarred me with an ironic dose of reality. She is a physician in the 1990s. While working with a white physician trained in my father's era, she and the white physician had a professional disagreement. The white physician left the operating room muttering the words "crazy nigger." The spirit and racism of the past affect African-Americans who have presumably made it today, regardless of whether they are successful physicians or famous athletes.

Scholarship

With this background in both sports and race, it was difficult to write from the more distant perspective of a scholar about the confluence of these issues. Today, as a professor, I specialize in the business of sports at the Wharton School of the University of Pennsylvania. I have endeavored to use the traditional tools of a scholar, but my background necessarily has found its way into this work as well. Indeed, this book represents the intersection of two areas that have had a tremendous impact on my life. And if one steps back, the reality is that both race and sports significantly affect most Americans.

My goal in writing this book was to focus on evenhanded methods of addressing a continuing problem that likely will not disappear. This is reflected in the majority of the interviews I conducted. I did not ask merely, "What problems exist?" but rather, "What solutions are applicable?" and "How can we make things better?" The interviews were both formal and informal; they were informational and thus served to balance the personal biases I admittedly bring. I spoke with team owners, presidents, vice presidents, general counsels, league officials, college athletic directors and coaches, sports agents, college athletes, professional athletes, former athletes, consultants, and fellow scholars. The interviewees were men and women, African-Americans and whites, old-timers and newcomers. Where people requested, the interviews were off the record. But whatever the level of formality, I attempted to synthesize the views of all with whom I spoke into something more than a critique. I also made the effort to explain why change is important.

I suppose I could duck behind my Wharton professor title and write about the business of sports without openly injecting my background. My belief is that the realities I and those close to me have encountered and the effort I have made to confront my own biases add value to this work. I have been influenced by my experiences both in and out of sports. But I am also a scholar. Years of research have gone into my understanding of the legal, business, and sociological aspects of sports presented here. I hope this work helps push us toward a societal goal of confronting racism directly and removing racism—but not, at this point, race—from employment decisions at all levels.

As I completed this manuscript I telephoned Clifford Alexander, whom I had met in the early days of the Baseball Network. I asked him for any final advice he might have. His sage words were to remember and acknowledge that a lot of progress has been made, but there remains so much to do.

A Note on Content and Terminology

Many specific race and discrimination problems are beyond the scope of this book. For instance, the race problems of Latinos in sports provide much material for deliberation.[4] Hockey aficionados will point to the salary discrepancies that favor U.S. and Anglo-Canadian players relative to French Canadians and Europeans.[5] Jewish athletes also suffer from discrimination, ranging from harassment to being barred from sports organizations.[6] Abroad, the Hawaiian-born sumo wrestler Salevaa Atisanoe, known as Konishiki, has faced racism in Japan as he has attempted to move up in that conservative sport.[7]

Although the discrimination problems relative to all of these groups and to others will, on occasion, be touched upon, the chief focus of this work is African-Americans in or striving for management and other "power positions" in sports. I have decided to make this a bipolar—black and white—racial analysis, with a complete awareness of the debate, in the academy and elsewhere, over a two-sided view of race. The history of sports, however, sets it apart from any other institution in America. Baseball is most illustrative of the special discrimination blacks have faced. The history of the game is filled with blacks passing or attempting to pass as Native Americans or Latinos because those racial groups were allowed to play the game and manage. One of the earliest blacks, frustrated in his attempts to play in the white world of organized sports, said at the time, "If I had not been quite so black, I might have caught on as a Spaniard or something of that kind. . . . My skin is against me."[8] The history of racism for African-Americans in sports is distinct. Even more narrow, the focus in this book is primarily on African-American males.

What constitutes "power positions" is loosely defined, but holders of these posts are generally the people who have responsibility for, as well as benefit financially from, the performance of athletes. Some, such as coaches, general managers, and owners, hold what are referred to generically as "front office positions." Others include athletic directors and sports agents. Racism exists in ancillary areas of sports as well, particularly in broadcasting and print media. This is exemplified by the small number of African-American sports columnists, reporters, and radio and television executives. Illustrative of this, of nearly sixteen hundred daily newspapers in the United States, only seven had full-time African-American sports columnists in 1993.[9]

This book does not attempt to cover every issue relative to African-Americans in every sport. Auto racing, and the difficulty African-American drivers such as Willy T. Ribbs have had in finding sponsors, is certainly one area that deserves attention. The representation and development of African-Americans in other individual sports such as golf, tennis, gymnastics, swimming, and martial arts merit particular attention. In the sport of rowing, for instance, cities are beginning to recognize the effect of the private-club nature of boathouses and regattas, where minorities are usually not participants.[10] Although not directly addressed in the book, much that is written on other sports is applicable to these issues.

Hockey, the fourth major team sport in the United States, is not included either. Hockey is a sport played largely by Canadians and others in cold-weather, nonurban areas. These are regions not highly populated by blacks. Race issues in the National Hockey League are magnified by the historic lack of involvement of African-Americans in the sport, not only as players but as spectators, and certainly on management and ownership levels. Additional reasons for this are obvious—equipment is expensive, and it has never been a very visible sport to African-Americans.[11]

With regard to terminology, *minorities* is probably an inappropriate word to use to describe African-Americans and Latinos in sports. In the National Basketball Association and the National Football League, those groups represent the majority while whites are in the minority. I use the term *minority* to indicate those groups traditionally viewed as the minority in American society at large.

Similarly, although the preferred usage herein is African-American, not all blacks in sports are Americans, particularly in baseball. Issues regarding "black" Latinos are often reflected in the discussions of African-Americans herein. At most of these junctures I use the term *black* instead of African-American.

Acknowledgments

On both a formal and an informal basis, many involved in the business of sports assisted my research for this book. Those currently or formerly in the business who have aided my thinking include, among others, Mark Alarie, Leslie Alexander, Jerome Allen, Mason Ashe, Dusty Baker, Brent Benner, Lucien Blankenship, John Carlos, Donn Clendennon, Marvin Cobb, Mary Davis, Doug Glanville, Harold Henderson, Lal Hennigan, Mannie Jackson, Newton Jackson, Billy "White Shoes" Johnson, Bill Johnston, Ted Leland, Will Miles, Rob Moor, Cheryl Nauman, Peter O'Malley, Kevin Ramsey, Jerry Reinsdorf, C. Lamont Smith, Jimmy Lee Solomon, Bob Steiner, Bill Strickland, Ralph Stringer, David Sussman, Jay Weiner, Bill White, and Kellen Winslow. Thanks also to those who chose to speak to me in confidence.

Those outside the world of sports who assisted in various ways include, Elijah Anderson, Timothy Davis, James T. Gray, G. Richard Shell, and Paul Weiler, who all reviewed various versions of the manuscript. For research and editorial assistance, my thanks go to Cheryl Butler, Jennifer Fox, Bryan Glass, Amanda Gross, Roslyn Levine, Rafael Rodriguez, Scott Rosner, Melissa Shingles, Sarbjit Singh, and Mekita Toliver.

Thanks for the early clerical and administrative assistance of Rae Goodman and the longer-term assistance of Lisa Kmetz.

Thanks to my agent Denise Stinson for her extraordinary efforts and support. Thanks also to Niko Pfund for quickly and confidently bringing the support of NYU Press behind what he perceived to be an important project.

For discussions on sports and race issues over the years I give thanks to many. I relied on all for assistance ranging from lifelong conversations to some long forgotten remote reflections. In addition to those already named, an incomplete list includes, Eric Ajaye, Clifford Alexander, Michael Alston, Ray Anderson, Darius Anthony, Phil Asbury, Lacey Atkinson, Kenneth Bacon, Keith Barnes, Toni Barnes, Herman Beavers, Freda Berman, Paul Birden, Marcia Boddie, Gary Bostwick, Lauren Boulware, Jacqui Bowles, Todd Boyd, James Brockenbury, Aubrey Brown, Carl Brown, Frank Brown, Reggie Brown, Jerry Bryant, Robert Bryant, Bill Burke, Keith Calhoun-Senghor, Madelyn Cobb, Tim Cobb, Wayne Collette, Ennis Cooper, Lois Corrin, Ron Crawford, Anita DeFrantz, Carl Douglas, George Duncan, Susan Dunnings, Gerald Durant, Stephan Earl, Harry Edwards, Joan Evans, Donald Eversley, John Finley, Velett Finley, Carl Fletcher, Darryl Fraser, Darrell Gay, Bart Giamatti, Bill Gould, Allen Green, James Hamilton, James Hardin, John Haydel, Tony Hill, Michael Hollingsworth, Marvin Holmes, Tim Jefferson, Mae Jemison, Bob Johnson, Lynn Johnson, Sherrie Johnson, Josetta Jones, Michael King, Stanley King, Joe Knight, Tetteh Kofi, Melanie Lawson, Felix Leatherwood, Tony Lecour, Peter Lewis, Charles Lowery, George Madison, George McKenna, Mora McLean, Ralph Moore, Warren Morrison, Bill Moultrie, John Murphy, Tommy Myers, Brenda Neal, Rich Nichols, Lee Nunnery, Charles Ogletree, Dion Peronneau, Allen Perry, Loretta Polk, Ricky Roberts, Harvey Schiller, Bryant Seaman, Warner Sessions, Teddy Shaw, James Sherrard, E. R. Shipp, Robert Smith, Donald Stevenson, Ewart Thomas, Jerry Thomas, Winston Thompson, Henry Tillman, Douglas Toomer, Reggie Turner, Peter Ueberroth, Peter Vaughan, Mel Vines, Darrell Walker, Rickey Walker, Fred Washington, Gary Watson, Rena Wheaton, Arlene Williams, Terrie Williams, Gerald Wilson, Solomon Young, and Aaron Youngblood.

The *Hastings Law Journal*, the *University of Colorado Law Review*, and the *Marquette Sports Law Journal* were kind enough to publish articles that ultimately evolved into portions of this book in volume 47 of the *Hastings Law Journal*, "Merit, Ol' Boy Networks, and the Black-Bottomed Pyramid" (1996); volume 67 of the University of Colorado Law Review, "Diversity, Racism and Professional Sports Franchise Ownership: Change Must Come from Within" (1996); and volume 6 of the *Marquette Sports Law Journal*, "Sports Agents and Race Conscious-ness" (1996). I express my appreciation to all of them.

I also want to give special acknowledgment to my wife, Diane, the true athlete in the family. I thank you for taking the time to read the manuscript, to give me time, and for allowing me to share some of your life in this work. Also to my older brother, Claudius, thanks for leading the way for me through life and for insights as coach and athlete on the issues herein. Finally, to my mother, Jane, thanks for everything including sending clippings that always find their way into my work. Especially thanks for the letter sent to my father from Peoples Hospital set forth in the Preface. That letter allowed him to have a tangible presence in this book as well.

Introduction: The Realities of Racism and Discrimination in America

> We have no solutions to the problems faced by minorities in attaining equitable employment status—other than to simplistically expect that persons who hire be race and gender blind.
> —Bob Steiner, director of public relations, Los Angeles Lakers

> Must I strive toward colorlessness? But seriously and without snobbery, think of what the world would lose if that should happen. America is woven of many strands; I would recognize them and let it remain so.
> —Ralph Ellison, *Invisible Man*

Racism in the United States

C. L. R. James has written eloquently on the role of race in sports. Players of all races and classes could come together and participate in a game, such as his beloved cricket, without regard to race or class. Race was rarely an issue among the players once on the field. But in James's West Indian cricket world, racism kept black players from playing for some clubs, from being captains of the ones for which they could play, and from involvement in the overall management of the sport. Race problems in America today similarly impact on the business of sports. Thus the race problems in America at large cannot be ignored in an analysis of the business of sports. It is the race issues in society that are the framework for this book.

The prospects for solving the race problems of the United States, particularly discrimination against African-Americans, are dismal. The 1992 Rodney King case in Los Angeles, wherein a suburban jury acquitted white L.A. police officers of using excessive force on King, an African-American, despite a videotape of the beating, cast the fundamental racism of the American criminal justice system in stark, violent relief yet again—a searing reminder to those who believed such inequities were behind us. Hidden cameras also reveal that discrimination still exists in housing, lending, and even retail.[1] The videotape makes those otherwise unaware cognizant of the reality of discrimination in the United States.

The initial Rodney King case verdict is one of the most prominent contemporary exhibits of American racism. That event, however, was overshadowed by the aftermath of the verdict in the murder trial of O. J. Simpson in Los Angeles in 1995. The former professional football player, Heisman Trophy winner, and Hall of Fame member was found not guilty of killing his ex-wife and her friend. Simpson is black. Both victims were white. During the trial police misconduct and racism were found. These corruption problems surfaced alongside strong circumstantial and scientific evidence against Simpson. Visions of African-American groups cheering the verdict and whites looking stunned are ingrained in all who observed the post-trial event. The reactions clearly illustrated the distance between blacks and whites. There was no videotape of the murders. But the trial was, in effect, a yearlong videotape for all to watch. The reactions to the long-running tape were apparently impacted by the background of the viewer. No sector of society is free of the malady. In reported legal opinions from the not-too-distant past, black patrons were segregated on the second floor of a motel,[2] a black businessperson agreeing to rent an office was later told by the landlord that it was unavailable;[3] and an accusation of theft was made against a black traveler who was simply seeking a refund on his bus ticket.[4] Examples of this type of racism are seemingly endless.

In Boston in 1990, police readily believed Charles Stuart when he said a black man had murdered his pregnant wife. Stuart, later found to be the perpetrator, initially was not even a suspect.[5] In a 1994 action brought by the United States Department of Justice against the Chevy Chase Federal Savings Bank, an $11 million settlement was reached because the suburban Washington D.C. bank had no branches in predominantly black neighborhoods.[6] In Milwaukee the police allegedly refused to take seriously the complaints of the black and Asian neighbors of mass murderer Jeffrey Dahmer.[7]

The incidents are not simply regional. Nationally, the image of Willie Horton pushed white voters away from presidential candidate Michael Dukakis to George Bush in 1988. In 1994, Denny's Restaurants paid 54 million dollars to settle race bias suits filed by thousands of black customers, with complaints ranging from being refused service to being asked to pay in advance.[8] Also in 1994, a study commissioned by the United States Office of Personnel Management found that black federal workers are fired at approximately twice the rate of whites.[9] The federal government is the largest employer of African-Americans in the country. Even allowing for over twenty factors, including differences in age, education, and job performance, the study concluded, with great clarity, that this discriminatory practice existed.[10] Blacks made up 17 percent of the federal workforce but 39 percent of those fired during 1992, the year studied.[11] And sadly, around the country the numbers of hate and bias crimes and segregated schools have increased as well.[12]

The laws have changed to outlaw discrimination, yet discriminatory practices continue. Racism is ingrained in our culture and our national psyche. One commentator has appropriately stated the view of many that "racial progress in the United States is characterized by an evolutionary process that has yet to work through its final stage."[13]

The Use of Statistics to Prove Racism

Paralleling society, attempts to end all but the most rigid and institutionalized racial inequalities in the business of sports have been generally unsuccessful. According to one 1995 study, African-Americans constituted the following percentages in the top-level positions in professional sports: 0 percent of the majority owners and commission-

Table 1: Racial Composition of Players

		NBA		NFL		MLB
White	1990–91	28%	1990	39%	1991	68%
Black		72%		61%		18%
Latino		0%		0%		14%
White	1991–92	25%	1991	36%	1992	68%
Black		75%		62%		17%
Latino		0%		2%		14%
White	1992–93	23%	1992	30%	1993	67%
Black		77%		68%		16%
Latino		0%		<1%*		16%
Other*		0%		1%		<1%*
White	1994–95	18%	1994	31%	1995	62%
Black		82%		68%		19%
Latino		0%		0%		19%

*There were twenty-two Pacific Islanders playing in the NFL during the 1992 season.
s o u r c e: Richard E. Lapchick, ed., *1995 Racial Report Card* (Boston: Northeastern University, Center for the Study of Sport in Society, 1995).

ers; 7 percent of the team presidents in the National Basketball Association (NBA) and 0 percent in the National Football League (NFL) and Major League Baseball (MLB); 12 percent of the team vice presidents in the NBA, 4 percent in the NFL and 5 percent in MLB; and 19 percent of the NBA head coaches, 7 percent in the NFL and 11 percent in MLB.[14] As Table 1 illustrates, on the court or field it is a different story: in 1995, while comprising 12 percent of the population of the United States, African-Americans made up eight out of every ten players in the NBA, 68 percent of the players in the NFL, and 19 percent of the players in MLB.[15] Although some argue that the on-the-field percentages are an indicator of equality, equal achievement has not occurred in terms of success at the highest levels.[16]

Labor and employment law scholars caution that in using statistics to show an underrepresentation of African-Americans in a certain occupation, the selection of the correct denominator is a key element. Is discrimination implied when the group being considered is not employed at a percentage level commensurate with their representation in the *general* population? No. The correct legal focus is on how many from a pool of the *qualified* population are employed at the position in question. The qualified pool is the relevant "population" number.[17] This point regarding the accuracy of the denominator cannot be overemphasized. The large number of African-American athletes is certainly a telling factor. It is, however, difficult—even impossible—to know who in these large numbers has the requisite skills to assume front-office positions. What constitutes that denominator in reality is certainly somewhere lower than the total number of athletes who play or have played the game but higher than the current number of African-Americans holding positions of power in the front office. It is similarly important to note, at the outset, that players are a significant pool for sports leadership positions but not the only pool. That denominator also includes African-American attorneys, accountants, physicians, and others. These non-athlete African-Americans are often overlooked when conversations regarding the underrepresentation of African-Americans in sports take place.

The use of statistics to prove or even to allege racism quite frankly makes many people nervous. As an example of the nerves their use strikes, I received several negative responses to an editorial I wrote on the day the first African-American head coach in the NFL was fired and the third was hired.[18] I simply pointed out (at least, I thought) that the percentages of African-Americans in head coaching positions were not reflective of the number of African-Americans with experience playing the game and presumably qualified to coach. I offered no solutions, not quotas or affirmative action. One letter in response to my views read:

Lani [Guinier, presumably] will be so proud. A quota king has finally emerged. What a blessing that the [Philadelphia Inquirer] is available to print this trash.

I wonder if you ever stop to think that 13 percent of the population holding 65 percent of the playing jobs is also pretty one-sided. The NBA also manages to go along with this trend in that 80 percent of the NBA players are African Americans. How disappointing for thousands of young white men who leave college every year and are unable to find jobs in the NBA. If this trend continues can you imagine the despair of these youngsters as they are forced to (gasp) find a job and go to work. Maybe they will be forced into lives of crime, welfare or even worse, graduate school. How about this for a quota, 50 percent of the opinion in the *[Philadelphia Inquirer]* must be on the conservative side. Run that by Lani and let me know what she thinks. In the meantime try Prozac. Cheers.[19]

I was a bit taken aback by this response, and by others like it. Quotas are not generally the answer, but ensuring that racism does not keep qualified people from opportunities should be the goal. If anyone is stopping qualified white athletes from taking Shaquille O'Neal's job, changes should be made at that level as well.

Years of debate in race discrimination cases have taught us that statistics alone, as staggering as they may be, are not enough legally to prove the existence of discrimination. Apart from determining the correct denominator (or qualified pool), representation below the level statistics might project is not proof of the existence of racism or discrimination. Supreme Court Justice Sandra Day O'Connor warns, regarding the use of statistics as evidence of discrimination, "It is completely unrealistic to assume that individuals of each race will gravitate with mathematical exactitude to each employer or union absent unlawful discrimination."[20] Statistics do not tell the whole story and generally do not legally make the entire case—but the vast disparities indicated by these percentages in sports suggest that, regardless of what precautions one takes in the use of statistics, racism and discrimination at an undefined level permeate American sports.[21] When the numbers of minorities are low in a particular occupation, the assumption of discrimination is reasonable but not self-validating. As one commentator has phrased it, "There are two possibilities. Either the low numbers are due to discrimination or they are not."[22]

In this regard, my analysis of the sports industry embraces three key themes from the critical race theory literature.[23] The first, incorporated throughout, is the view of the impact of color-blindness and the failure of such policies in addressing existing race problems. Racial inequalities cannot be resolved unless race is, in fact, taken into account. Second, an important element amplifying this need to eliminate color-blind theories for resolving discrimination is the existence of unconscious racism.[24] To move forward in solving our problems, we must recognize that unconscious racism exists in all of us. Finally, this book also embraces Derrick Bell's concept of the permanence of racism in America.[25] An understanding of these three concepts will provide greater clarity to the reforms discussed herein.

Race Consciousness and Permanence

Color-blindness

One clearly stated goal of American civil rights law is color-blindness. Today, Dr. Martin Luther King, Jr., is held up as the leading visionary of America as a color-blind society. His much-quoted desire was for the content of our character, not the color of our skin, to be the yardstick by which we are measured. Legal scholars point to Justice John Marshall Harlan's dissent in *Plessy v. Ferguson* as the source of the normative principle of color-blindness.[26] It is this ambition toward an absence of race consciousness—toward "unconsciousness"—that has hindered support by both blacks and whites for appropriate, color-conscious interim strategies to combat racism.

The sports business provides an example of why we are not yet ready for color-blind policies. Few, if any, of the people in power in sports in the United States are color-blind, and few make employment and other management decisions without regard to race. The color-conscious decisions, however, primarily advance the careers of whites, not blacks. Tony Dungy for several years has been a leading African-American contender for a head coaching position in the National Football League. Recently, when unsuccessful in obtaining the top job, he acknowledged that he did not have the appearance of the older, middle-aged, white male that the owners—and all others, for that matter—were accustomed to seeing as a professional football head coach. Asked to describe a head coach, Dungy said, "Cerebral guy, Bill Walsh; Vince Lombardi, disciplinarian. Is it Bill Parcells? Is it Joe Gibbs? Is it Paul Brown, George Halas, Weeb Ewbank? Go back for eons, and no matter what characteristics you think of the guy, you think of a somewhat older, white man. Those are two classic characteristics."[27]

The word color-blind is a rhetorical strategy often used to deflect an allegation of racism or discrimination against a particular individual. The proclamation of one's color-blindness is often inappropriately viewed as a way to prove one's actions are race-free. If all people in sports were color-blind, then the statistical underrepresentation of African-Americans in management positions could be explained away by justifications other than racism. The focus of this and other discussions could be on matters such as how to prepare African-Americans for these positions or how to interest African-Americans in these jobs. But African-Americans are prepared and interested. Color-blindness is not the reality. One would be hard pressed to find this truly color-blind person in society at large and in sports—especially in the front office. Color-blindness is not only an unrealistic societal goal—particularly in the short term—but one that fails to place value on the benefits of diversity. As T. Alexander Aleinikoff wrote:

Colorblindness puts the burden on blacks to change; to receive "equal" treatment, they must be seen by whites as "white." Hence, the "compliment" that some whites pay to blacks: "I don't think of you as black." Colorblindness is, in essence, not the absence of color, but rather monochromatism: whites can be colorblind when there is only one race—when blacks become white.[28]

In sports, as in other businesses, an owner may assume that he or she is conducting the business in a color-blind fashion and that such conduct is good. But this innocent conduct of business may be accompanied by an ingrained view that the person to hire should look like the previous white males that were hired. In 1987, during a period of particular focus on racial discrimination in baseball, Edward Bennett Williams, the late owner of the Baltimore Orioles, told the Associated Press, "I will take second place to no one in the United States on my sensitivity to racial justice. I am embarrassed—really embarrassed— that our front office has such a horrible ratio of minority workers. I can guarantee you it did not come about because of any form of bigotry. I think . . . we have just gone along with a colorblind hiring policy."[29] Chicago Bulls and White Sox owner Jerry Reinsdorf was similarly astounded when he reviewed the hiring of minorities for front-office and high-level positions by his teams in the late 1980s.[30]

But is not this form of color-blindness a form of racism as well? Maybe it is not conscious racism, but it supports unconscious racial beliefs.[31] Acknowledging the race of those you hire *is* important. The incorporation of color consciousness into our antidiscrimination laws is a subject of ongoing debate. Owen Fiss long ago proposed that antidiscrimination laws benefit African-Americans only in a limited way by prohibiting discrimination based on race.[32] To benefit African-Americans, the law has to be color-conscious and allow employers to be color-conscious. Fiss concluded in 1971 that "a law that does no more than prohibit discrimination on the basis of race will leave that desire [to improve the economic position of blacks], in large part, unfulfilled."[33]

What blinds many to the pervasive racism of American sports is the strong presence of African-Americans on the field of play. Even Andrew Hacker, in his much-acclaimed work on race *Two Nations*, praises sports as an industry of racial success.[34] The sports success story, however, has not yet progressed much beyond athletes playing the game.

Unconscious Racism

There is a need for recognition that racism exists in all of us. Charles Lawrence points to the deep psychological grounding of racism in all Americans as a reason for its permanence, if solely at an unconscious level:

Americans share a common historical and cultural heritage in which racism has played and still plays a dominant role. Because of this shared experience, we also inevitably share many ideas, attitudes, and beliefs that attach significance to an individual's race and induce negative feelings and opinions about nonwhites. To the extent that this cultural belief system has influenced all of us, we are all racists. At the same time, most of us are unaware of our racism. We do not recognize the ways in which our cultural experience has influenced our beliefs about race or the occasions on which those beliefs affect our actions. In other words, a large part of the behavior that produces racial discrimination is influenced by unconscious racial motivation.[35]

Racism is a historic reality in this country and in sports in particular; plans for change must be made with this reality in mind. What may work in sports in addressing racism may not work in other industries. Some of the changes I suggest in this book may be viewed as already failing in other sectors of society, or they may have been rejected for other reasons.

Racism's Permanence

It might seem unnecessary to define racism. But with conservative declarations that racism in the United States no longer exists, that merit alone is the determining factor in employment decisions, it is useful to identify what is meant by this commonly invoked "ism." From the standpoint of the individual, racism is a hatred of a specific group of people based on difference in skin color.[36] The level or degree of hatred held or expressed may vary and may be exhibited in a number of ways.

Often expressions of racism are subtle. In the business context, choosing not to hire or promote an individual based on his or her race is an example. Not admitting an individual into a business partnership because of the individual's race is another. Not using the services of a particular professional because of race is a further depiction. No announcement need be made; taking the action is enough. A racist may also use the "I don't feel this way but others may" excuse: "I don't think we should hire 'B' (an African-American) as our new athletic director because the alumni will not receive her well and that will negatively impact on fund raising," or, in another circumstance, "I don't know how well 'C' will be able to communicate with white players and management."[37] These forms of racism may exist in varying degrees as well. These versions of racism, however, may be denied publicly. It may be only the business decision maker who knows that his or her action was affected by the race of the individual or individuals in question.

The Reverend Arthur Williams, an Episcopalian bishop and a coauthor of a 1994 Episcopalian pastoral letter condemning racism, defines racism as prejudice coupled with power. He goes on to assert that "if you're going to attack it [racism] or eradicate it, you really have to look at the dominant race. In this country, of course, that would be white persons."[38] In sports some degree of power rests with African-Americans, causing an interesting variation to the conclusion by Wil-

liams and a need to look at both blacks and whites. The power definition of racism raises some unique issues in the sports context, particularly with regard to the discussion of sports agents in chapter 6.

The key point here is that the present cannot help but be tainted by
the racism of the past. Hence attempts at reform must take into
account its presence from the historical foundations of the sports
business. According to Derrick Bell, racism is a permanent part of
every American institution, and that element cannot be changed:

Black people will never gain full equality in this country. Even those herculean
efforts we hail as successful will produce no more than temporary "peaks of
progress," short-lived victories that slide into irrelevance as racial patterns
adapt in ways that maintain white dominance. This is a hard-to-accept fact
that all history verifies.[39]

Bell is not alone in his predictions of permanence. Thomas Jefferson
also once said, "'Deep rooted prejudices entertained by the whites'
. . . and 'ten thousand recollections, by the blacks, of the injuries they
have sustained,' combine to make equal, peaceful coexistence between
blacks and whites impossible."[40] Historian John Hope Franklin's 1993
reflection on William E. B. Du Bois's observation that the problem of
the twentieth century is the problem of the color line is particularly
relevant:

Without any pretense of originality or prescience, with less than a decade left
in this century, I venture to state categorically that the problem of the twenty-
first century will be the problem of the color line. This conclusion arises from
the fact that by any standard of measurement or evaluation the problem has
not been solved in the twentieth century, and this becomes a part of the legacy
and burden of the next century. Consequently, it follows the pattern that the
nineteenth century bequeathed to the twentieth century and that the eigh-
teenth century handed to its successor.[41]

American Race Unconsciousness

Nicknames as Racism Without Ill Intent

Many "nonblack" issues provide background on the racial sanctu-
ary status sports has attained. Each day, racism creeps into sports

pages in the names of professional and collegiate teams. None is quite so glaring as the Washington Redskins football team. The team name has remained even while other institutions have appropriately changed the use of what the National Congress of American Indians, the oldest and largest American Indian organization representing about 150 tribes, calls a racial slur. According to the Rainbow Coalition for Fairness in Athletics:

The term "redskins" is from an era when there was a bounty on Indian people and they were skinned and scalped. Eighty cents for a man's skin, 60 cents for a woman's skin and 20 cents for a child's skin. . . . It is the most derogatory term that exists for Native Americans in the English language.[42]

The casual use of headdresses, face paint, chants, and dancing, promoted among and practiced by the football team's fans, is considered sacrilege to the religion of Native Americans.[43] The "tomahawk chop" hand gesture adopted by Atlanta Braves baseball fans is offensive in this regard as well. The 1995 World Series between the Atlanta Braves and Cleveland Indians, with their own offensive logo, was a prime-time display of American race unconsciousness. If one is conscious of the offensiveness of the chop gesture and the logos, sitting in the stands surrounded by fans who have such ill regard for history is extraordinarily uncomfortable. But obviously, many Braves fans see nothing offensive in their actions. Braves fans are not alone in being blind to the racism in their actions.

At Stanford University, I once encountered a white alum who had attended the school when the Stanford Cardinal was the Stanford Indians. His attitude reflected the views of many: "The Indian was a strong, proud symbol. The sharply chiseled nose. The war dance he performed, what was wrong with that?" Then came the inevitable rhetorical query: "Should we get rid of the Fighting Irish, too?" This encounter stands out in my mind because, drunk or not, the alum's assumption was that *everyone* missed the "Indian" mascot. He had no insight into the sensibilities of those of whom the mascot made a mockery.

The lack of sensitivity in the team name area is difficult to explain. But there exists an unfortunate African-American insensitivity in this regard as well. I remained ignorant of the offense until I was years removed from the blinding school spirit. My high school team's nickname was the "Dons," a reference to the Spanish land barons of California. Our mascot was a stereotypical "sleepy Mexican," wearing a huge sombrero and poncho with head down and eyes shut. The high school was nearly 100 percent African-American and none of us ever complained about wearing the uniforms emblazoned with the mascot, or about the African-American elected by the student body to parade around as the mascot with the huge sombrero. It was all in good fun, and it was only a mascot. Across town, in Compton, California, a nearly all African-American high school used the nickname "Tarbabes." The school was seeking to connect itself with the Compton College Tartars, and the "Tarbabe" name must at one time have been thought cute.

White Race Consciousness

I do believe that blatant racism often is not the reason for mascot and team name and other race problems in sports. A white colleague brought this in full focus for me. While discussing the lack of African-American faculty and administrators at the university where we teach, he confided, "I could walk around here for years, seeing only other white males, and not even notice the problem unless you raise it. I mean no ill will, but a 'color survey' is not on the average white guy's list of self-initiated concerns."[44]

My colleagues' lack of focus on racial issues is not unique. As one author explained:

White people externalize race. For most whites, most of the time, to think or speak about race is to think or speak about people of color, or perhaps, at times, to reflect on oneself (or other whites) in relation to people of color. But we tend not to think of ourselves or our racial cohort as racially distinctive. Whites' "consciousness" of whiteness is predominantly unconsciousness of whiteness. We perceive and interact with other whites as individuals who have no significant racial characteristics. In the same vein, the white person is unlikely to see or describe himself in racial terms, perhaps in part because his white peers do not regard him as racially distinctive. Whiteness is a transparent quality when whites interact with whites in the absence of people of color. Whiteness attains opacity, becomes apparent to the white mind, only in relation to, and contrast with, the "color" of nonwhites.[45]

This kind of ignorance of the seriousness of discrimination can be illustrated through countless anecdotes in relation to sports. In 1994 a major sports-race controversy hit the city of Philadelphia prior to the annual Dad Vail Regatta, held in the city-owned Fairmount Park on the Schuylkill River. The city parks commissioner publicly expressed his concern about the absence of minority involvement in the event. He suggested that if things did not change, perhaps the city should no longer support the competition. From the mayor on down, most of white Philadelphia was outraged by the African-American official's comments. Consider one published letter to the editor of the *Philadelphia Inquirer:*

I agree with Park Commissioner Richard Gibson that the Dad Vail Regatta, Boathouse Row and boating in general should all be abolished in this city because African Americans are underrepresented in this sport. I also believe hockey should be axed for the same reason. Goodbye, Flyers.

Basketball, too, should be assigned its painful place in history as an example of reverse discrimination due to the fact that the majority of this country, Euro-Americans, are sorely underrepresented. Goodbye, 76ers.

Baseball? Isn't what was done to the Chinese during the building of this nation's railroad system bad enough? Do we really need a sport in which there are virtually no Asian Americans represented? Goodbye, Phillies. Football. Oh boy, how many football players have names like Juan Carlos Rivera? I can't think of one. Goodbye, Eagles.

Enough is enough of this nonsense. What I really believe is that we need a new park commissioner. Goodbye, Gibson.[46]

Gibson did resign some days later.

The Realities of Racism in Sports Hiring

In my role as a professor, I have for the past several years seen different versions of a particular scenario all too frequently. The story goes something like this: an African-American student and a white student—similarly qualified, the only obvious difference being their race—visit my office and tell me about their interest in a career in the sports business. They approach their search with seriousness and a keen awareness that sports is the twentieth largest industry in the country, grossing nearly one hundred billion dollars per year.[47] When they ask about getting "into the business," I inform them (as so many counselors advised me), "It's tough." I then offer some suggestions: write the teams, attend the league meetings, and so forth. Both students heed my advice.

The two students return with contrasting results. The white student—after some back and forth over the phone and through the mail—ends up "selecting" a job as the assistant general manager of a minor league baseball team in the Midwest. The African-American student reports to me that he felt lost at the annual meetings, that he could barely initiate any conversations, and that he came away with nothing: no leads, no hopes for an interview, and certainly no job. (On a related note, Tracy Lewis, an African-American woman and president of the minor league Savannah Cardinals from 1985 to 1987, recalls, "I walked into the winter baseball meetings last year and it was overwhelming, absolutely amazing. I thought, 'There's no black people in this lobby. There's no women in this lobby.' ")[48]

This type of incident is not an isolated one in the business world of sports. The selection of the right person for a position in sports, both on and off the field of play, is extraordinarily subjective. It is thus impossible to say with certainty that race was the determining factor. But race is almost always a pivotal factor. In 1988 I was on a public television broadcast, *Another View,* along with two other African-American panelists.[49] We were asked if the lack of minorities in management positions in sports was attributable to racism. None of us gave an outright yes. "Yes" would have certainly been the simplest answer, but it is one subject to criticism if given without support. It was not that we did not believe that racism was the main reason the problem existed. We were all lawyers and, without a "smoking gun" reference to a specific event or empirical evidence, we did not want to state an absolute. My answer today would be different. Quite simply, race is a determining factor for the absence of blacks in the positions of power in sports.

In 1987, then NFL commissioner Pete Rozelle, trying to explain why, at that time, there was not an African-American head coach in his sport, stated, "Choosing a head coach is like choosing a wife. It's a very personal thing."[50] Social relationships play an important role in sports, often outweighing objective qualifications. Probably more than in any other business, people in sports tend to hire their friends. Examples include Dallas Cowboys owner Jerry Jones's hiring his Arkansas teammate Jimmy Johnson to coach and even Los Angeles Raiders owner Al Davis's hiring his longtime player and assistant coach, Art Shell. In any industry characterized by long work hours, it may be human nature to want to spend those long hours with friends. And in contemporary America people tend to have friends of the same race. Throughout the book, this phenomenon will be referred to as the "network" or the "old boys' network" explanation for the racial inequality in sports management.

A Microcosm of Society

The business of sports provides a useful paradigm for studying many of the problems of society at large. As the late commissioner of baseball and former Yale University president A. Bartlett Giamatti wrote, "It has long been my conviction that we can learn far more about the conditions, and values, of a society by contemplating how it chooses to play, to use its free time, to take its leisure, than by examining how it goes about its work."[51]

Even racial problems in sports have been, and continue to be, brushed aside as "nothing unique," the explanation being that sports are just a microcosm of society. C. L. R. James, in fact, saw cricket as one of the purest reflections of Trinidadian society and its problems. He wrote of the close connection between self-government of the country and self-governing in cricket, particularly with respect to black team captains. Until the 1960s no black had served as captain of the West Indies team that played in international competition. In James's words, "The intimate connection between cricket and West Indian social and political life was established so that all except the wilfully perverse could see."[52]

Something special about sports in America exists that makes its race problems different from those faced at a major corporation, a university, or the post office. This microcosm of society not only reflects but sometimes also seems to influence the racial direction of the country. As harsh as some criticisms of the industry may seem, Northeastern University's Center for the Study of Sport in Society in Boston, which issues annual grades on the racial performance of the various sports leagues, consistently awards the leagues higher grades than society at large.[53] Further, shortly after Jackie Robinson integrated Major League Baseball, the United States Supreme Court integrated public schools in the landmark 1954 decision *Brown v. Board of Education*.[54] But the world of sports is not society at large and begs for unique solutions. The various chapters of this book explore a range of race problems in sports. Combined, they point to the existing sports power structure as the cause for continued racial injustice as well as a potential remedy to the problem. But others must bear the burden of reform as well.

Chapter 1 provides a brief historical overview of the major race issues in sports. The review is meant not to be an exhaustive history but to place the problem in historical context and perspective, to establish for the reader the source of prejudice that exists in sports culture today. The chapter will establish that race is a permanent fixture in the thinking of sports leadership and that racism has been a part of the culture of American sports from the beginning.

Chapter 2 addresses the lack of African-American ownership in modern day professional sports leagues, establishing what obstacles exist to legal action intended to bring greater diversity to the ownership ranks. The chapter also prescribes methods by which representative African-American ownership might arrive and what a difference such ownership might make. The key is leadership on the part of management and star athletes.

Chapter 3 ponders the current state of antidiscrimination law and its effects on any changes in the management infrastructure of professional sports. The chapter distinguishes the sports industry from others in asserting that voluntary affirmative action programs are clearly legal in sports.

Chapter 4 expounds on the shortage of African-Americans in management and on-the-field coaching positions in the major sports. This chapter proposes aggressive affirmative action methods to increase the numbers of African-Americans in those positions. The chapter also addresses the trepidation most Americans feel about affirmative action programs and clearly defines the type of affirmative action needed in the sports context and perhaps in other sectors of society.

Chapter 5 details the particular racial issues that exist in college sports, including the rules that bar access to athletic scholarships based on standardized test scores. College athletes represent the largest pool of players for the professional ranks and subsequently for the power positions in sports. The chapter critiques the role of these eligibility rules and proposes other rules to improve the plight of the African-American student-athlete. The chapter also calls for National Collegiate Athletic Association (NCAA) and individual, school-based affirmative action programs to remedy the absence of African-American head coaches and athletic directors at the college level and discusses mechanisms for increasing those numbers.

Chapter 6 explains the role of sports agents and the absence of a prominent role for African-Americans in this lucrative and influential field. The chapter presents proposals for a more prominent role for African-American agents as well as for increasing the role of African-American agents at predominantly white firms.

Chapter 7 explores the direction in which we as a society must move to accelerate the progress that has occurred thus far in combating the problems of racism and discrimination in sports. The chapter also discusses the historic role played by the African-American and other athletes in social change, a role that we must revitalize.

While focusing on racial discrimination in the sectors of the business where control is maintained and decisions are made, it is essential to keep in mind the words of Hugh P. Price, the president of the National Urban League: "We must not let ourselves, and especially our children, fall into the paranoid trap of thinking that racism accounts for all that plagues us."[55] In this regard, reform strategies must recognize the existence and omnipresence of racism but also that racism is not the sole culprit. In all sectors of society, but particularly in sports, existing social networks, regardless of race, play an important role, especially in who receives employment opportunities.

One final introductory point: In other sectors of society strong arguments are often made regarding the scarcity of qualified African-Americans for various positions. Whether the qualification is an advanced degree, years of experience, or some other defined measure of merit, these elements may well be lacking in the African-American community for particular positions. For African-Americans in the business of sports, however, lack of merit is not an issue. Although this is the case, and has been for some time, the percentages in top-level management positions in sports have remained relatively unchanged. This is certainly not to say the percentages on the playing field should match the percentages in the front office. But the gap between the percentage of African-Americans that play the game and the percentage that serve in the front office should not be as wide as it is. This raises the key issue: If there is no merit issue in sports yet inequality still exists at top-level positions, what will happen if merit issues are ever eliminated in other business sectors? Answers to the sports problem could well assist the rest of America in the future.

When Jackie Robinson integrated Major League Baseball in 1947, that event was hailed as the biggest civil rights success since the Civil War. The year 1997 will mark the fiftieth anniversary of Robinson's debut. There has been much progress on the field but not in the front office. Although this work initially focuses on describing the existence of race problems, its true value lies in its prescriptions for reform in the law, the sports industry, and society.

ONE

The Roots of Racism and Discrimination in Sports

Everybody wants to get to heaven but nobody is willing to die.
— A recurring sermon from the African-American pulpit

Right now, in our country, not just in athletics, there's a great deal of talent we let go unnoticed. Coming from an ethnic background, you see it. You see talent not being derived, not being noticed, not showing what it can really do. There are a lot of people who could be doing the job I'm doing, given the opportunity.
— Tyrone Willingham, Stanford University head football coach

The Lawn Jockey Mentality

Lawn Jockeys

Small statues of black jockeys, usually dressed in bright red coats and holding a ring or lantern have for decades been a status symbol on the lawns of suburban homes in the United States. The approximately three-foot-high lawn ornaments often feature oversized lips and flared nostrils. The origin of the lawn jockey is uncertain, although there are numerous stories explaining its history. The director of education for the Smithsonian's Anacostia Museum, Zora Martin-Felton, relates a version of its origin in which the statuettes grew out of a story told about the frozen figure of George Washington's eight-year-old slave "Jocko." According to the anecdote, the slave froze while holding the reins of George Washington's horse after the crossing of the Delaware River in 1776.[1] Other legends point to a slave frozen as he held the horse of his master while the master and friends drank inside a tavern.[2] A less common explanation is that the statues are a salute to the formerly dominant African-American jockey in horse racing.[3]

The negative racial connotations of the lawn jockey have caused most of these degrading caricature statues to disappear. Some of the existing figures have been painted white—perhaps to conceal the racism of the image. But many remain. One could be in an otherwise pristine setting and encounter rustic homes on whose manicured lawns the black-faced lawn jockeys greet visitors. Obviously, some people see nothing wrong with the statues. Much the same frame of mind allows teams in professional sports to have names or caricatures that degrade Native Americans.

The Racist Statements

■ *Al Campanis.* Public statements by prominent sports figures over the past few years reveal that a "lawn jockey" mentality permeates several sectors of sport.[4] Probably the most publicized statement of this genre occurred on a show honoring the fortieth anniversary of Jackie Robinson's integration of Major League Baseball. In 1987, Al Campanis, then an executive of the Los Angeles Dodgers, had the following exchange with Ted Koppel on ABC's *Nightline:*

> *Koppel:* Why are there no black managers, general managers or owners? . . . Is there still prejudice in baseball today?
> *Campanis:* No, I don't believe it's prejudice. I truly believe that they may not have some of the necessities to be, let's say, a field manager or perhaps a general manager.
> *Koppel:* Do you really believe that?
> *Campanis:* Well, I don't say that all of them, but they certainly are short. How many quarterbacks do you have, how many pitchers do you have, that are black?
> *Koppel:* Yeah, but I got to tell you, that sounds like the same kind of garbage we were hearing 40 years ago about players.
> *Campanis:* No, it's not garbage, Mr. Koppel, because I played on a college team, and the center fielder was black, and in the backfield at

NYU with a fullback who was black. Never knew the difference whether he was black or white. We were teammates. So it might just be, why are black men or black people not good swimmers? Because they don't have the buoyancy.[5]

With that, ABC and Koppel took a station break.

Campanis was confirming what seemed to be otherwise unverifiable: that racism permeated sports. The Dodgers executive was simply stating what he believed the world knew as fact. Like many who profess to conduct business in a color-blind manner, Campanis exhibited some deeply held beliefs. In his initial words, and the words of those who spoke for him after the fact, there was no racial ill will intended. This was just what he believed to be true.[6] It was 1987, and we were not accustomed to hearing blatant admissions of racism. Discrimination, after all, was no longer legal in America. School desegregation became the law of the land in 1954, and the final sets of laws outlawing discrimination were put in place in the mid-1960s. But Campanis made clear once again that racism cannot be outlawed.

When the network returned from commercials, Koppel gave Campanis the chance to clear things up. Campanis sought to rehabilitate himself by remarking that blacks were "outstanding athletes . . . very God-gifted . . . wonderful people . . . gifted with great musculature and various other things. They're fleet of foot."[7] The outrage over Campanis's statements was nearly universal. After an initial hesitation, the Dodgers fired him.

Campanis's remarks were particularly ironic from a Dodgers executive because of the history of that organization. The Brooklyn Dodgers had become the national team for many African-Americans when Jackie Robinson became the first African-American to break the modern-era sports color barrier. My grandfather, who was born in Kansas in 1893 and spent most of his adult life in Oklahoma, remained a staunch Dodgers fan until his death in 1993. Forget that, particularly in recent years, the majority of the blacks on the Dodgers were Latino and other teams could more respectably bear the title of "black America's team;" the Dodgers were the team Jackie Robinson played for, and my grandfather and others of his generation never forgot it. Now, in 1987, the Dodgers were again part of a significant moment in baseball history.

■ *Jimmy "the Greek" Snyder.* Jimmy "the Greek" Snyder also achieved notoriety by making a grossly inappropriate statement on an important date in African-American history. On Martin Luther King, Jr.'s birthday in 1988, a Washington, D.C., television reporter, Ed Hotaling, asked Snyder about the role of blacks in football, in the context of a Martin Luther King story on which Hotaling was working. Snyder at the time was a featured commentator on professional football for the CBS television network and presumably qualified to speak on the matter. In response Snyder remarked:

The difference between blacks and whites goes all the way back to the Civil War when, during the slave period, the slave owner would breed his big black [man] with his big [black] woman so that he could have a big black kid— that's where it all started. The black is a better athlete to begin with because he's been bred to be that way because of his thigh size and big size. [They] jump higher and run faster.

All the players are black; the only thing that the whites control is the coaching jobs.[8]

Snyder picked up, in a sense, where Campanis left off—blacks cannot swim but they are bred for all other sports. Snyder, like Campanis, presumably had no ill will in his words. He was not conscious of the racist interpretation that could be given to his words. Just as happened after the Campanis incident, many commentators spoke of how they did not believe Snyder to be a racist and how he had never exhibited any attitudes of racism in the past. CBS followed the Dodgers' example, however, and fired Snyder based on his statements. Although Snyder made no direct attacks on African-American intellect, as did Campanis, he verbalized an oft-unspoken white fear of losing power to the black man. Interestingly, some jumped to defend portions of Snyder's analysis.[9]

■ *Marge Schott.* In 1993, Marge Schott, the owner of the Cincinnati Reds baseball franchise, made several comments behind closed doors that offended Americans of many races and religions. The comments came to light when a wrongful dismissal lawsuit was brought against the Reds by a former employee. Statements Schott allegedly made include: referring to two star black players as "million-dollar niggers" and stating that she would "rather have a trained monkey working for me than a nigger."[10] Schott also allegedly referred to Jews as "Jew bastards" and "money-grubbing Jews" and noted that "Hitler had the right idea for them, but went too far." At a later time, she equated athletes who wore earrings to "fruits."

Schott was fined $25,000 by her fellow owners for her racist and anti-Semitic declarations and suspended from operating the club on a day-to-day basis for one year.[11] She was permitted to return to the team a few months early after voluntarily attending diversity training. Schott's words were certainly offensive. One could, however, argue that racist talk in private, while offensive, should not be punished. Probably the more offensive fact was that only one in forty-five Reds front-office employees was black.[12]

Schott's statements are certainly more extreme than those of Campanis and Snyder. The Campanis and Snyder statements might be explained as a revelation of a racist belief, without any ill will—offensive, but only for the ignorance of the logic of each man's respective conclusions. Schott, in contrast, exhibited malicious racism, with no pretense of logic. She was, presumably, completely conscious of her words and their meaning. A key distinction is that Schott probably assumed that her audience in each instance held the same beliefs as she did and that there would be no subsequent reporting of her words. But obviously, she was wrong.

When It Was a Game: Jim Crow and Sports
Reluctant Integration

With all three of the figures just examined there was a sense on their part that "certainly everyone, at least everyone white, feels this way." Where do Campanis, Snyder, Schott and others get these ideas? History partially answers that question.

My grandfather, the Dodgers fan Leroy G. Moore, attended Southwestern College in Kansas shortly before World War I. As he used to phrase it, "I was the only colored boy on the football team." He was a running back. The racial hatred that flowed in his direction from other teams was never lost on him. He used to tell about how it did not take long for the Southwestern squad to determine how best to use his talents: although he was by far the fastest and most skilled runner on the team, he was used as a decoy. The taunt of opposing teams was "tackle that nigger"—whether or not he had the ball. He was a superb decoy. Race determined his role in sports. Neither coaches nor administrators sought to stop the discriminatory acts of the players. He would laugh and sadly shake his head as he told and retold the story over his ninety-nine years of life.

African-American All-American Paul Robeson described a similar experience on his first day of football practice at Columbia University in 1918: "On the first day of practice, I was attacked by twenty-one guys. All the guys on defense, and all the guys on my team. They put me in the hospital for two weeks. And you know, they did me a favor. From then on I was wary of my teammates as well as my opponents, and nobody was ever going to catch me like that again."[13] Fritz Pollard, one of the first African-Americans to play professional football, adopted a technique when tackled of rolling over on his back and flailing his legs bicycle-style to prevent piling on.[14]

Probably the earliest example of this type of discrimination comes from a halfback named Jewell, who played for the University of Michigan in 1892. In a game against Purdue, the crowd shouted, "Kill the coon!" When Jewell was carried off the field unconscious early in the game, the crowd, on its feet, cheered.[15] Similarly, Robert Higgins, a pitcher for the Syracuse Stars in the International Leagues in the late 1800s, had to endure chants of "Kill the nigger."[16] And when it came time for the team photo, one of his teammates said, "I am a Southerner by birth, and I tell you I would rather have my heart cut out before I would consent to have my picture in the group."[17]

This is just a snapshot view of a few of the African-Americans and their early roles and the treatment they received in college and professional sports in America. They were treated differently, with hostility many times, and when they were allowed to play on teams, the acceptance was often reluctant.

A broader view of the role of African-Americans in sports at a slightly later time is provided by nostalgic films on baseball. Every year, at the beginning of baseball season, the cable television channel Home Box Office (HBO) broadcasts a production titled *When It Was a Game*. Composed of jumpy eight- and sixteen-millimeter home movies, the show's intent is to have the viewer reflect on the good old days of baseball, from the years 1925 through 1961. When I first saw the program, I focused on what had largely been missing from the screen for much of the first forty-five minutes or so. Only a few black ballplayers were shown with the other jagged figures going across the screen. There was nothing discriminatory on the part of the filmmakers; blacks were not "allowed" to play in Major League Baseball during most of this era.

The motion picture *Field of Dreams* portrays a similar era. It was a movie with vivid hues but a lack of color on the field (other than the off-the-field role of Terence Mann played by James Earl Jones). But it, too, was a reminiscence of a different time.

My grandfather's, Robeson's, Pollard's, Jewell's and Higgins's experiences, juxtaposed with the HBO-*Field of Dreams* view of baseball, illustrate how we got where we are today. There has long been a recognition of the talent of black athletes. Displaying black athletes on the field, even reluctantly, has at various times been acceptable under changing racial codes. Some sporting events have been integrated since before the twentieth century. But at the beginning of the twentieth century, integrated sports leagues disappeared almost completely. Society at large was in the process of defining the post-Civil War role of blacks in America. When Jim Crow laws split the country in two, sports were not exempted. The "happy days" visions of *When It Was a Game* and *Field of Dreams* reflect this era when blacks were kept out of the game.

Today, the management of sports leagues keeps African-Americans from occupying representative numbers of sports leadership positions, thus guarding against the fear awkwardly articulated by Jimmy "the Greek" Snyder. The vestiges of the past are largely responsible for African-American exclusion from power positions today.

The 1800s saw long periods of integrated sports competitions. John W. (Bud) Fowler was the first black professional baseball player.[18] From 1872 until the beginning of the next century, Fowler made a living playing professional baseball.[19] Ironically, Fowler was born in the mythical birthplace of baseball and the home of its Hall of Fame, Cooperstown, New York.

Moses Fleetwood Walker, a bare-handed catcher for the old American Association franchise in Toledo in 1884, was the first black to play at the major league level.[20] He was also the last black to play baseball as a known African-American at the major league level for any significant length of time, until Jackie Robinson in 1947. It is not known how many blacks "passed" or were passed off as white, Latino, or Native American. A general distaste for the "Negro's" involvement in the integrated version of the sport was clear even at this early stage. The manager of the Toledo franchise received the following letter prior to a game in Richmond, Virginia, where Walker was to play:

We the undersigned do hereby warn you not to put up Walker, the negro catcher, the evenings that you play in Richmond, as we could mention the names of 75 determined men who have sworn to mob Walker if he comes on the ground in a suit. We hope you will listen to our words of warning, so that there will be no trouble; but if you do not there certainly will be. We only write this to prevent much bloodshed, as you alone can prevent.[21]

Later in life Walker became a columnist, urging blacks to go back to Africa.[22] He wrote that all they could expect in America was "failure and disappointment."[23]

In his history of the African-American athlete, *A Hard Road to Glory*, Arthur Ashe noted that in the earliest years of this country, cycling, horse racing, boxing, baseball, boat racing, and pedestrian events were the major sports; by the Civil War, blacks participated and excelled in all of them.[24] Illustrative of Ashe's account is the prominent role that African-Americans played as jockeys at the turn of the century. In the first Kentucky Derby in 1875, fourteen of the first fifteen jockeys were black. Ten of the Kentucky Derby's first seventeen winning riders were black, including the first American jockey to be inducted into the Racing Hall of Fame, Issac Murphy.[25] Many of the jockeys were slaves, extensions of the horses, riding much like the animals for their owners.

Segregation

The Jockey Club was formed in 1894 to license riders, and it mandated that jockeys be licensed. The club "systematically denied the relisting of blacks. The ebony-skinned riders were just too good and made too much money to suit the whites in charge."[26] After the Civil War, horse-racing promoters desired to make the sport more marketable; it had formerly been a sport of largely unsavory characters in the southern United States. According to David Horne, "That's when they started looking for things to sell the sport. A white rider getting roses, kissing the owner's daughter looked a lot better in the newspapers."[27]

One less racially motivated reason has been suggested for the end of the dominance of the sport by African-American jockeys. The curator of the Kentucky Derby Museum cites change in diet as the evolutionary factor: "I think this is a real good example of what happens to people when you start feeding them regularly."[28] The view of the curator is that the African-American just got too big physically to ride in horse races.

In boxing as well, two blacks had fought for the heavyweight title prior to the Civil War.[29] The disappearance of African-Americans from boxing occurred after the reign of African-American Jack Johnson as heavyweight champion. Johnson partially instigated the disappearance of blacks from the championship ranks by flaunting his romantic relationships with white women, perhaps the biggest social taboo of the era. After his defeat of Jim Jeffries, the "Great White Hope," there were race riots in many of America's major cities.[30] From 1915 to 1937 no black held the heavyweight boxing title, or was even allowed to fight for it.[31]

Similar moves were made in other sports—some with formal laws, some through gentlemen's agreements.[32] As baseball became more popular after the Civil War, demands that blacks be banned from the game increased. The National Association of Base-Ball Players was formed in 1858. The sport became professional in the 1870s, and the direct banning of blacks in this league was formalized in a statement by the league's Nominating Committee:

It is not presumed by your committee that any club[s] who have applied are composed of persons of color, or any portion of them; and the recommendations of your committee in this report are based upon this view, and they unanimously report against the admission of any club which may be composed of one or more colored persons.[33]

These notions provided the framework for the *Field of Dreams* era and most of the *When It Was a Game* period.

Reintegration

Not until Jackie Robinson joined the Brooklyn Dodgers in 1947 did Major League Baseball see another African-American player. Ironically, Robinson was initially signed to play in the Dodgers farm system for their Montreal franchise in the International League, which was the last of the integrated leagues when Fleetwood Walker closed out his career there in 1889.[34] Five years prior to Robinson's signing, Major League Baseball Commissioner Kenesaw Mountain Landis said, "There is no rule, formal or informal, or any understanding—unwritten, subterranean or sub-anything—against the hiring of Negro players by the teams of organized baseball."[35] Today's evidence puts the veracity of that declaration into question. Hall of Famers from the Negro Leagues such as Josh Gibson and James "Cool Papa" Bell were not signed by any team in organized baseball, although any of these players could have been signed to a contract at a relatively inexpensive price. It was under Landis's rule as well that Major League Baseball stopped maverick owner Bill Veeck from purchasing the last-place Philadelphia Phillies and replacing its players with African-American stars.[36] It was not until a new commissioner came into office, Albert "Happy" Chandler, that Major League Baseball allowed African-Americans to enter the League.

Professional football was a relative latecomer in U.S. sports history. For most of the twentieth century, college football was much more popular than the game in the professional leagues. At various levels African-Americans were members of both the early college and the professional franchises. But in the 1920s, African-Americans were phased out of the professional football ranks, much as they had been in heavyweight boxing.[37] For a twelve-year period, from 1934 through 1946, no African-Americans played on or were allowed to try out for teams in the NFL. In 1934 white players complained about job competition, and the NFL subsequently barred blacks. The dozen or so blacks in the league were not invited back for the next season.[38] Writer Stephen Fox places the blame for the banishment of blacks on the influential owner of the Washington Redskins at the time, George Preston Marshall:

> The NFL went lily-white not for general historical reasons but because of the overwhelming personal influence of one man, George Preston Marshall. Of border-state origins and racial sensibilities, Marshall had entered the league in 1932. Five years later he moved the Redskins from Boston to his home city of Washington and began a Confederate marketing strategy, aiming his radio broadcasts and publicity at the white South—which still lacked any NFL teams of its own. When the Redskin band played "Dixie" at halftime, the symbolism was inescapable. Given these circumstances, Marshall would not abide an integrated NFL. By deploying his noisy assertiveness at league meetings, and because of his crucial friendship with [the powerful Chicago Bear owner] George Halas, Marshall usually could impose his will on other league owners. Apparently no formal agreement was ever necessary. Everyone knew how Marshall felt, and nobody risked a public fight about it. The NFL faded to white.[39]

In 1946, Kenny Washington, a one-time roommate and teammate of Jackie Robinson at the University of California, Los Angeles, was the first African-American to play in the NFL with the Los Angeles Rams. Woody Strode also signed with the Rams in 1946, as Ben Willis and Marion Motley did with the Cleveland Browns.[40] Competition from the All-American Football Conference, which did hire blacks, was probably the economic motivation for the change.[41]

Basketball has less of a history of segregation than baseball. Just as in football, some blacks played basketball at white universities from the turn of the century up until World War I.[42] The sport had several coexisting leagues prior to the formation of the National Basketball Association (NBA) in 1949.[43] If one of the black-owned teams, the Renaissance, had survived one additional season, they would have been a part of the original NBA. The original Harlem Renaissance folded when they lost their following after moving to Dayton, Ohio.[44]

In 1950, just after the formation of the NBA, Chuck Cooper was selected in the second round of the National Basketball Association draft by the Boston Celtics. The New York Knicks subsequently bought the contract of Nat "Sweetwater" Clifton from the Harlem Globetrotters, and the Washington Capitols drafted Earl Lloyd. Lloyd was actually the first of the three to play in the NBA, starting a day before Cooper.[45] The first African-American coach of a team in a major professional sports league was Bill Russell of the Boston Celtics in 1966.[46]

The Permanence of Racism in Sports

Two factors are generally cited to explain the segregation of sports in the first half of the twentieth century. The most obvious is simply the desire of whites not to associate with African-Americans. George Preston Marshall exemplifies this factor. In the years after the Civil War and Reconstruction, there was much turmoil in the United States regarding the appropriate role for African-Americans in society. Historian John Hope Franklin has written: "In the nineteenth century white Americans, determined to maintain racial segregation, discrimination, and degradation even as chattel slavery ended, would argue that social and economic conditions dictated that sharp distinctions of every conceivable kind be made between white Americans and African-Americans."[47] Segregation was the route adopted by America and this included sports. Jim Crow laws were meant for all.

Associated with this desire for separation was the primary reason for the desire, the other broad explanation: a view that African-Americans are inferior. This view, of course, finds its roots in slavery and provided a common excuse for separation of the races. Consider the words of two of our most famous presidents; first, Thomas Jefferson:

The first difference which strikes us is that of color. Whether the black of the negro resides in the reticular membrane between the skin and scarf-skin, or in the scarf-skin itself; whether it proceeds from the color of the blood, the color of the bile, or from that of some other secretion, the difference is fixed in nature, and is as real as if its sear and cause were better known to us. And is this difference of no importance? Is it not the foundation of a greater or less share of beauty in the two races? Are not the fine mixtures of red and white, the expressions of every passion by greater or less suffusions of color in the one, preferable to that eternal monotony which reigns in the countenances, that immovable veil of black which covers all the emotions of the other race? . . . There are other physical distinctions proving a difference of race. They have less hair on the face and body. They secrete less by the kidneys, and more by the glands of the skin, which gives them a very strong and disagreeable odor. . . . They seem to require less sleep. A black after hard labor through the day, will be induced by the slightest amusements to sit up till midnight, or later, though knowing he must be out with the first dawn of the morning. They are at least as brave, and more adventuresome. But this may perhaps proceed from a want of forethought, which prevents their seeing a danger till it be present.[48]

Although the views of Thomas Jefferson may appear extreme, it was against such views that African-Americans in sports have had to fight from the beginning in the United States. President Abraham Lincoln made the following comments in a speech while in office:

I will say then that I am not, nor ever have been in favor of bringing about in any way the social and political equality of the white and black races [applause]—that I am not nor ever have been in favor of making voters or jurors of negroes, nor of qualifying them to hold office, nor to intermarry with white people, and I will say in addition to this that there is a physical difference between the black and white races which I believe will for ever forbid the two races living together on terms of social and political equality. And inasmuch as they cannot so live, while they do remain together there must be the position of superior and inferior, and I as much as any other man am in favor of having the superior position assigned to the white race.[49]

Certainly, much has changed in sports since the days of Jefferson and Lincoln, and even since the early days of integration. However, as the words of Campanis, Snyder, and Schott indicate, much has remained the same in the minds of some. Racism is ingrained in the sports culture. Although the racial percentages of those on the playing fields have changed over time and the formal and most of the informal agreements against discrimination have disappeared on the field, racism is prevalent in the front office.

I present these conclusions not so the battle against racism in sports will be abandoned but to provide a proper perspective for seeking prescriptions for the problem. There will always be some degree of racism present in the cultural belief system of sports, if only at a subconscious level. It is not possible to eradicate racism so that in some future year it will be regarded as a formerly dreaded disease, like polio. Even with polio we have found in recent years that it is necessary to keep a constant vigil to ensure that the vaccine is being utilized—or the disease will reappear.

Shortly before he passed away, Arthur Ashe maintained that the struggle against racism "is twenty-four hours a day. . . . It is something you have to plug into your daily computer and figure, 'Now how am I going to work around this today?' "[50] Any solution to the race problem in sports must take into account both this permanence and the need for persistence. Just as one of those lawn jockeys may appear on the lawn of a home or establishment today, a Campanis, Snyder, or Schott may make a public statement that shocks us by its blatant racism—but in fact has historical groundings. Many in power positions in sports today became involved when their leagues were segregated. Others learned the business from those from the segregated area. The permanence of racism in sports is exposed when the lawn-jockey mentality in the statements or actions of the leaders in sports are revealed to the public at large.

The onus of resolving the problems of racism in sports does not lie in dealing with any particular outspoken individual. As the University of California sociologist Harry Edwards has said, "Marge Schott is not the problem; she is a 64-year-old smoker and drinker with a weight problem. That's a problem that's going to take care of itself."[51] Campanis, Snyder, and Schott to varying degrees simply represent the presence of racism in American culture. A recognition of the persistent existence of racism at conscious and unconscious levels is essential to improving the situation in American sports.

In Search of a Solution

Following the Campanis statement, Major League Baseball Hall of Famer Reggie Jackson wrote in *Sports Illustrated,* "Because of the unfortunate things Mr. Campanis said, the time has come to break down the wall between whites and blacks. The time has come to say *we* have a problem and to address it. Together."[52]

Overwhelming change has not taken place to mitigate racism and discrimination in sports for much the same reason that problems of racism and discrimination persist in other industries in the American rank and file. For African-Americans to attain a greater role in the power positions in sports, a representative role, some people—*white people*—will have to give something—white power—up. In sports what must be sacrificed is the right of whites, primarily white men, to appoint top-level management positions and sell franchises to their white friends. Since the beginning of sports in this country, private personal networks have controlled the power positions. The sacrifice is not so much giving up one's own job as it is giving up the power to give a job to someone else.[53] This power has real, practical importance when the economy of the sports industry is taken into account. The business of sports is not downsizing but expanding. Each year at least one of the professional sports leagues adds or contemplates adding a new franchise. Jobs continue to emerge in sports while they disappear from other industries. To begin to do business in a different way is an almost unthinkable sacrifice. All of the parties need to remove their color blinders and recognize the harm of discrimination and the positive value that diversity brings.

And once more African-Americans enter the industry, another problem may develop—the one undiplomatically presented by Snyder, phrased in another way by sports industry consultant Ralph Stringer:

Eventually, at some point, you're going to have some people who are going to feel threatened, because all of a sudden you're going to see these sharp minorities coming in here, and some people are going to start to look and they're going to find out that not only are they sharp, they're sharper than some of the people that are training them.[54]

Although many I interviewed disagreed, times and people have changed. Ty Cobb was once suspended from baseball for attacking a disabled fan in the stands who called him a "half nigger."[55] The suspension was eventually lifted when the rest of Cobb's teammates refused to play until he was allowed to return. The attitude of Cobb's teammates was "What else would you expect someone to do who had been hurled such an insult?"[56] The reaction by Cobb's teammates was a function of the sports culture. Today, if the beliefs of the players have changed, they should take affirmative steps to bring about change—just as they did in Cobb's day.

The first epigraph at the beginning of this chapter speaks to the need to sacrifice in order to reach desired goals. To make the changes that most perceive as right, sacrifices have to be made at a high level by a diverse group of people. These sacrifices and the benefits that all, including the parties that give something up, will receive are outlined in the following chapters.

TWO

Sitting in with the "Good Old Boys": Ownership

[Washington Redskins owner Jack Kent] Cooke . . . kept a "lawn jockey" statuette—with a black face—at the front of his Virginia estate.   —Peter Perl, *Washington Post*, January 31, 1993

White men can't jump? They don't have to. They own the team.
                                        —Paul Mooney, comedian

The Problem: A Lack of Diversity in Professional Sports Management

One possible path for decreasing actual or perceived racism against African-Americans in any business setting is increased African-American ownership. The broad assumption accompanying this remedy is that increased diversity in the ownership of an industry will decrease occurrences of discrimination.[1]

Table 2 illustrates percentages of team ownership by race.

Clearly, diversity, a much discussed and analyzed concept, is absent from the ownership power centers of professional sports just as in other sectors of society.[2] In 1994, of the 275 individuals with ownership interests in the professional sports leagues of baseball, football, and basketball, only 7 were African-Americans. As table 2 reveals, none of the seven holds or combines with any of the others to hold a controlling interest in a franchise.[3] Although some argue that the on-the-field percentages are an indicator of equality, equal achievement has not occurred in terms of success at the highest levels.[4]

Table 2: Majority Owners of Professional Sports Teams, 1995

	NBA	NFL	MLB*
White	100%	100%	97%
Black	0%	0%	0%
Latino	0%	0%	0%
Asian-American	0%	0%	0%

*The Seattle Mariners are owned by Hiroshi Yamauchi, a resident of Japan.

General Benefits of Diversity in Ownership

What would be the primary benefits of greater minority ownership in professional sports? Two would be (1) the social value of diversity and (2) the financial value of diversity, in terms of allowing minorities access to a piece of the lucrative sports ownership pie and expanding the individual franchise revenues by attracting more fan support and attendance from minorities and achieving equity in player salaries without regard to race.[5]

The Social Value of Diversity

Meaningful sports-franchise ownership by African-Americans would symbolize a narrowing of the equality gap in the sports industry and with regard to race issues in general. In the bluntest terms possible, the common occurrence of minority ownership would to some degree negate what can be viewed—and in labor and other disputes often is viewed—as the last business akin to slavery, with owners buying, selling, and trading people.[6] Admittedly, while some of the social values of diversity are real, others are difficult or even impossible to validate.

■ *The Actual Value of Diversity.* Events in the United States Senate over the past decade have served as reminders to Americans of the importance of diversity. The absence of diversity on the Senate Judiciary Committee during the 1991 confirmation hearings of now Supreme Court Justice Clarence Thomas was the major force behind the accusation that the white, male Senate "just didn't get it."

Quite a difference could be seen after Carol Moseley Braun was elected as the first African-American female member of the U.S. Senate in 1992.

According to the *New York Times*, it took a "daughter of slavery"— as the headline called Senator Braun—to advise the primarily white, male Senate on a race issue that otherwise would have gained the Senate's approval without any commentary.[7] At issue was the petition of the United Daughters of the Confederacy to have a patent renewed on their association symbol, which included a replica of a Confederate flag. Leading the battle for what was primarily symbolic congressional approval (the renewal of a patent is largely a prestigious measure bestowed on a small number of groups, such as the American Legion) was North Carolina Senator Jesse Helms. It took an impassioned presentation by Senator Braun to defeat the measure.[8] Although largely without malice, her fellow senators were not conscious of the racial implications of their action.

A similarly strong presence could be felt in the Senate in 1994, when it debated allowing Admiral Frank B. Kelso II to leave the military with full retirement honors.[9] Kelso was the top naval officer during the U.S. Navy's Tailhook sexual harassment scandal. He had agreed to step down, although convicted of no wrongdoing, provided the government gave him a highly visible display of full support. This public exhibition of support included allowing the admiral to retire at the four-star rank with a pension of eighty-one thousand dollars per year.[10] The seven female senators called for Kelso to retire with only two stars and a lesser pension. Although they were unsuccessful, in a six-hour debate they expressed views that otherwise might not have been heard. Once again, the consciousness of the Senate was raised, with any subconscious feelings on the matter brought to the conscious level for the senators.

A further instance of the benefits of diversity, or of the problems when there is not diversity in an enterprise, is the cover photo for the O. J. Simpson case that was selected and artistically revised by *Time* magazine in the summer of 1994.[11] The white-dominated editorial board of the magazine picked a darkened version of the Simpson mug shot with, as was later reported, no ill intent.[12] Apparently no one in that boardroom thought of the racial implications of darkening Simpson's image.

The relevance of these events to sports ownership is not difficult to grasp. Once diversity is introduced into any setting, those accustomed to a monochromatic institution also must change. Both blatant and unconscious acts of racism are more likely to be addressed by a diverse group. People with diverse backgrounds generally will provide a varied perspective and encourage more thoughtful viewpoints from others.

An example from my personal experience may help clarify my view. As an employee of the Los Angeles Olympic Organizing Committee, I was in charge of hiring people from across the country who knew how to run an amateur boxing competition. We needed about fifteen hundred employees for the two-week competition. One exchange during my three years of working at the committee stands out.

I answered the phone while my secretary was fielding another call. "Mr. Shropshire?" the caller inquired.

"Yes?" I replied, not recognizing the southern drawl.

"This is R. I applied for one of those positions and I haven't heard from you yet." I recognized the name, since he had previously inquired in writing.

"Mr. R, we're moving as rapidly as we can," I responded, regretting having answered the phone. "We'll get to you as soon as possible."

Then, in his most courteous voice, seeking presumably to assure me that he was a good fellow, he began "Now, I don't want to stir up any niggers in the woodpile or anything. . . ." R did not know who or what race I was. The last person who could have any power over him would be a black man. "But I'm really anxious to get out there this summer," he continued. "Boxing has been my whole life." The sport had been his whole life, yet he had no respect for the primary participants in the sport: African-American boxers.[13] R also was certain that an African-American could not be in charge.[14]

■ *The Perceived Value of Diversity.*   In a more colloquial sense, diversity means empowerment rather than powerlessness. In the African-American community, a large share of the analysis of sports takes place in barbershops on Saturday afternoons. Nike shoe commercials of the early 1990s that featured NBA stars such as George Gervin illustrated this. The conversations and interactions are more institutionalized than in white barber- and beauty shops: the customers at black barbershops historically have sought more than haircuts. The discussions contain a blend of fact and fable. Some of the conclusions on race and sports reached in this venue and in similar ones may seem a bit harsh—maybe even racist in their own right. For those who gather in black barbershops on Saturday afternoons, as long as there is racism and white team owners wield the power, African-American athletes may not always get a fair shake. Beyond a deficiency of sensitivity due to a lack of diversity in the decision-making rooms, there also remains a level of favoritism toward the white athletes that leads to little favor toward the black athletes. So apart from the reasons for African-American ownership noted initially, there is also a view that long-term African-American ownership would have the power to "make things right." In barbershop lore, the source of most of the problems with sports franchises as they exist today is the "white man" running the team. Often the team owner is perceived as the guilty party.

In the African-American barbershop, the evidence is clear. Several cases in the last few years illustrate that in their handling of personnel issues the white management and hierarchy in professional sports tend to be more lenient with white players than with black players. For example, the only spots reserved on teams for "project" players seem to be for whites. The college football star quarterbacks Major Harris of West Virginia, Tony Rice of Notre Dame, Charlie Ward of Florida State, and Marvin Graves of Syracuse, all African-American, had somewhat routine, minor deficiencies in their games cited as major reasons for being drafted very late or not at all. Owners and management will not "waste" a pick on an African-American athlete who cannot just step in and play for a team. In basketball, seven-foot, six-inch Shawn Bradley was drafted by the Philadelphia 76ers as the second overall pick after having played only one year of college basketball and being two years removed from his last game. The prospect of a white superstar player in the league with a Larry Bird type following surely can be seen as a factor in management's decision to draft Bradley and then sign him to a $42 million guaranteed contract. His first two years in the league, even as a project, were disappointing. "A nice white guy getting chances a black player could never expect to see," I recently heard one patron say, while others in the barbershop nodded. These same patrons miss the similarity in the drafting of the African-American high school player Kevin Garnett. Without a single minute of college play he was the fifth pick in the 1995 NBA draft.

Another instance of the perception of owner power that grew out of the 1980s is the drug abuse leniency that has been shown to New York Yankees pitcher Steve Howe. Howe has violated Major League Baseball policies regarding drug use an unprecedented seven times, and each time he has been allowed back into professional baseball.[15] The barbershop conclusion is that no black athlete would ever be given that many chances. Right or wrong, that is the prevalent perception. Further, an African-American owner would be more inclined to give his or her African-American employees second chances. Never mind that African-Americans—Darryl Strawberry and Michael Ray Richardson are notable examples—have had second chances; a white athlete, Steve Howe, has had the most. More important, an African-American owner would be more likely to give both white and African-American employees equitable treatment; just look at the African-American manager Dusty Baker, who gave such a chance to Darryl Strawberry. Strawberry was released by the Los Angeles Dodgers for substance abuse problems in 1994. The San Francisco Giants, with Baker out front, signed Strawberry shortly after he left a rehabilitation clinic.[16] But even Baker could not give Strawberry another chance. It took an owner, the Yankees' George Steinbrenner, to take that step.[17]

Harlem Globetrotters owner Mannie Jackson, an African-American, acknowledges that minority ownership may not necessarily bring about any of the changes discussed above. He emphasizes that although one would hope that an African-American owner would be more sensitive to issues of racism and discrimination, whether or not he or she has greater sensitivity is a function of the individual.[18]

Despite these concerns, a minority owner is much more likely to recognize the benefits of diversity in management than an all-white ownership group.

The Financial Value of Diversity

■ *Owner Revenues.* With increased participation, African-Americans could share in the ever more lucrative ownership pie in professional sports. Regardless of the moaning and groaning that takes place in labor and salary negotiations, it is indisputable that owners of professional franchises often reap large financial rewards.

Ten years ago, the top sales price for a baseball franchise was only forty-three million dollars.[19] The values now have nearly quadrupled. Eli Jacobs purchased the Baltimore Orioles baseball team for $70 million in 1989. Four years later, Jacobs sold that same franchise for $173 million, a gross profit of over one hundred million dollars in only four years. That type of return on investment is not unusual for the sale of a sports franchise.[20] As a further example, when Norman Braman sold his Philadelphia Eagles football team to Jeffrey Lurie in 1994, the sales price was $185 million for a team for which Braman paid sixty-five million dollars just nine years before.[21]

■ *Attendance and Player Salaries.* However, a broader issue exists for the owners of professional sports that pertains to how the African-American athlete is valued in terms of the compensation he is paid. This issue is integrally related to game attendance. In large part, African-Americans do not attend sporting events. When there was talk of the Reverend Jesse Jackson's leading a boycott of baseball to protest the absence of minorities in top positions in 1993, one commentator wrote, "I sympathize fully with Jackson's goal, but question whether his methods will work. African-Americans have already been boycotting baseball—for about 40 years."[22] *Boycotting* is an extreme term, but other than for the NBA, attendance by African-Americans is moderate. In 1988 a study by Simmons Market Research Bureau of New York found that the percentage of black attendance at Major League Baseball games was 7.5 percent; at NFL games, 8.1 percent; and at NBA games, 15.7 percent.[23]

John Holway, the same commentator who observed the "forty-year boycott," sought to explain how this low level of African-American attendance came about. In the sport with the worst African-American attendance record, baseball, Holway and others point to the perception that baseball is a "white man's game." Yet this poor attendance was not always the case. The early 1900s were witness to a proliferation of teams and fans in professional black baseball on the East coast and in the Midwest. In Chicago during that era, Rube Foster, the masterful manager blessed with superior baseball knowledge and business skill, saw his team, the American Giants, build up such a following in the city that they often outdrew both the Cubs and White Sox on Sundays.[24] The annual black all-star game at Chicago's Comiskey Park would draw fifty thousand fans in the 1930s and 1940s.[25] When Jackie Robinson joined the Dodgers, the "colored" sections designated in all ballparks were filled to capacity. The day Jackie Robinson made his debut at Ebbets Field, there were twenty-six thousand fans in attendance and more than half of them were black.[26]

With integration in the sport, black attendance at Major League Baseball games increased while the number of those at Negro League games declined. "We couldn't draw flies," Buck Leonard, a former Negro Leaguer, stated about his team, the Homestead Grays.[27] In Newark, the Eagles had drawn 120,000 fans in 1946 but drew only 35,000 in 1948.[28] The Negro League folded in 1950, and then, Holway writes,

the lily-white ownership of the American and National Leagues lost interest in black fans. Indeed, beginning in the late 1950s, owners sought to escape black fans by moving from the old downtown stadiums near black neighborhoods to the white suburbs, a trend that only stopped recently. At the same time, the allegiance of the black community began shifting to basketball, a sport where black contributions, tradition and style are more honored.[29]

Sports-franchise owners can point to the lack of African-American impact on fan attendance to justify paying African-Americans lower salaries on average than whites. For example, one of the leading studies on racial discrimination in pay in basketball concludes that in many instances when there are black and white players of equal ability, the black players are paid less than their white counterparts:

We find that although black and white players earn comparable average salaries, when we control for performance, league seniority, and market related variables, blacks are paid less than whites by about 20 percent, or about $80,000 per year. . . . Regarding fan attendance, when we control for other influences on attendance, we find that white players add fans. Replacing a black player with a white player who performs equally well raises home attendance by 8,000 to 13,000 fans per year. This finding suggests that at the margin, *fans would rather see white players.*[30]

In 1991 professional basketball player Charles Barkley made a public comment relating to the role that race plays in ownership business decisions. The heart of his statement was that as the final cuts approached on the Philadelphia 76ers roster (his team at the time), the one player who was safe was the lone white athlete remaining on the roster, Dave Hoppen: "I don't think [team owner Harold Katz] is racist, but I said it would surprise me if we had an all-black team."[31] Many commented on the racism of Barkley in asserting such a thing. The Barkley observation was the lead story on Philadelphia television and in newspaper sports sections for several days. In fact, Hoppen did remain on the 76ers' roster in the end.[32]

The *Village Voice* ran a brief piece indicating that Barkley's belief was not unfounded. No team had ever won the NBA title without at least two white players on the roster.[33] The same *Voice* article went on to raise another, broader issue that indicated why owners may be reluctant to allow a team to become entirely black. At that time, the last all-black team had been the 1979-1980 New York Knicks. Although the team improved its previous record by eight wins, the attendance at Knicks games that year dropped to a thirteen-year low.[34] The owners of multimillion-dollar sports franchises did not get where they are without an awareness of this type of demographic information. The bottom line for most owners is increasing profits.[35]

Some sports-franchise owners may sincerely be torn between the logical financial decision based on players' attendance impact and paying based on player talent alone. These owners are not alone in making marketing decisions apparently based on race. Super Bowl Most Valuable Player (MVP) award winners Joe Montana and Troy Aikman, who are white, have been quite successful in the endorsement market. But African-American Super Bowl MVP Doug Williams received few endorsement opportunities after his victory. In fact, the $175,000 Williams earned in endorsements was considerably less than the $1,000,000 and $750,000 paid to the prior two white Super Bowl MVP quarterbacks, Jim McMahon and Phil Simms.[36] White Olympic gold-medal decathlete Bruce Jenner found his face on the Wheaties box almost instantly. Multiple Olympic gold-medal heptathlete Jackie Joyner-Kersee, an African-American, initially received few endorsement opportunities reflective of her accomplishments (although this probably speaks to sexism in marketing as well). It also took years for the two top-ranked African-American, female tennis players Zina Garrison and Lori McNeil to profit from any commercial endorsements.[37] There are some exceptions, of course, and basketball's Michael Jordan is the most obvious and striking, often leading the lists of those receiving the largest amounts in endorsement incomes and ranking with such stalwarts as golfers Arnold Palmer and Jack Nicklaus.[38] Nonetheless, whites still far outstrip minorities in the endorsement game. The African-American success in this area has been for participants in team sports, like Jordan, Shaquille O'Neal, and Emmitt Smith.

Diversity in the ownership ranks would arguably help eliminate questions of whether salary decisions are race-based in nature. The issue is a genuine conundrum. Diversity as a solution to these salary disparities presumes either that African-American owners will ignore any impact on attendance statistics in making salary determinations or that African-American owners will seek to attract greater numbers of African-American fans, thus eliminating any potential economic arguments for salary discrimination. For greater financial gains, it would seem beneficial for owners in general to strive to cultivate the African-American market. There are not, however, adequate instances of modern-day African-American sports-franchise ownership to verify that greater equity will actually arrive with diversity.

■ *Hiring.* A final issue is the prospect of an African-American owner hiring greater numbers of African-Americans at the management level.[39] Studies from other industries in the late 1980s indicate that black employment increases at firms owned by blacks.[40] For those who fear that the quality of sport would decline under black owner-ship, the studies also assert that performance of the firm is not at all negatively impacted on by black ownership. Subsequent studies have also found that the market value of a company increases as its diver-sity increases.[41] These studies did not focus on the sports industry, so the findings are not fully transferable. The implications, however, certainly point toward greater chances of meritocratic employment for African-Americans in professional sports while maintaining business stability and prosperity. What is missing is a long-term experience in integrated sports ownership to test this theory.

Specific Examples of African-American Ownership

What impact would increased African-American ownership have in the sports world? As Mannie Jackson pointed out, it certainly would not be the panacea for all of the racial ailments of professional sports leagues.[42] Complaints would still be heard from black barbershops and other quarters.

Determining the specific benefits of African-American ownership of professional sports teams is difficult precisely because actual occur-rences of it have been limited. Apart from a smattering of minor league experiences, one short-term experience in the National Basket-ball Association, and a few minority interests in other leagues, the ownership history of African-Americans in professional sports is not extensive.

The Negro Leagues

Negro League baseball was big news, both financially and socially. The league provided a view of the success African-American sports enterprises might have. Both the financial performance of the teams and the hiring of African-Americans by the owners evidence this.[43] The black teams developed at the end of the nineteenth century as a result of the banning of blacks from Organized Baseball, and initially they barnstormed independently throughout much of the eastern half of the United States.[44] Many leagues started and failed prior to the formation of the National Association of Professional Baseball Clubs in 1920.[45] This league, commonly referred to as the Negro National League, was disbanded in 1930. Apart from the Kansas City Monarchs, a franchise owned by J. L. Wilkinson, all of the owners and management were black; the league leadership insisted on this. The demise of this league chiefly was due to the declining health of its founder and motivating force, Andrew "Rube" Foster. The league was revitalized in 1933 by Gus Greenlee and several other blacks, who made money, for the most part, from illegal activities such as "numbers."[46] In 1937, the Negro American League was launched.

The Negro Leagues generated about $2 million in revenues per year per team. But not all of the teams were profitable. By the late 1920s, financial difficulties had beset most teams. The true cause of these difficulties lay in the declining economic status of the black population. With the onset of the mid-decade industrial depression, blacks in Philadelphia and other cities began to lose the economic gains achieved during World War I, and the always fragile foundation of black baseball began to crumble.[47] Once integration occurred, black sports-team ownership completely disappeared.

Baseball's integration did not have to occur the way it did. No merger occurred, and there were few payments for talent signed out of the Negro League. According to Holway:

The estrangement of blacks from baseball is rooted in the way the major leagues were desegregated four decades ago. Integration, a godsend for black players, was a disaster for black owners, who were defenseless even to protest. Branch Rickey, the Brooklyn Dodgers owner who broke baseball's color line, was so anxious to grab black players that he forgot to grab his checkbook to pay for them. Rickey never paid a nickel for the contracts of Robinson, Roy Campanella or Don Newcombe—talents who had been nurtured by the owners of the Negro League. Cum Posey, owner of the Homestead Grays, muttered on his deathbed, "It's like coming into a man's store and stealing everything off the shelves."[48]

The successful organization of Negro League baseball, despite facing unfavorable conditions that plagued nearly all African-American business enterprises during segregation, represented a significant achievement in African-American economic self-development.[49]

The Professional/Major Leagues

The instances of any type of African-American sports-franchise ownership since the time of the Negro Leagues have been few. In the second half of the twentieth century, Peter C. B. Bynoe and Bertram C. Lee, two African-Americans, spent three years in a unique position. From 1989 to 1992 they owned as much as a 37.5 percent interest in the Denver Nuggets of the National Basketball Association, during which time Bynoe served as the managing general partner of the franchise. Their partner in the venture, and the party to whom they eventually sold their interest in 1992, was COMSAT Corporation. The franchise was purchased by the Bynoe-Lee-COMSAT ownership group in 1989 for a reported $54 million.[50]

This was a brief example of minority ownership, but not much of a track record was left behind. One African-American hired during their tenure, Bernie Bickerstaff, did become the only African-American president of a professional sports franchise in 1995.[51]

The Bynoe-Lee tenure was also highlighted by a unique negative result from their ownership. The Denver Nuggets were sued because a former assistant coach believed he had been fired by African-American management because he was white. Doug Moe, Jr., filed a suit that included a charge of reverse discrimination against Bertram Lee and Peter Bynoe. Moe alleged that the team's "acts in terminating were without cause and were motivated, in part, by . . . race."[52] Moe later dropped the suit, which seemed baseless when the Nuggets hired Paul Westhead as head coach and Jim Boyle as an assistant, both of whom are white. Included in Moe's lawsuit was the claim that "Bertram Lee, a general partner, has stated that he wants all assistant coaches and other employees to be black."[53]

The Minor Leagues

The ownership experience of Bynoe and Lee concerned ownership of only a minority interest. There is, however, a modern-day example of full African-American ownership of a minor league franchise. The Savannah Cardinals were an example of African-American ownership increasing African-American employment. The franchise was purchased in 1985 by Tom Lewis, an African-American and owner of Inter-Urban Broadcasting, at the time a conglomerate of seven radio stations. This purchase made Lewis the first African-American owner of a baseball team since the disappearance of the Negro League in 1954. No special affirmative action programs or schemes put Lewis in position to purchase the team; he saw an advertisement in the *Wall Street Journal* that offered the franchise at a sales price of $285,000, and he bought it. Most sports-franchise acquisitions are not so simple.

Minority ownership of the Savannah Cardinals did not last long, from 1985 only through 1987. But the president of the team was then twenty-five-year-old Tracy Lewis, Tom's daughter. Lewis's "management team" was made up primarily of African-Americans. In fact, the lone white member of the group was frequently asked, "How come you're not black?"[54] As exemplified by Tom Lewis, once minority owners join the ownership ranks, they are best positioned to make changes and hire traditionally excluded individuals into the sports management structure.

Legal Recourse: Can the Law Compel Diversity?

With the social and financial benefits of diversity outlined above, the question naturally arises of whether existing law provides any possible causes of action to increase diversity and African-American ownership in professional sports management. The conclusion is that present law can play only a very limited role in mandating increased African-American ownership in professional sports. This mirrors the limited role the law has played in discrimination in private sector business transactions in general.[55]

Legal Recognition of Diversity

The U.S. Supreme Court has acknowledged the importance of diversity in two frequently cited cases. While neither mandates diversity in the sports industry, both are important in delineating the value of diversity in varied industry settings.

■ *Metro Broadcasting, Inc. v. FCC* and *Adarand Constructors v. Pena.* In the now much maligned case of *Metro Broadcasting, Inc. v. FCC,*[56] the Court examined minority ownership in the broadcasting industry and concluded that with representative minority participation the industry will produce "more variation and diversity than will one whose ownership is drawn from a single racially and ethnically homogeneous group."[57] The Court's view was that minority ownership in the broadcasting industry would give greater assurance that programming representative of the interest of minorities would be presented over the airwaves. The broadcast message delivered would not be exclusively that of white male owners.

Adarand Constructors v. Pena[58] overruled much of *Metro*. *Adarand* specifically held that the applicable standard of scrutiny by courts in reviewing any government affirmative action program, whether local, state, or federal, is strict scrutiny,[59] thus narrowing the occasion when affirmative action programs will be upheld. But the court also stated specifically that *Metro* is only overruled to the extent that it is inconsistent with the level of scrutiny to be applied in cases where there is a governmental actor.[60] To amplify this point, as well as the importance of the diversity portion of the *Metro* decision, Justice John Paul Stevens wrote, dissenting in *Adarand*, "The proposition that fostering diversity may provide a sufficient interest to justify such a program is not inconsistent with the Court's holding today—indeed, the question is not remotely presented in this case—and I do not take the Court's opinion to diminish that aspect of our decision in Metro Broadcasting."[61] Thus there remains much value in the *Metro* decision, and arguably, in *Adarand* as well.

Analogizing *Metro* to sports ownership relies on viewing the sports industry as a form of entertainment that has a societal impact similar to that of the broadcast industry. The *message* that sports presents would have to derive some of the same benefits from diversity as does the programming presented by the broadcasting industry.

Certainly sporting events deliver many messages. The youth who sees only whites as owners, officials, and quarterbacks gains an understanding of who the leaders are in society, as well as of who the leaders are not. This reinforces both the conscious and unconscious beliefs regarding race held by all who watch. This message delivered by sports franchises—that is, who occupies leadership roles—is determined in large part by the owners. Thus the philosophy is the same as that behind the congressional determination that minorities will send out messages in broadcasting that are more sensitive to minority groups than will white owners.[62]

This broadcasting-sports analogy runs into difficulty, however, as the holding in *Metro* was indebted to a federal statute promoting diversification of broadcast programming.[63] Moreover, no matter what message is sent by increased diversity in sports, it is probably not speech that is protected by the First Amendment, as in *Metro*. The message in sports is not derived from a miniseries, sitcom, or news-related programming but rather from images on the field or the images of the people in charge of the hugely successful sports industry.[64] Although much of the spirit of *Metro* is applicable to the African-American sports ownership discussion, the case is not directly on point. But the case does clearly support the principle of diversity.[65]

■ *Regents of the University of California v. Bakke. Regents of the University of California v. Bakke*[66] is an even earlier Supreme Court case that emphasizes the value of diversity. In this case, Justice Lewis Powell wrote that an affirmative action program to attain a diverse student body was justifiable because of the benefits delivered by bringing diverse ideas to the classroom, which in turn results in educational excellence.[67] Regarding *Bakke* and similar cases, the argument certainly could be made that diversity in a university setting is more valuable than elsewhere.[68] The university is where society expects people representing a wide variety of viewpoints to generate and discuss ideas. However, the same generation-of-ideas argument is not ideally transferrable to sports. For a legal argument in support of diversity to be successful, it would have to be constructed by amplifying the role of diverse images and ideas from sports in society. The law supports the concept of diversity but offers no strong precedent for legal action in sports ownership.

Moreover, Justice Powell was the lone author of that portion of the written opinion broadly in support of diversity.[69] Powell is no longer a member of the Court, and it does not appear that justices of similar viewpoint have replaced him.[70]

The Limits of the Law's Impact on Private Business Associations

It is difficult for anyone to become a sports-franchise owner simply because one has the desire and the adequate finances. Tom Lewis's situation with the minor league Savannah Cardinals was exceptional. Even being positioned to compete with the offers of other bidders for teams does not ensure that a party will be able to make the purchase. A group that included African-American Earvin "Magic" Johnson lost out in its effort to gain an NBA franchise in Toronto in 1993.[71] Similarly, in 1993 a group headed by Jean Fugett, an African-American businessman and then chief executive officer of the largest African-American business in the world, decided not to bid to purchase the Baltimore Orioles baseball franchise.[72] A group that included the Chicago Cub Hall of Famer Ernie Banks was not able to put a bid in for the Chicago Cubs baseball franchise because of a prior commitment to the Tribune Company.[73] And yet another group including former New York Mets All-Star Donn Clendennon met a similar fate when it attempted to purchase the Oakland Athletics.[74]

Potential white owners have been snubbed on franchise purchases as well. The law is clear that the owners in a given league may sell or grant franchises to whomever they choose, and provided nothing in their decision-making process violates any other laws, no legal action can force the existing owners to sell to a particular group.[75] Two lawsuits set forth the law in the area of the awarding of sports franchises. The plaintiffs in both of these cases based their actions on antitrust laws, arguing the anticompetitive nature of a league not accepting them as franchise owners.

In the first lawsuit, Irving Levin desired to purchase the NBA's Boston Celtics. Although he was financially well positioned to do so, the NBA owners voted against him.[76] In this case the concern was that Levin would align with an owner with whom the majority of the other NBA owners disagreed. After Levin brought suit, the court ruled in

Levin v. NBA that the owners had the right to choose their ownership partners and that they could reject ownership applications for any reason or no reason at all, provided the reason is not illegal. One party testified regarding the reasons for rejecting the prospective owner:

You are with Sam Schulman. He has been a craw in the throat of these owners. He's a renegade and a rebel, a troublemaker, and he just doesn't play their game, and they are obviously worried that you fellows, being close to Sam, are going to be siding with him on any matters that come up before the NBA.[77]

In the second case, *Mid-South Grizzlies v. NFL*,[78] the owners of the Memphis World Football League franchise the Memphis Southmen, who redubbed themselves the Mid-South Grizzlies, sought to have their team taken in as an expansion franchise in the National Football League. When the NFL owners refused, the owners of the franchise sued in federal court. The Memphis owners lost on the same principles articulated in *Levin*[79]—the decision to expand and on who receives an expansion franchise is that of the existing NFL owners alone.[80] The court ruled that the NFL could not be compelled to expand into Memphis.

In both the existing-franchise purchase area and the expansion area, the choice of which potential owners to bring on board is that of the respective league owners. Just as in any other business, courts are reluctant to compel sports-franchise owners to take on new partners.[81] As long as the reason for rejection is not illegal, courts are not likely to intervene.[82]

Title VII and Section 1981

The introduction of race into the equation may improve a plaintiff's position. Arguably, barring African-Americans from franchise ownership is similar to those cases where a person is denied partnership in a law firm based on race. The law most applicable in law-firm partnership cases is Title VII of the Civil Rights Act of 1964.[83] But Title VII is not applicable to the sports ownership scenario because that antidiscrimination law is applicable only to employer-employee relationships.[84] In other words, that law is applicable only where there is the preexisting relationship, not where a relationship is being sought. Sports owners generally do not have preexisting employment relationships with the various leagues. Also, unlike law firms, there are no "associates" employed and waiting to be considered as "partners." Presumably, athletes playing in the various leagues would have difficulty making an argument that the move from player to owner is a mere promotion. In fact, such a transition is the exception.

Another possible mechanism of legal recourse is the Civil Rights Act of 1870.[85] In its present form, the Civil Rights Act of 1870, as codified in volume 42 of the *U.S. Code*, section 1981, provides that "All persons within the jurisdiction of the United States shall have the same right in every State and Territory *to make and enforce contracts,* . . . as is enjoyed by white citizens."[86]

Section 1981's scope of coverage is wider than that of Title VII; it applies to the making and enforcing of all contracts, not just employment contracts.[87] The Supreme Court also has held that the section applies to both public and private discrimination.[88] Consequently, Section 1981 may provide relief whenever an individual is denied admission to a partnership on account of his or her race, since a partnership is a contractual agreement.[89] If an individual is denied the opportunity to become a partner because of race, he or she is denied the opportunity to make a contract, in violation of Section 1981.[90] Thus if the plaintiffs in *Mid-South Grizzlies* or *Levin* had been denied membership to their respective leagues because of their race,[91] they would have had a cause of action under Section 1981. However, to bring this type of action successfully, a plaintiff would have had to establish racial motivation, not just the absence of African-American ownership or other comparable statistics.[92] Absent the unlikely event of owners publicizing that they have denied an individual a sports franchise on the basis of his or her race, the use of Section 1981 will not bring about change.

Although under both Title VII and Section 1981 a court of equity can mandate the adoption of an affirmative action program[93] in awarding franchise opportunities, courts likely will not mandate that a franchise or league admit equity owners it does not wish to admit.[94]

First, courts have been hesitant to provide analogous relief, such as reinstatement, under Title VII in upper-level employment discrimination cases, even when actual discrimination has been found.[95] For example, in *EEOC v. Kallir, Philips, Ross, Inc.*,[96] a federal court denied reinstatement to a high-level employee. The court reasoned that reinstatement was not appropriate since the employee's job "required a close working relationship between plaintiff and top executives of defendants [employer]. . . . The Court is convinced that after three-and-a-half years of bitter litigation the necessary trust and confidence can never exist between plaintiff and defendant."[97]

Second, hiring criteria for high-level employees tend to be very subjective.[98] The courts are hesitant to second-guess the validity of such subjective criteria. The "courts in upper level cases often profess a lack of expertise and [thus] refuse to assess an applicant's qualifications."[99] This logic would be amplified for the admission of fellow owners in a sports league.

Finally, compelling admission of partners or equity owners may interfere with the present partners' freedom of association.[100] For example, in *Hishon v. King & Spalding*,[101] the U.S. Court of Appeals affirmed the lower court's conclusion that Title VII did not apply to the selection of partners because a professional partnership was like a marriage and to compel admission of unwanted partners under Title VII "resemble[d] a statute for the enforcement of shotgun weddings."[102] On appeal, the U.S. Court of Appeals stated that "the essence of a partnership [was] voluntary association."[103] Although the U.S. Supreme Court reversed, it did so on the ground that plaintiff's promotion was a "term or condition of employment."[104] It left untouched the presumption established by the two lower courts that freedom of association prevented the applicability of Title VII to the selection of partners. This conclusion is supported by Justice Lewis Powell's concurring opinion, in which he made clear that the Court's decision "should not be read as extending Title VII to the management of a law firm by its partners."[105] His reason was that "the relationship among law partners differs markedly from that between employer and employee—including that between the partnership and its associates [i.e., employees]."[106] In short, although freedom of association is not a defense in the employer-employee context,[107] it may be a defense outside the strict employer-employee context.

It cannot be disputed that for a sports league to be effective and successful there must be trust and confidence between and among the partners or fellow owners in the league. A bad choice can doom the partnership. There are thirty or fewer franchises in each of the professional leagues.[108] Consequently, individuals who enter into partnership or who expand their partnerships are very selective of whom they permit to join, and the courts are aware of this selectivity. The necessary trust and confidence will not exist if the partnership is compelled by force of law to admit an individual whom the partnership does not want. On the contrary, there will likely be much bad blood and distrust.[109] Once legal action is initiated, the possibility that this individual and the other partners could work together in peace and harmony is almost nil, and the forced admission of the individual could jeopardize the partnership. This is why reinstatement is not a favored remedy for high-level employees in both employment and partnership contexts.[110]

The Impact of Litigation and Litigation Threats

As the analysis above indicates, increasing minority ownership through litigation may be the most difficult transition to make in solving the problem of the underrepresentation of African-Americans in sports management. Increased minority ownership through legal recourse is most likely to come from consent decrees and other similar agreements with civil rights organizations. The 1994 actions by the Denny's restaurant chain are illustrative of what a compound legal effort might bring about.[111] Further, an interesting social intersection involving the Denny's actions probably helped to add one African-American to the ownership club in the National Football League, albeit with a minority interest. The incidents of alleged discrimination by the restaurant chain may have affected the decisions of the individual who was granted an NFL franchise in Charlotte, North Carolina.

There were several allegations of discrimination against Denny's, but the most publicized involved six African-American Secret Service officers. In an Annapolis, Maryland, Denny's the six officers received agonizingly slow and rude service while their fifteen white colleagues were served rapidly. After complaining to a waitress over a fifty-minute period, they complained to the manager, who provided no satisfaction. According to one of the six African-Americans, "His attitude was so nonchalant, you knew where he was coming from."[112] The six Secret Service officers filed a lawsuit for the discrimination they suffered.[113]

The chief executive officer of Flagstar Companies, the holding company for Denny's, is Jerry Richardson. At the time this event and others were occurring, he was seeking the rights to an NFL franchise in Charlotte, North Carolina.[114] For Richardson, the timing could not have been worse.[115]

Two events occurred, relevant to the ownership discussion. First, as a result of class action lawsuits filed by the NAACP (National Association for the Advancement of Colored People), the Secret Service litigation, and several other public accommodation and different race-related lawsuits, Richardson entered into a settlement agreement. Eventually the agreement led to the granting of a number of Denny's franchises to African-Americans.[116] Second, Richardson brought an African-American, Bill Simms, into the sports franchise ownership group. This made Simms the first African-American owner in an NFL franchise since two of the original owners of the New Orleans Saints in 1967. The *New York Times* called the Simms-Richardson relationship a shotgun wedding.[117] As part of a "fair share" agreement that Richardson entered into with the NAACP, he promised to include an African-American investor.

Some might argue that the ownership interest given to Simms was simply another example of affirmative action, an unfair advantage where whites, too, were denied franchise ownership.[118] Simms expressed little concern over this type of allegation. According to Simms, "I don't mind the people saying this is an affirmative action deal. The reason why a lot of us are where we are is because people like Dr. King backed people against the wall and made them open the door."[119]

Will It Happen? Need for Voluntary Efforts

The previous section indicates that a court is not likely to interpret existing law as a mandate to compel professional owners to admit minorities into their league ownership ranks. What is likely to be much more effective—at least in the short term—is increased commitment from existing owners and players to recognize the important benefits that diverse ownership in sports can bring. Apart from an occasional racist statement by an owner or management person, the racism in sports-franchise ownership is nowhere near as overt as at Denny's.[120]

The Role of Existing Owners and Commissioners

League commissioners can play a greater leadership role in increasing minority participation in ownership. NBA Commissioner David Stern, for instance, showed that a sports commissioner can exert some power in bringing about minority deals. Stern was reportedly instrumental in putting the majority investor together with Bynoe and Lee when it appeared that their deal for the Nuggets was falling through.[121]

Additionally, the NFL acted positively by including African-Americans in their two most recent expansion franchise groups.[122] Certainly, the commissioner of baseball and future commissioners in other sports could take similar stances to increase or develop African-American ownership in sports.

In Major League Baseball, a group that may have a long-term impact is the league's Equal Opportunity Committee. The committee is comprised of owners, colleagues who may be able to have an impact on their fellow owners. Unfortunately, at this point the committee consists entirely of white males.[123]

The Role of Athletes

Power obviously plays a role in who may have the leverage to obtain a franchise. As Simms's inclusion in the Richardson group indicates, timing is important as well.[124] The African-American parties best positioned to obtain franchises are the current active athletes. Who has the greatest leverage in obtaining a franchise or ownership interest—a retired Magic Johnson or Walter Payton, or either of these players in his prime? An active athlete asserting a desire for ownership would not be without precedent. Isiah Thomas reportedly negotiated such a deal with the basketball team he was playing for, the Detroit Pistons, but later decided against it.[125] After retiring, he ended up with the Toronto Raptors as part owner and general manager.[126] Although not an active player at the time, but uniquely positioned, former Los Angeles Lakers basketball player Earvin "Magic" Johnson became a part owner of that franchise.[127] In yet another instance, former American Basketball Association (ABA) and NBA star Rick Barry (who is white) successfully negotiated to obtain a 15 percent stock interest in the corporation that owned the ABA Oakland Oaks.[128] (The league was an upstart, and the franchise is now defunct.) Thus precedent exists for the assertion of this sort of power by the superstar athlete.

Not all present or former African-American athletes have an interest in sports-franchise ownership. Those who do, however, should recognize the value of timing in asserting their interest in ownership. Once retired, their leverage has all but disappeared. Making ownership—to whatever extent—a part of contract negotiations at a prime point in an athlete's career would be the most powerful use of player clout.

The present athletes must play a greater strategic role in bringing about this change. The athletes, maybe more than anyone else, are keenly aware of the power the owners of sports franchises assert. The owners control the lives of that primarily African-American group of athletes on the fields and in the arenas. They are responsible for any disparities in salaries that exist.[129] The owners also control who will serve in the powerful management positions.

Throughout the ownership and other issues explored herein runs an important theme: who has the greatest stake in the sports industry? In the studies of corporate governance, the roles that parties other than management and shareholders play in the running of a business have been analyzed.[130] Often, the key stakeholders in an industry are the employees. A classic example of the power that employees can wield is the long-term labor saga of United Airlines pilots.[131] Their struggle led to employee ownership of the corporation. In sports the athletes comprise the largest and most powerful employee group. Athlete-owned leagues existed early in sports, and the concept arose again during the baseball strike of 1994.[132] Moreover, the athletes resemble the airline pilots in at least two other respects: both groups are highly compensated, and their livelihoods depend on the success of the business.[133]

Conclusion

African-Americans confront many difficulties when attempting to join the ownership ranks in professional sports. The chief obstacles are not financial but structural.[134] The sports-franchise owners themselves must somehow be compelled to desire change. Furthermore, the owners suffer from the same levels of conscious and unconscious racism as are present in the rest of society.[135]

A key barrier to change is the legally sanctioned clubbiness of the owners, who enjoy the exclusive right to select their co-owners.[136] There is no requirement, unless self-imposed, that the owners accept the best financial offer. As a group, the owners of any league certainly could mandate that any multi-owner group seeking a franchise must include African-American investors. The NFL took a step in this direction with the new Jacksonville, Florida, franchise, in which African-American and former NFL player Deron Cherry has an ownership interest.[137] Similarly, African-American businessman Bill Simms is part of the ownership group for the NFL's Charlotte franchise.

As ownership opportunities do become available to African-Americans, the economic benefits must be analyzed carefully by prospective owners, since the prices of teams have inflated to their current extraordinary levels. One commentator analogized some of the opportunities for purchasing teams that are available today to buying a dilapidated house in a great neighborhood—except that the purchaser must pay far more for that run-down house than did the purchasers of the neighboring, high-quality houses. According to Mannie Jackson, "Unless you have a billion dollars or so just sitting in the bank, it's hard to make the numbers work in the deals that are being offered today."[138] To realize the huge profits discussed at the beginning of this chapter, a new owner must have the cash flow to operate the franchise, perhaps even at a financial loss in the short term, while waiting for its value to inflate.

The law in the area of franchise ownership is difficult to use in compelling greater African-American ownership. In *Metro*, the diversity-in-broadcast-ownership issue is coupled with congressionally directed issues on speech and First Amendment concerns.[139] In *Bakke* and other related cases, the goal is diversity in the university setting.[140] There is no congressional action on the need for increased African-American ownership in sports; nor is there a speech argument similar to that of *Metro* for the ownership of a sports franchise. The strongest existing arguments are those for the benefits of diversity. In this regard, if Justices Anthony M. Kennedy and Antonin Scalia thought that "broadcast diversity" was trivial, how would they rule on a program that sought to encourage more diversity on the ownership side of sports?[141] It probably would not be difficult for them and for other justices to trivialize the importance of such diversity.[142]

The burden therefore is on league leaders and the athletes to achieve such change. There needs to be a recognition that cooperation, not conflict, will foster growth and prosperity for all involved. As summed up by Ed Bolden, the visionary African-American manager and organizer of the Hilldale Field (Baseball) Club, over seventy years ago, "Close analysis will prove that only where the color-line fades and co-operation [is] instituted are our business advances gratified. Segregation in any form, including self-imposed, is not the solution."[143]

The Front Office and Antidiscrimination Law

> In order to get beyond racism, we must first take account of race.
> There is no other way. And in order to treat some persons equally,
> we must treat them differently.
> —Justice Harry Blackmun, dissenting
> in *Regents of the University of California v. Bakke*

The Conundrum of Antidiscrimination Law

Whether techniques are implemented to broaden the field of African-American candidates or the more extreme measure of counting race as a plus factor is taken, both are forms of affirmative action. All affirmative action programs must comply with the law. Competing tensions in antidiscrimination law create a conundrum that will not easily be solved. Unquestionably, this is not merely a sports issue but one for the populace at large. On the one hand, any form of affirmative action, even with regard to recruitment alone, may be viewed as reverse discrimination and a violation of the law.[1] On the other hand, racial preferences designed to remedy the effects of past discrimination, even societal discrimination, may be benign and legal.[2] The sports industry faces pressure from both sides.[3]

The Supreme Court of the United States has cautioned that the use of racial preference in any situation covered by the law probably must be reviewed under strict scrutiny.[4] According to Justice Byron White, "Any preference based on racial or ethnic criteria must necessarily receive a most searching examination to make sure that it does not conflict with constitutional guarantees."[5] In the same vein, Justice John Paul Stevens has written, "Racial classifications are simply too pernicious to permit any but the most exact connection between justification and classification."[6]

The law is interwoven with any effort to bring about change in an industry troubled by discrimination. One of the earliest descriptions of the ideal goal of antidiscrimination law in employment was presented in a book by Michael Sovern.[7] Sovern perceived effective antidiscrimination law as twofold: first, to prohibit racial discrimination, and second, to improve the economic condition of African-Americans.[8] Even accepting these aims as correct, legal actions that could force sports leadership to change would be difficult to mount with success, absent an act of almost malicious discrimination. The law allows primarily for remedial steps in cases of specific, individual discrimination. The emphasis of antidiscrimination law is on specific events of discrimination in that particular industry, not on discrimination in society at large. As has been noted, and as Owen Fiss wrote in 1971, the law does much to bar discrimination on the basis of race once it is detected but little, if anything, to change the economic plight of African-Americans.[9] The efforts of the law are not focused on ensuring that African-Americans attain positions at the highest levels in sports, or any other industry for that matter.

The Statutes

Most discrimination claims brought at the federal level against private or nongovernmental entities are made either under Title VII of the amended Civil Rights Act of 1964 or under the Civil Rights Act of 1870 as codified at volume 42 of the *U.S. Code* in section 1981.[10] Individual state antidiscrimination laws may be applicable as well. Plaintiffs commonly challenge an employer's hiring practice in one of two ways, alleging either disparate treatment or disparate impact.

Disparate Treatment

"Disparate treatment" is the legal reference to intentional discrimination against an individual. The key issue in disparate treatment cases is *intent*. The disparate treatment intent to discriminate is shown when an employment opportunity is denied because of race. This intent can be evidenced in any of three ways. The first method of proof is through direct evidence. This would be the rare "smoking gun" event, where the employer says, for example, "We don't want to hire you because you are black." The second method of proof would be comparative evidence, where there is no direct evidence. The plaintiff would show that the employer treats similarly situated white employees or prospective employees differently than nonwhite employees or prospective employees. By comparison, the non-white employee may show negative treatment. Third, the Supreme Court, in *McDonnell Douglas Corp. v. Green,* approved a formula to show illegal discriminatory intent, if it can be shown that the plaintiff is a person of color; the plaintiff applied for a position; the position was vacant; the plaintiff was qualified for the position; the employer rejected the plaintiff; and the employer continued to accept applications.[11] In all of these cases of proving intent, the employer may rebut the proof of intent by proving it false or by establishing that there was a non-discriminatory reason for the hiring decision.[12]

Disparate Impact

The other manner by which a plaintiff may challenge an employment practice is by showing "disparate impact." Under this cause of action, an employment practice has a general negative effect on a particular race or on some other legally protected class. Here the key factor is the *effect* of the employment practice, regardless of whether its intent is discriminatory. Courts determine on a case-by-case basis what constitutes disparate impact. Some courts have used an 80 percent or four-fifths rule, holding that disparate impact is present if the plaintiff's class has a success rate with the employment practice of less than four-fifths or 80 percent of the success rate of whites.[13]

Examples of disparate-impact employment practices include standardized tests and educational requirements.[14] An employer may attack the plaintiff's evidence by disproving the statistics or by arguing that the employment practice is a business necessity, for example requiring that candidates possess the ability to drive a specific type of vehicle or to speak a foreign language with clients.

Application of Antidiscrimination Law to Sports Front Offices

The statistical composition of sports management's upper echelon would seem to implicate at least one of these legal theories. A key problem, however, lies in the informal nature of hiring practices in the sports industry. Disparate treatment is a tough evidentiary case to make. Regarding disparate impact, Title VII addresses "unlawful employment practices" and in most instances has been judicially interpreted to require the identification of a specific discriminatory hiring practice.[15] This has evolved through early interpretations of the act, especially in *Griggs v. Duke Power Co.*, where discrimination could be found even if it was not overt or intentional.[16]

According to a study conducted by the NAACP in 1994, the majority of the professional sports associations or teams do not have specifically identifiable hiring or promotion practices that can be pointed to as either intentionally discriminatory or resulting in disparate treatment of or impact on minority candidates.[17] Employers in sports tend to use a series of subjective criteria that vary among employment decisions, with no elements necessarily being weighed more heavily than others. With no unique employment practice to target as discriminatory, it is difficult to bring an action under Title VII, no matter what the statistics show regarding the underrepresentation of any group at any job level.[18]

The nature of the law indicates that the most viable suit for individuals is one brought by a party denied a job opportunity on the basis of race or a discriminatory selection device or hiring practice. Thus if there is no party wronged, no person denied employment based on discriminatory criteria, then no viable cause of action exists. Federal law makes it unlawful for an employer "to limit, segregate, or classify his employees or applicants for employment in any way which would deprive or tend to deprive any individual of employment opportunities or otherwise adversely affect his status as an employee . . . because of such individual's race, color, religion, sex, or national origin."[19] When those in power tap a friend or family member for a job opening, it is difficult to prove that a particular African-American candidate has been denied an opportunity for employment; in an industry run through contacts and word of mouth, it is likely that there were no other applicants. So, very often, no individual is harmed when a management position goes to yet another white male, because there were no other applicants who could prove that they were denied the job on the basis of race. And in many instances, race was not a factor in that specific hiring decision at all—at least, not a conscious factor. The *McDonnell Douglas* formula is wholly inapplicable because the African-American candidate rarely even gets into the pipeline. The positions also do not remain "unfilled," as required under the *McDonnell* test.[20] The hiring decision in question just followed the existing pattern in the industry. With no plaintiff, no one satisfies the constitutional requirement of standing. Therefore, no one exists to bring suit.

One lawsuit on this issue was lost when the prospective employee's proof of discrimination was apparently inadequate.[21] In that case, an African-American alleged that he was not hired as an assistant football coach by the NFL's New York Giants because of his race. Lance Hamilton, a former Pennsylvania State University player, brought the suit on both breach of contract and racial discrimination grounds. A New Jersey Superior Court judge found the action to be frivolous.[22] The ruling was based on a conversation between Hamilton and Giants head coach Bill Parcells, secretly recorded on tape by Hamilton. There was no clear promise made to Hamilton and no evidence that race was a factor. The judge ruled that "the allegations in Hamilton's complaint were false, [that his lawyer] knew or should have known that the action was frivolous, [and that] the case should never have been commenced."[23]

Employers in most industries have evolved from the simpler days when employment decisions were made based on specific criteria, such as a high school diploma and a written exam, as in *Griggs*, to a wide-ranging series of subjective criteria. The hiring practices in sports resemble what Senator Edward Kennedy referred to, in hearings leading to passage of the Civil Rights Act of 1991, as a "black box mush."[24] The reference is to employers who combine a number of practices in an inseparable manner and reach the employment decision out of that "mush." If race is a factor in that mush, it may be difficult to single out for legal purposes.

The statistics indicating the low numbers of African-Americans in power positions are not enough alone to make a case. What appears to be the final nail in the coffin with regard to basing a case on statistical proof alone was driven in by *Wards Cove Packing Co. v. Atonio* and the Civil Rights Act of 1991.[25] In *Wards Cove*, the United States Supreme Court stated that "statistical proof can alone make out a prima facie [disparate impact] case."[26] But it is also necessary, *Wards Cove* held, to show that the statistics emerged from a specific discriminatory employment practice and that the statistical disparity between whites and nonwhites hired was not caused by a shortage of qualified minorities in that particular marketplace. The Civil Rights Act of 1991 codified this into the 1964 act.[27]

Complicating the difficulty in forming a successful discrimination lawsuit against the hiring practices in professional sports is the fact that at the management level, particularly in sports, many employment decisions rest significantly on factors not objectively quantifiable.[28] Judges typically are reluctant to override an employer's decision and impose their own judgments of a candidate's qualifications, especially when the criteria are highly subjective. The instances of judges professing a lack of expertise and refusing to step in and overrule hiring decisions for high-level employment positions are legion in case law.[29]

The sports industry has the added patina of unique talent-identification criteria, particularly for coaching and general manager positions. Courts have been particularly reluctant to interfere with purely sports-related decisions of private sporting enterprises, such as which driver won an automobile race[30] and which team should have been selected to participate in a collegiate championship playoff.[31] Whether a specific African-American would be a better coach than the white applicant hired is not an issue in which a court is likely to become involved.

Case law does indicate that it is possible to attack an employment process rather than a specific hiring device, although the latter is likely to be the more successful case. In *Wards Cove*, the case involved plaintiffs who were Asian-Americans of primarily Filipino and Alaskan ancestry.[32] The workers filed their action under Title VII, alleging both disparate impact and disparate treatment in hiring and promotion practices. They argued that they tended not to get the higher-paying "noncannery jobs" at the company because of separate hiring channels, no objective hiring criteria, nepotism, and not promoting from within. The noncannery workers were recruited by white supervisors through word of mouth. This may sound similar to the hiring mechanism in America's sports leagues, but the end result was even worse. The company established separate dormitories and mess halls, segregating the white cannery workers from the non-white cannery workers.

The sports business is able to distinguish itself from the Supreme Court's decision in *Wards Cove* in another way. The Court found that the statistical evidence of underrepresentation of minorities at the higher levels at Wards Cove was not enough to make a case. Justice Byron White wrote, "It is . . . a comparison . . . between the racial composition of the qualified persons in the labor market and the persons holding at-issue jobs . . . that generally forms the proper basis for the initial inquiry in a disparate impact case."[33] In the national labor market for management positions in sports there is no shortage of qualified minorities. Again, the size of the qualified pool is not the same as the number of players on the field, but that number is significant. The "racial composition" comparison in a sports discrimination case would weigh more favorably for a plaintiff there than in *Wards Cove*.

The whiteness of upper-level sports management seems to be the result of the white men in power hiring their (generally white) associates. This is easily defined as an unconscious omission, of the nature described by Charles Lawrence, rather than an overt, conscious act of discrimination.[34] Still, it would appear that the compositional imbalance in management itself would be enough to evidence discrimination. But as has been discussed, the law, particularly Title VII, has been interpreted to regulate employer behavior and does not impose an affirmative obligation on employers to seek minority candidates for job openings or to employ a racially diverse workforce. The Supreme Court of the United States has stated succinctly that "statistics can never in and of themselves prove the existence of a pattern or practice of discrimination, or even establish a prima facie case shifting to the employer the burden of rebutting the inference raised by the figures."[35] The Civil Rights Act is prospective, not retrospective,[36] and there is little burden imposed on employers to remedy statistical imbalance in the workforce.[37] Title VII has always been an antidiscrimination statute, not a proportional representation statute.[38] Compositional imbalance alone will not support a discrimination suit when there is no specific hiring practice to attack or wronged plaintiff. In sports a plaintiff would be able to incorporate in his or her argument the discriminatory impact of the lack of a defined hiring practice. With the difficulty in bringing legal action to compel change, what are the legal opportunities to promote change through voluntary affirmative action on the part of management?

The Supreme Court and Voluntary Affirmative Action Plans

United Steel Workers v. Weber

In industries where a lack of representation of minorities has existed at various employment levels, affirmative action plans have been implemented to correct the disparity. The law permits the development and implementation of private affirmative action plans, but such plans are subject to judicial review. In *United Steel Workers v. Weber*, the Supreme Court upheld a private affirmative action plan developed by the Kaiser Aluminum and Chemical Corporation.[39] The plan reserved half of the spaces in a training program for minority job applicants.

Five justices held that the Kaiser program was in line with the goals of Title VII, since the plan aimed to "break down old patterns of racial segregation and hierarchy."[40] The Court found merit in the plan because, among other things, it did not "unnecessarily trammel the interests of the white employees" or "require the discharge of white workers" or "create an absolute bar to the advancement of white employees."[41] Also, the Court was impressed that the plan was a "temporary measure [that] is not intended to maintain racial balance, but simply to eliminate a manifest racial imbalance."[42] Although subject to much criticism, the ruling in this case—and the subsequent one in *Johnson v. Transportation Agency*—still stands for the proposition that temporary, voluntary affirmative action plans are legal, provided they comply with the guidelines set forth in case law and affirmative action related legislation.[43]

Johnson v. Transportation Agency

The *Johnson* plan established a long-range goal for the employer to attain a workforce reflective of the demographic distribution in the geographic area. The plaintiff in this case was Mr. Paul Johnson, who applied for a promotion to a dispatcher position. Ms. Diane Joyce applied for the promotion also. Johnson received a score of 75 on his interview, and Joyce received a 73. A passing score was 70. As a result of the affirmative action plan, the female Joyce was promoted and Johnson was not. The court upheld the plan as a "moderate, gradual, approach to eliminating . . . imbalance in [the company] work force."[44] The Court also noted the limited impact on nonminorities by stating that the plan "visit[ed] minimal intrusion on the legitimate expectations of other employees."[45]

Affirmative action plans have been labeled as—and in the strictest sense, are—discriminatory. The fact is that they favor one group over another. If none of the benefits of an affirmative action plan is conveyed within the plan's literal, discriminatory form, then the criticisms gather strength. The message conveyed by *Johnson* and *Weber* is that if equal treatment and integration are the goal of a firm's "discrimination" and ill will and bias are not, then the affirmative action plan may survive legal attack.[46]

Even where these positive-purpose messages are conveyed, condemnation of affirmative action continues. In a harsh criticism of private affirmative-action plans Larry Alexander wrote, "Private affirmative action is potentially a highly toxic form of remedy for the negative effects of disparate impact. Its own negative effects may be worse than those of group inequality. It is not intrinsically immoral, and it is currently legal, but it may be extrinsically immoral."[47]

City of Richmond v. J. A. Croson Co.

An additional case that must be examined and complied with when utilizing racial preferences is *City of Richmond v. J. A. Croson Co.*.[48] Although the case involves governmental affirmative action and not a private voluntary program, the views of the Court may be applicable in future affirmative action cases. *Croson* found preferences to minorities in city contracting to be illegal. Lacking in that case, although a strong dissent by Justice Thurgood Marshall disagreed, was past discrimination that would make such a remedial program necessary.[49] In that same case Justice Harry Blackmun wrote in his dissent:

I join Justice Marshall's perceptive and incisive opinion revealing great sensitivity toward those who have suffered the pains of economic discrimination in the construction trades for so long.

I never thought that I would live to see the day when the city of Richmond, Virginia, the cradle of the Old Confederacy, sought on its own, within a narrow confine, to lessen the stark impact of persistent discrimination. But Richmond, to its great credit, acted. Yet this Court, the supposed bastion of equality, strikes down Richmond's efforts as though discrimination had never existed or was not demonstrated in this particular litigation. Justice Marshall convincingly discloses the fallacy and the shallowness of that approach. History is irrefutable, even though one might sympathize with those who— though possibly innocent in themselves—benefit from the wrongs of past decades.[50]

Adarand Constructors v. Pena

In a 1995 Supreme Court opinion, this time focusing on the use of affirmative action in federal government contracting, the legal opportunities for using affirmative action were narrowed even further. *Adarand* requires that any preference program instituted by any governmental entity be subject to strict scrutiny.[51] The previous standard at the federal level was intermediate scrutiny.

Again, although *Adarand* is not directly applicable to a private enterprise such as a sports league or franchise, the Court has shown that it will retreat from previously approved less restrictive standards. This certainly gives the good businessperson reason to develop affirmative action plans with caution, rather than placing full reliance on the precedential value of *Weber* and *Johnson*.

The 1991 Civil Rights Act

Murkiness over the continued existence of racism was in place for the majority of justices in *Croson* and amplified in *Adarand*. For some, there is also murkiness in the current federal statutory law, even though Section 116 of the 1991 Civil Rights Act specifically states that nothing in it should be interpreted to affect "court ordered remedies, affirmative action, or conciliation agreements that are in accordance with the law."[52] In this regard, Senator Robert Dole points to Section 107 of the act, which was written to create liability in discrimination cases where there are motives in the employment action in addition to race. That section of the law creates liability when race is a motivating factor. Senator Dole harks back to the old saw that race-conscious affirmative action plans are just the type of action that incorporates race as the motivating factor.[53] Still, Section 116 of the Civil Rights Act would seem to control implementation of the act, as long as the guidelines in *Adarand*, *Croson*, and *Weber* are followed.[54]

The Role of Governmental Intervention in Sports

Consent Decrees

Another potential legal vehicle to compel the creation of league-wide affirmative action plans in sports, one being pursued by the Rainbow Coalition for Fairness in Athletics (RCFA), is action by the

United States Department of Justice. The RCFA has been compiling statistics, particularly of the underrepresentation of minorities at the collegiate level, and forwarding that information to Attorney General Janet Reno and Assistant Attorney General for Civil Rights Deval Patrick.

The goal of the RCFA is to encourage the department to investigate, to pinpoint the discriminatory act or acts, and to bring appropriate action and pursue consent decrees incorporating affirmative action plans, as it has done in other problematic industries. In the past the Justice Department has followed a similar course with regard to other industries where it has found a "pattern and practice" of discrimination.[55] A public example of this strategy is the 1994 settlement reached with the Chevy Chase Federal Savings Bank mentioned in the introduction.[56] In 1994 the Justice Department instructed the Department of Labor to investigate alleged discriminatory hiring in college sports, brought to the Justice Department's attention by RCFA.[57]

Finding State Action in the Major Leagues

One additional legal route to reform that might be pursued is to attack individual franchises through state-action theories based on the teams' playing in government-owned stadiums. Under Title II of the 1964 Civil Rights Act, the argument would assert that the private and discriminatory hiring practices of a franchise become "state action" because the state or local government leases the facility and also derives some financial benefit—such as a percentage of revenues from concessions or parking. In a case that adequately tied the discriminatory actions of a private party with the action of the state, the Supreme Court ruled regarding the decision's applicability to other cases, "Only by sifting facts and weighing circumstances can the nonobvious involvement of the State in private conduct be attributed its true significance."[58] Hence this would probably be a difficult case to make, even though most professional sports franchises play in government-owned facilities.[59]

A similar argument was successfully made in a sex discrimination case by female sports reporter Melissa Ludtke, who was barred from the locker room of the New York Yankees in Yankee Stadium. Yankee Stadium was found to be "maintained and improved" by public funds.[60] This level of governmental involvement constituted state action within the contemplation of the Fourteenth Amendment.

Conclusion

In summary, the uneven legal and political setting causes employers to move cautiously in putting strong affirmative action plans in place. For more meaningful plans to be implemented, internal as well as external pressure will need to continue on the sports industry. Short of investigation, it is probably unrealistic to hope for any other type of government intervention at the professional level—particularly not corrective legislation.[61] Without the specific proof that discrimination is ongoing, the concept of past discrimination is probably not adequate to prompt legislative action. Supreme Court Justice Sandra Day O'Connor has written:

A generalized assertion that there has been past discrimination in an entire industry provides no guidance for a legislative body to determine the precise scope of the injury it seeks to remedy. . . . An amorphous claim that there has been past discrimination in a particular industry cannot justify the use of an unyielding racial quota.[62]

This is coupled with a general reluctance, particularly at the federal level, to pass any legislation related to sports. It is rare that politicians find it beneficial to introduce a bill on sports (with the exception of when a sports franchise threatens to leave town), particularly when there are problems such as world hunger, homelessness, health care, and crime that constituencies would prefer to see their politicians resolving.[63]

The most viable route to increasing diversity at the management level seems to be to pursue the voluntary options discussed. Because employers have no affirmative obligation to employ a racially diverse workforce, the way to ensure that more minorities attain management positions in the sports industry is to make sure there is a broad pool of applicants to fill each position. When there are many minority candidates to choose from, there is a greater chance that some will be hired and less of a chance that minorities will be edged out on the basis of difficult-to-challenge subjective criteria.[64] The present informality of hiring transactions makes the provision of notice to minority applicants difficult, and the solution seems to be a more aggressive posture toward seeking employment opportunities in sports management on the part of minorities.

The sports industry has unique characteristics that cannot be disputed. Off the field, the evaluations for whom to employ are always subjective. There is a documented history of discrimination. In fact, it is these distinct industry characteristics that make aggressive affirmative action programs legal in the sports industry while problematic in other industries. Further, most large companies conducting business in the United States have some form of affirmative action program.[65] The sports industry should as well, certainly in a more public way than currently exists. The next chapter sets forth some viable industry options.

"Fear of a Black Planet": The Front Office

> I'm against affirmative action. . . . That probably might be illegal,
> too.   —A sports franchise owner

> America refuses to deal with the drumbeat of bigotry that comes
> from every principal power cluster in our country.
>   —Clifford Alexander, sports industry consultant

The Front Office and the "Natural" Transition

The most visible nonplaying personnel in sports are those who reside in the front office. These parties include chief executive officers, team presidents, general managers, and the head coach, who straddles the line between the field or court and the administrative offices. The front office also includes such professionals as team doctors, lawyers, and accountants.

Hiring decisions in the sports world are often difficult to understand. In 1987, Dr. Harry Edwards, a professor of sociology at the University of California at Berkeley, was hired by then Commissioner of Baseball Peter Ueberroth to help identify African-Americans for the front-office positions for which Al Campanis said they lacked the "necessities." Edwards's hiring made sense in many ways, given his long background in sports civil rights.[1] Edwards, did not, however, have a background in baseball, and many former baseball players felt that a person with a baseball background would have been a better selection.[2] Edwards then hired Campanis to assist. "Al Campanis has

Table 3: Physicians

		NBA		NFL		MLB
White	1994	95%(59)	1994	97%(71)	1994	95%(36)
Black		2% (1)		1% (1)		2% (1)
Latino		2% (1)		1% (1)		2% (1)
Other		2% (1)		(0)		(0)

SOURCE: Richard A. Lapchik and Jeffrey R. Benedict, eds. *1994 Racial Report Card*, (Boston: Northeastern University, Center for the Study of Sport in Society, 1994)

been in baseball for 40 years and has a tremendous store of knowledge," Edwards said at the time. "He will be very valuable in preparing me for dealing with those people in baseball. We're going to have to deal with the Campanises in baseball, and it's good that I have a person in-house who knows how they think."[3]

Just as Campanis was valuable to Edwards, it would seem natural and valuable for a former athlete—in the manner that the star salesperson becomes the vice president of marketing and eventually president of a manufacturing firm—to move from the field to coaching and on to the front office.[4] And while retired athletes are the prime candidates for on-the-field management, other front-office positions should certainly be potential employers of African-American professionals who have not played the game. For example, as Table 3 shows, in 1994 there was only a single African-American team physician in each of the major sports leagues. The team physician is an ideal position about which to ask, "What is the proper denominator?" If most team physicians are orthopedic surgeons, then that is the proper qualification to consider. If most are former athletes, then that is a further narrowing consideration. But one would expect to see a greater number of African-Americans.[5] This barrier to the sports industry for nonathlete African-Americans is an important indicator of the nature of the problem.

For those athletes who do desire a career in management after their playing days, the transition up the sports-management business ladder is possible for some but generally not for African-Americans. White athletes such as Pete Rose and Larry Bowa became managers in baseball shortly after retiring from playing the game. A management position was also given in 1993 to Kansas City Royals star George Brett; the day that Brett announced his retirement he also announced that the next year he would become the Royals' vice president for baseball operations.[6] Rarely are such retirement-day promotions included in the articles featuring African-American athletes.[7] Concurring with this is former baseball All-Star and now Atlanta Braves executive Hank Aaron: "They think the only thing that blacks can do is just go out and hit the baseball, run the bases, and after that, you know, when you ride in the front seat of the bus for 10 years and after your career is over with, then they flop you right in the back of the bus again."[8]

Historically, there has been consistent underrepresentation of African-Americans in the three major sports, as the statistics cited earlier have shown and as is outlined below. The manager position in baseball and the head coaching positions in football and basketball are illustrative. Major League Baseball established the early precedent.

Baseball

Baseball has the oldest professional sports league in this country, and also the longest history of discrimination in the front office. Dave Anderson of the *New York Times* researched the roots of ignoring the African-American athlete as an on-the-field managerial candidate. The first obvious prospect to manage in Major League Baseball was Jackie Robinson. Anderson wrote that the owner of the Dodgers, Walter O'Malley, and the general manager, Buzzie Bavasi, "never particularly liked Robinson, whose combative nature was just what most club owners look for in a managerial or front-office candidate."[9]

When O'Malley was asked about the potential for Robinson in management he said, "Robinson can't manage himself, how can you expect him to manage 25 ballplayers?"[10] O'Malley was proven wrong about Robinson's management skills, at least as they emerged in a non-baseball capacity. After retirement from baseball, Robinson became an executive in the Chock Full o' Nuts restaurant chain and chairman of the board of Harlem's Freedom National Bank. The precedent was set; in Major League Baseball there was not a black manager until the Cleveland Indians hired Frank Robinson in 1975. Even today, the reluctance continues.

After Frank Robinson's hiring, one reason that was given for not hiring African-American managers was their lack of success relative to that of their white counterparts once managerial opportunities were given. *USA Today* challenged this premise with a concise statistical study.[11] Prior to the Campanis event three African-Americans had been managers: Frank Robinson, Larry Doby with the Chicago White Sox, and Maury Wills with the Seattle Mariners. According to the newspaper's analysis, "The three blacks who were hired to manage in the major leagues were given garbage teams whose records continue to pale when they were returned to Caucasian direction. . . . The black managers were 512–572 (.472). The whites who came next were 423–561 (.430)."[12] Cito Gaston later completely exploded the myth of the incompetent black manager in baseball. In the 1990s Gaston, the black manager of the Toronto Blue Jays, led the team to two consecutive World Series championships.

Football

The NFL's hiring record at the head coaching position, the rough equivalent of the baseball team manager, has not been as diverse. Until Art Shell was hired as head coach of the Los Angeles Raiders in 1989, there had never been an African-American head coach in the modern era National Football League.[13] The last black head coach in the League, Fritz Pollard, held the position in 1926. The same day that Art Shell was fired by the Raiders, Ray Rhodes, another African-American, was hired as the head coach of the Philadelphia Eagles.[14] As of 1995, Rhodes and Dennis Green of the Minnesota Vikings were the only African-Americans holding the head coaching position in football.

Hall of Fame football coach Bill Walsh says, in regard to hiring for coaching positions in football, "It's a very fraternal thing. You end up calling friends, and the typical coach hasn't been exposed to many black coaches."[15] There is nothing unique about Walsh's view. In the nonsports industry the old boy network is reality as well. Jason

Wright, a black vice president at RJR Nabisco, Inc., said about the business world, "The reality of life in America is that if you're white, most of the people you know are white. If someone says to you, 'Do you know anyone for this job?' the people you recommend will probably be white."[16] Sports, in this respect, is much like the rest of society.

Basketball

The National Basketball Association has been at the other end of the spectrum in numbers of African-American coaches hired. The league is generally able to hire and fire black coaches without much commentary in the press or elsewhere regarding the coach's race.

But the NBA has been subject to periodic criticism. In 1992, National Basketball Players Association Executive Director Charles Grantham wrote a commentary in the *Chicago Sun Times* titled "NBA: A Land of Unequal Opportunity."[17] There Grantham observed that although 75 percent of the league's players were black, the NBA had not hired a black head coach in two years. In that two-year span, twenty-five head coaches had been hired, and all of them were white. Grantham went on to note, "Not only were [the positions] all filled by whites, but in most of these cases the most qualified black prospects weren't even offered interviews for the vacancies."[18]

Why the Need for Representative Numbers of African-Americans in the Front Office?

Many of the same issues that make African-American ownership important also apply to front-office management.[19] The value of diversity, for example, is just as important at these non-ownership levels. There are other strong managerial arguments in addition to diversity for increasing the number of African-Americans in front offices.

In coaching in particular there have been psychological reasons cited by African-American athletes and those who have studied them for favoring African-American coaches. A study of football players conducted during a three-year period from 1984 to 1986 by sports psychologist Mark H. Anshel concluded:

The subjects indicated unequivocally a preference toward the use of more subdued and individual mental preparation strategies than is usually experienced on a team basis. Rather than demonstrate the proper psychological state with boisterous vocal responses in the locker room, the black players in this study preferred to behave in a calm, low-key manner. Moreover, requiring all team members to prepare themselves for the game with identical mental strategies (e.g., a full-team mental imagery session or locker room cheering for psyching up) ignored individual needs.[20]

The basic point is that a person with similar life experiences, another African-American, is likely to have a better understanding of the African-American athlete on a personal level than is a white coach.

Alan Wertheimer would urge that one proceed with caution in jumping to this type of race-conscious hiring conclusion, even where possible managerial outcomes dictate otherwise.[21] Legal guidelines also scorn using race as a bona fide occupational qualification.[22] If the conclusion is that an African-American coach should be preferred due to studies such as the one cited, then where is the line drawn as to when race should be considered on a job application and when it should not? Wertheimer calls this race element a "reaction" qualification and lists several examples, including the following: "A shoe store owner must choose B (black) or W (white) as a salesman. B can fit shoes better, but because many customers are hostile to blacks, W will sell more shoes."[23] Wertheimer distinguishes between reaction qualifications and technical qualifications. He lists technical qualifications as including such "ordinary" qualifications as "strength, ability to solve problems, and coordination."[24]

The uneasy question raised by Wertheimer, an ongoing issue in addressing policies to deal with discrimination, is when is race consciousness appropriate—that is, when should the race of a candidate be taken into account? In sports the race factor should be recognized as the positive that it may be. This does not mean it automatically gives the edge to the African-American candidate over the white candidate; there are both white and black athletes who will benefit more greatly from the decision to hire a particular white coach. It is enough that sports grow to view the race of any coaching candidate not as negative but as potentially positive in psychological ways to

employees of the organization. This is the importance of color consciousness, as compared to color blindness. In other words, race consciousness in this selection makes sense particularly where the historic
underrepresentation of African-Americans in head coaching and managing positions exists. In the bundle of qualifications to consider in a
management candidate, race should be one of them. Race has always
been a factor, but one where being white was positive and African-
American negative. This reformed view would assist those African-
Americans striving for top positions in sports, where the perception of
the positive image is the "older white man." [25]

Wertheimer discusses whether hiring the best qualified candidate
ever means including the party's race as a factor. He observes that "a
preference by a member of a victimized group for members of that
group seems more legitimate . . . than a preference by members of a
dominant group for members of that group." [26] Wertheimer points to
history as the justification for allowing this preference, noting that "a
black's preference for a black policeman seems comparatively legitimate because there is a history of brutality by white policemen against
blacks." [27]

The end result should be a view that has been expressed by former
professional football player and present coach Bobby Hammond:

I think you need coaches who understand how players operate. I think that's
the key. White, green or indifferent, I hear about a guy who players love and
they play for him, that's what I want to hear. I don't want to hear because he's
black, he gets along with players. Well, what about the white players? What
about the Indian players? [28]

This level of diversity with an African-American in charge has been
illustrated at the NFL's Philadelphia Eagles. Prior to the hiring of
African-American Ray Rhodes as the head coach, the team had only
one African-American assistant coach. Under Rhodes, the staff includes three African-Americans, the most of any NFL franchise. [29]
Rhodes took no extreme actions in hiring, but the percentages are now
more representative of the NFL player population.

The same race consciousness should apply to off-the-field management personnel as well. These are the people who make the decisions

that impact the players, including who will be the head coach. The number of African-Americans in front offices will not increase, however, until the informal hiring networks are expanded to include African-Americans.

Affirmative Action as a Solution?

The Problem of Breaking Down Networks

The old boy networking cycle is not one that is readily broken. It will take some affirmative steps to bring greater diversity into the hiring networks. According to Mary Davis, the vice president of Human Resources for the NBA's Washington Bullets, "If you're starting off with a predominantly white male workforce and who they know and who they network with is predominantly other white males, that's what I think has happened in this business years ago and even now, but that just continued and they gave each other breaks, and up the ladder."[30]

But systems to break down this key barrier are not easily implemented. Even top level management has difficulty increasing diversity, particularly on the field. One Major League Baseball executive reported:

I can have a lot more influence, I do have a lot more influence about who we hire, and certainly about who we interview, for a front office job, including the manager, even at the upper level, than I would have over who's going to be our next first base coach. That is a, quote, baseball, close quote, decision, which means it's basically the general manager and ownership. And my own feeling is that the so-called old boy network is still—or remnants of it—is a lot stronger when you get into the true baseball positions.[31]

Affirmative action must be taken for more African-Americans to become a part of these hiring networks.

Public Opinion

The major problem with any affirmative action plan is the general lack of public support. A 1995 *Wall Street Journal*/NBC News poll found that the majority of Americans do not support such plans.[32] As Table 4 illustrates, 68 percent of all adults surveyed do not favor such plans.

There is no evidence indicating that the application of affirmative action to sports is viewed more favorably than its application in other sectors.

Forms of Affirmative Action

There are typically four forms of affirmative action: the concerted recruitment of an underrepresented group; the institution of training programs, such as diversity and sensitivity training; the modification of employment practices that promote the underutilization of underrepresented individuals; and the most popular conception of affirmative action, the preferential hiring and promotion of underrepresented groups.[33] Any of these forms or combinations of two or more may constitute an affirmative action program. The last and most extreme version is not needed in sports at this time. What are needed in sports are strategies to open the hiring networks.

Similar to the issues involving minority ownership, there is, absent overt acts of discrimination, likely no legal action that can force the owners to change their hiring practices. But as with the ownership area, assuming owners do not act independently, a commissioner can take a strong leadership role. Increasing the numbers of minorities in management and coaching positions in sports could be the flagship item on a league commissioner's agenda. The presentation of a meaningful plan for change, one incorporating strong affirmative action principles, could be a part of such an agenda.[34]

Randall Kennedy has defined affirmative action as a form of "social justice" given "as rather modest compensation for the long period of racial subordination suffered by blacks as a group."[35] Any affirmative action plan would both signal that a league is serious about reform and provide a road map for those owners who are interested in bringing about change and promoting diversity in league and franchise management. As discussed above, any such plan would have to be in place and pass legal scrutiny before race could be viewed in the bundle of qualifications.

Table 4: Affirmative Action Views

"Do you favor or oppose eliminating affirmative action based on race or gender in deciding admissions to state universities, hiring for government jobs and awarding federal contracts?"

Favor:	White Men	68%
	All Adults	61%
Oppose:	White Men	28%
	All Adults	32%

SOURCE: The *Wall Street Journal*/NBC News Poll, *Wall Street Journal*, January 24, 1995, A24.

One such plan was offered not by a league commissioner but by the Rainbow Coalition for Fairness in Athletics (RCFA). The Reverend Jesse Jackson and the RCFA presented the ten-point affirmative action plan, outlined in Table 5, to Major League Baseball in 1993.

The RCFA plan has much to offer. Without attempting to micromanage, it establishes a strong framework for change. It points the way for further development by the league and the teams, and establishes steps to increase diversity in the league. It is these specific, numerical mandates that may subject the plan to its greatest criticism. Even setting aside the merit question as applied to African-American candidates, the use of specific, numerical goals represents the type of affirmative action Americans largely disfavor. Increased diversity, individual-franchise affirmative action plans, and specific training are certainly moves in the right direction. The plan's outline lacks the methods of monitoring and enforcement, but the basic standards have merit.

By contrast, a plan made public by Major League Baseball owners shortly after the RCFA version was received, presented in Table 6, lacks the specificity in the RCFA proposal.

What is remarkable about this plan is that its eminently sensible contents should ultimately be acted on and not require a specially drafted agenda. Any successful plan must not merely be symbolic but also have actual substance, not the loosely stated goals presented by Major League Baseball. The Major League Baseball plan would be much more effective if it provided specific mandates regarding increasing the numbers of minority candidates and provided sanctions

Table 5: Rainbow Coalition for Fairness in Athletics Ten-Point Affirmative Action Plan

---

1. Plan community development programs and youth leagues.
2. Add three minority or women members to each team's board.
3. Develop three- to five-year affirmative action plans for team and league posts, including for umpires and broadcasting.
4. Purchase at least 20 percent of all goods and services from minority- or women-owned vendors.
5. Develop three- to five-year affirmative action plans for manufacturing, marketing, and merchandising through major league properties.
6. Form a committee to seek possible minority team ownership.
7. Include at least two minority candidates for all executive and managerial jobs.
8. Provide personal development and financial management training for players.
9. Provide "diversity and humanities training" for all owners and executives.
10. Appoint a vice president for organization development and diversity.

SOURCE: "Comparison of Baseball Affirmative-Action Plans," *USA Today*, March 30, 1993, 5C.

for teams that do not comply. Both the RCFA and Major League Baseball plans are examples of broad affirmative action policy.

Sports Affirmative Action Compared with That of Corporate America

The uniqueness of affirmative action in sports is that there so clearly is no basis for the white societal presumption of African-Americans being less qualified than whites. Affirmative action in sports should be concerned with access for those that do not normally have it. This is a question not of lack of merit but rather of a lack of opportunity.[36]

The rest of corporate America has been under pressure to have equality in hiring since the Civil Rights movement and legislation in the 1960s and 1970s. Some companies responded after legal action; others responded voluntarily for moral reasons or as part of a public relations program. Even with years of this type of activity, however, one still will not find an African-American chairman of a Fortune 500 corporation.[37] A March 1995 *New York Times* report shows that only 8 percent of high-level managers in corporations are African-American.[38] Although the percentages in sports management are similar, one should remain cognizant of the higher percentages of African-Americans in the sports industry as a whole. From a legal standpoint,

Table 6: Major League Baseball's Plan Regarding Minority Issues

1. Include minority candidates for jobs throughout their organizations "within a reasonable time frame."
2. Attempt to attract minorities as investors and have "appropriate minority participation" on their boards of directors.
3. Seek minority-owned vendors, including doctors, lawyers, and bankers.
4. Insist nonminority vendors be equal opportunity employers.
5. Make new efforts to attract minorities as fans.
6. Have their employees undergo sensitivity training "unless clearly unnecessary."
7. Increase community and charitable activities.

SOURCE: "Comparison of Baseball Affirmative-Action Plans," *USA Today*, March 30, 1993, 5C.

the larger numbers relative to other industries prepared to move into management are significant. The denominator is higher.

Methods for Opening Sports Hiring Networks

Organized Networking

■ *The Baseball Network.* As was noted in the Preface, after the Al Campanis commentary, a group called the Baseball Network was formed to attempt to inject minorities who normally would not be a part of the old boys' network into that networking structure. The organization attempted on an ad hoc basis to make the various teams aware of minority candidates whenever job opportunities opened so that those who normally would not have been considered (not being close friends or having a previous relationship with the decision maker) would be at least a step closer to an interview. The informal, not-for-profit organization lost much of its drive when its executive director died in an automobile accident in 1989. But its goal, a formalization of the normally excluded in networking, would serve the interests of all of the professional sports leagues.

■ *The Achieving Coaching Excellence Conference.* Another organized networking success was the conference "Achieving Coaching Excellence," presented by Stanford University and its football team's head coach Bill Walsh in 1994. The stated goal of the four-day conference was to enhance the teaching skills of black football coaches, as well as their career ambitions. The informal goal was greater exposure of talented African-American coaches to networks that would lead to head coaching positions, including contact with those who make hiring decisions. The end result was the hiring of five participants as head coaches at the college and professional levels within a year after the conference.[39]

■ *NFL Coaches Fellowship Program.* With a similar aim, the National Football League in the late 1980s instituted a coaching internship program. The program now brings entire coaching staffs primarily from historically black colleges and universities, to work with NFL staffs. As a result of this league-instituted program, approximately twenty of two hundred participants have been hired by NFL franchises as assistant coaches. The internship is essentially a four-week interview.[40] The program has evolved to this more formalized state from its beginnings when the African-American participants were little more than fans with practice field privileges.

There is a negative associated with this or any type of internship program. One could ask, and some African-American college coaches have asked, "Why do I have to do this when my white counterparts don't?" This is a fair question that highlights the additional sacrifices African-Americans must make to attain their goals. Instead of spending four weeks with their families in the college off-season, it has almost become a requirement that they participate in the fellowship program, for little monetary compensation.

■ *PGA Tour Internship Program.* Another illustration of opening hiring networks to non-former pro athletes and coaches is the Professional Golfers' Association (PGA) Tour internship program. This program focuses on minority undergraduates who have an interest in a career in sports; no golf experience is required. The internship possibilities include work in public relations, communications, data processing, and on-site promotions. According to the consultant for the PGA program, Ralph Stringer, "The one thing that we really try to stress is the business opportunities that are being missed out on, because everybody thinks of it as just a game that they see on the television, but there's an awful lot going around there . . . marketing positions, the sales positions, promotions, that have been untouched."[41] Stringer attempted to convince other professional sports leagues to institute similar programs. None were interested.

■ *College Sports Management Programs.* Improvement can also come with greater involvement of African-Americans in college sports management and internship programs. Both are certainly feeders to higher-level positions. In many instances the sports management programs are where the teams and leagues go to look for interns. Thus increasing African-American enrollment in those institutions is particularly important.

■ *Involvement with African-American Professional Associations.* Along the same lines, members of sports entities can become involved with African-American business associations such as the local Black Chamber of Commerce, the NAACP, or the Urban League. The goal obviously is to bring in those who would not normally be in the informal networks and to increase the comfort level of those between whom there is no historical relationship.

Opening Networks with External Pressure

External groups such as the RCFA should take a lesson from the Reverend Leon Sullivan and his efforts against apartheid in South Africa.[42] In the 1970s, Sullivan drafted a list of principles focused on racial equality in South Africa. He approached individual companies and asked them to become signatories. The program was voluntary, and companies were graded, based on their compliance, at level 1, 2, or 3. Sullivan's efforts then focused on making known the names of those companies that signed on to fight against apartheid and those that did not. The Sullivan Principles were credited with prompting debate, compromise, action, and change.[43]

Similarly, if the RCFA is unsuccessful in getting an entire league to sign onto its or some other organization's plan against racism in sports, the appropriate step may be to approach individual franchise owners. Although the owners tend to be a difficult group to break apart, this may be an area where individuals would want to stand out as unique. As more sign on, none will want to be seen the lone holdout.

Opening up the networks may not compel change, but it certainly is the appropriate interim step. Brent Benner, an executive recruiter in the sports industry, explains, "Hire your best buddy but get exposure to others. I'm surprised at how many times people do not want to look at a resume. That's how it's done in other businesses. So what, so they interview a couple of more candidates."[44]

In an optimistic view, Jimmy Lee Solomon, an African-American who is the director of Major League Baseball's minor league operations, said:

Things will change when two things happen. First, about ten years from now there will be a bunch of athletes just forty years old or so with $30 to $40 million in their pockets, and they'll need something to do. They will then go back to what they love. They'll be involved in buying a team, and a management position like president or vice president will be part of the deal.

Second, in five to ten years there will be enough time for whites around the league to develop a comfort level with guys like me. After a period of years it won't be so tough.[45]

This all points to the need for commissioner and owner action. To change the reluctance on the part of these parties pressure must be brought, externally as well as internally from athletes with enough leverage to cause change. Unlike the ownership level with its problems of financing and the legal protections that protect clubbiness, much can be done fairly rapidly and with the help of strong leadership to increase the numbers of African-Americans in front-office management and coaching positions.

The Affirmative Action Debate in America: Its Applicability to Sports

The Quota Debate

A review of the corporate experience with affirmative action shows that the more successful organizations in terms of meeting affirmative action goals are those that have clear commitment from the top. This commitment is represented by the allocation of resources to affirmative action and the tying of success in accomplishing greater diversity to the organization's managerial-performance review and reward systems. Management must view affirmative action as a self-correcting mechanism that helps the entity to resist its own conservatism and biases regarding the employment of minorities, rather than as a process to hire minorities who are unqualified. Any program attempting to increase diversity within an organization must be designed to be promoted and executed as a plan that benefits the entire organization.

In the case of sports, it will not be enough simply to set goals; the plans must identify within each league and team the persons who will take responsibility and be held accountable for their implementation. The commissioners of the respective leagues, as well as the team owners, must anticipate the resistance to change that always lurks behind any sudden push forward, particularly with regard to race, such as that characterized by the negative responses to affirmative action offered by Walter Williams. Williams and others equate any affirmative action plan with a "quota system." The negativism associated with quotas has become one of the leading methods of attack against any corrective system. Williams writes:

The civil rights vision, calling for numerical equality through racial quotas, ignores some of the real impediments faced by blacks. It is also immoral and illegitimate in a free society, and it heightens racial antagonism. Racial quotas, like other forms of government allocation, are a zero-sum game, where one person's gain necessarily requires another person to lose. Poker is a voluntary example and theft an involuntary example of the zero-sum game. In either case, one person's benefit necessarily comes at the expense of another.[46]

One source of this fear of quotas is Justice Sandra Day O'Connor's opinion for a plurality in *Watson v. Fort Worth Bank & Trust*, where she stated:

Respondent and the United States are thus correct when they argue that extending disparate impact analysis to subjective employment practices has the potential to create a Hobson's choice for employers and thus to lead in practice to perverse results. If quotas and preferential treatment become the only cost-effective means of avoiding expensive litigation and potentially catastrophic liability, such measures will be widely adopted. The prudent employer will be careful to ensure that its programs are discussed in euphemistic terms, but will be equally careful to ensure that the quotas are met. Allowing the evolution of disparate impact analysis to lead to this result would be contrary to Congress' clearly expressed intent, and it should not be the effect of our decision today.[47]

Despite the words of commentators such as Williams, there does not appear to be a misunderstanding about the role of quotas and preferences in the law. In *Watson* again, O'Connor wrote that the use of the tandem of quotas and preferences "*can* violate the Constitution."[48] According to William Gould, the Court has used its judgment to approve quotas and preferences in some cases and to disapprove them in others.[49]

Gould's analysis and O'Connor's statement that quotas and preferences can violate the Constitution outline the present day parameters within which any affirmative action plan may operate. Any plan will be subject to scrutiny and, if challenged, may or may not be approved by a court. With this type of resistance in mind, the sports commissioners should be sure that these plans are not left at their door as their responsibility alone. The leaders in sports should assert as fervently as possible that the problems of racism and discrimination still exist, even in sports. Some of their owner colleagues and those in management have quotes on the record that show this to be true. The statistics confirm the existence of disparity as well.

The Role of Those in Sports Power Positions in the Debate

It is important that the commissioners and franchise owners see the hiring of more minorities not just as a social issue but also as a managerial one. By tying rewards to performance and by casting the new effort as a particular league's remedy to its own, rather than minorities', shortcomings, the changes stand a chance of being viewed positively, rather than as yet another minority entitlement. The response from the league and owners to quota arguments must incorporate the broad benefits of diversity, the realities of the skills and capabilities of African-Americans, and the cultural history of the sports industry.

In implementing meaningful affirmative action plans, sports leaders can prepare for one major problem that has confronted private industry: the inevitable unanswered question of how long the affirmative action plan must stay in place. The answer is problematic, since the law mandates that these programs be remedial and finite.[50] To comply with the law, as well as to confront claims that racism has ended or been corrected, the sports leagues should establish in advance that any plan adopted must stay in place for a lengthy period of time, at the same time avoiding nullification by courts because there is no finite time frame established. The plans should be designed as a constantly monitoring corrective measure—a slow intravenous drip for the sports business racism and discrimination problems.

Because affirmative action programs in theory should be ended some day, there has been much debate, led in many instances by African-American conservatives, about dismantling existing affirmative action programs immediately and not initiating any new ones.[51] In response Cornel West has written:

The new black conservatives assume that without affirmative action programs, white Americans will make choices on merit rather than on race. Yet they have adduced no evidence for this. Most Americans realize that job-hiring choices are made both on reasons of merit and on personal grounds. And it is this personal dimension that is often influenced by racist perceptions. Therefore the pertinent debate regarding black hiring is never "merit vs. race" but whether hiring decisions will be based on merit, influenced by race-bias against blacks, or on merit, influenced by race-bias, but with special consideration for minorities and women, as mandated by law. In light of actual employment practices, the black conservative rhetoric about race-free hiring criteria (usually coupled with a call for dismantling affirmative action mechanisms) does no more than justify actual practices of racial discrimination.[52]

Affirmative action plans must continue to be implemented in order to prevent a return to what has historically been the status quo. Thus the leaders in sports have a double sale to make: first, the affirmative action plans, and second, their long-term status. This battle will be difficult. These programs are subject to immediate criticism from other quarters in addition to those already cited.

North Carolina Senator Jesse Helms articulated the view of many regarding affirmative action in his come-from-behind defeat of Harvey Gantt in the 1990 senatorial elections in that state. In the final days of the campaign, Helms ran a political advertisement, which has come to be known as the "white hands" commercial, that displayed a white man's hand balling up an apparent rejection letter from an employer. The voice-over said, "You needed that job, and you were the best qualified, but it had to go to a minority because of a racial quota."[53] The forces fighting against the role of affirmative action in private industry are strong.

The fear articulated by the Helms advertisement and by other persons is that of unfair advantage. The idea that one group is getting something for nothing is the loftiest barrier against valid reparation programs. This fear, coupled with the presence of racism, makes any formal affirmative action program difficult to institute. Dr. Martin Luther King, Jr., had occasion to comment on this fear of unfair advantage and said:

Whenever this issue of compensatory or preferential treatment for the Negro is raised, some of our friends recoil in horror. The Negro should be granted equality, they agree; but he should ask nothing more. On the surface, this appears reasonable, but it is not realistic. For it is obvious that if a man is entered at the starting line in a race three hundred years after another man, the first would have to perform some impossible feat in order to catch up with his fellow runner.[54]

To promote affirmative action in sports, the commissioners and owners must articulate the historical diversity shortcomings of their sports, the fact that racism is deeply ingrained in the culture of sports. The view of Professor Charles Lawrence that permanent unconscious racism exists in all of us must also be conveyed.[55]

There is much in the scholarly literature on affirmative action to divide the two parties impacted on most by such regulations—white males as "innocent victims" and African-Americans as "victims of societal discrimination." The presumption is that the white male is the innocent victim because he was minding his own business when he had to pay for the historical discriminatory acts of another. Most persons in organizations where affirmative action plans have been implemented were not even adults when *Brown v. Board of Education* ordered the desegregation of American public schools in 1954. These innocent victims find it difficult to understand why they should have to bear the burden of the sins of those who lived in another time. They have further difficulty understanding why those who were not the victims of legal discrimination should be the beneficiaries of legal largesse. On this subject Patricia Williams has written:

When every resource of a wealthy nation is put to such destructive ends [dehumanization of blacks], it will take more than a few generations to mop up the mess. . . . Thus generalized notions of innocence and guilt have little place in the struggle for transcendence; there is no blame among the living for the dimensions of this historic crime, this national tragedy.[56]

The professional sports leagues have their own racially problematic histories. The familiar cry is "I never owned any slaves," or more specifically in sports, "I never discriminated against anyone." The African-American may not be able to show any direct, personal discrimination, but he or she has suffered from living in this country where there has been discrimination in the past. As a result of this type of analysis, Supreme Court Justice Potter Stewart pointed to providing benefits to African-Americans under affirmative action as "the creation once again by government of privileges based on birth."[57] One commentator analyzed this to mean, "By this analogy the black beneficiaries of affirmative action are like the European noblemen of the Old World, enjoying great and utterly unearned advantage at the expense of the whites, who are like the feudal serfs."[58] This is yet another barrier that affirmative action plans must overcome.

Affirmative action plans should be more palatable in sports than in other industries for a number of reasons. Any Snyderian fear of whites being forced out due to diversity programs is even more unrealistic in sports than in other industries. Jimmy "the Greek" Snyder's fear is reminiscent of Gunnar Myrdal's observation that "when the feed-box is empty the horses will bite each other."[59] But in sports the amount of feed is not decreasing. As was observed in chapter 1, while other businesses are downsizing, the sports industry continues to expand, with the addition of new franchises in all of the major sports leagues in recent years.[60] The number of jobs available in sports continues to increase; what needs to change are the traditional hiring practices used to fill these jobs. Strong affirmative action policies can encourage this change.

Implementing programs and bringing owners on board is a difficult balancing act. One of the problems that can occur if the owners feel "forced" to change was expressed by Tony Perez, the former manager of the Cincinnati Reds. He was hired shortly after the flap over Reds owner Marge Schott's statements, reported in chapter 1. Perez, a black Latino, was fired forty-four games into his first season. He said, "I feel I've been used. I don't know if I was used because I was a big name in town or a minority. But the way they did it, I'm not happy about it."[61] The benefits of diversity must be clearly understood, and those who take action must be active advocates of the process.

Any sports affirmative action plan must be carefully designed to actually work. Some affirmative action plans in other industries have been ineffective. This is true in the American experience of creating programs either to bring about or to preserve equity even at the end of the twentieth century.

■ *Countering "Reverse Racism."* The conscientious managers of sports enterprises can argue with merit for the need to move cautiously in establishing any affirmative action program. It is the nature of the law that it is illegal to discriminate against any race, and the argument that affirmative action programs are, in fact, a form of discrimination is not lost on their critics.[62] Contrary to the views expressed by some scholars that the antidiscrimination laws should be used to assist African-Americans specifically, the laws are generally intended and interpreted to disallow discrimination against any race. This creates the obvious problem of inventing ways to help one race without harming another. This situation is the source of the creation of the terms *reverse discrimination* and *reverse racism* in response to affirmative action plans that have not been constructed within the guidelines of the law.[63] Stanley Fish writes of those who view affirmative action plans as a form of reverse racism:

"Reverse racism" is a cogent description of affirmative action only if one considers the cancer of racism to be morally and medically indistinguishable from the therapy we apply to it. A cancer is an invasion of the body's equilibrium, and so is chemotherapy; but we do not decline to fight the disease because the medicine we employ is also disruptive of normal functioning. Strong illness, strong remedy; the formula is as appropriate to the health of the body politic as it is to that of the body proper.[64]

Both the disease of racism and the treatment might be considered bad medicine.

■ *Countering Paternalism.* Another criticism of affirmative action is that it is paternalistic and places a stamp of approval on the concept that African-Americans are inferior and need help to succeed. Some commentators hold the view that this image is too dear a price to pay, even if a few African-Americans do benefit from affirmative action programs. The programs create a "presumption" that any black who succeeds does so at the expense of a more qualified white and that, were it not for the program, the African-American would not succeed. T. Alexander Aleinikoff provides an example from the University of Michigan Law School student newspaper. He cites an article wherein a white student calls for the abolition of a program at the school that provides academic and nonacademic support to nonwhite students. The white student wrote that the program "implicitly brands every minority student with a scarlet 'D.' I can't believe so many bright people allow themselves to be insulted and stigmatized in such an obnoxious way." Broadening his attack to reach affirmative action programs in general, the student stated, "I see stirrings of resentment everywhere. If a black student makes a silly classroom comment (and we all do), some white students—not racists, mind you—will think in their heart of hearts about affirmative admissions policies."[65]

The truth is that the qualifications of African-Americans will always be questioned, whether formal programs in place or not. This is part of the nature of the racism and discrimination that have been present in this country since its earliest days and are a permanent part of our culture.

The Affirmative Action Experience in Education

One sector that has long been a testing ground for affirmative action is academia. The first major Supreme Court case addressing the issue of affirmative action was *Regents of the University of California v. Bakke.*[66] The case challenged the admissions program at the Medical School of the University of California at Davis, which specifically reserved sixteen spaces in its hundred-person first-year class for minorities.

In addressing preferential admissions programs, Shelby Steele has criticized undergraduate admissions efforts as having a lack of impact because of the low graduation rates for African-American students. He cites statistics showing that "a full six years after admission, only 26 to 28 percent of blacks graduate from college."[67] Additional problems in academia, particularly a program at Duke University, illuminate the affirmative action issue further.

Duke University moved forward with a program to increase the number not of black students (at least, not directly) but of black faculty members. The program, initiated in 1988, essentially mandated that by the fall of 1993, each of the academic departments at the university must have added an additional black faculty member. The school has fifty-six departments and sixteen hundred faculty members. This would have been a monumental step. When the fall of 1993 arrived, there was a total, net gain of only eight blacks on the university's faculty.[68]

The criticism of Duke's program has come from many sides. Certainly, the mere presence of a numerical goal is suspect to many. But that is probably the least of the problems with which the plan supporters are now confronted. The problem of a "royalty" status given to African-Americans is certainly present. The program has even resulted in a lawsuit involving an African-American faculty member in the political science department and one of his white colleagues, both of whom were denied tenure in the same year. In a unique affirmative action lawsuit, the white faculty member has said that he was denied tenure because the university desired to avoid the possible repercussions of granting it to the white and not to the African-American.[69]

The major distinction that can be drawn between Duke and other major universities on the one hand and the sports world on the other is that in sports there exists a huge pool of candidates, uniquely *qualified* candidates, whereas the pool of black, and especially African-American, Ph.D. holders is limited. Whereas internship and training programs for African-Americans are a somewhat distasteful proposition in sports, the same types of programs make sense in academia, to increase the numbers of Ph.D. candidates. The feeling of many African-American job candidates in sports—both athlete and nonathlete—is "Why should I have to go through some special training program when my white counterparts have moved in and out of the system for so long without such programs?" Again, the decision as to who gets the job in sports is largely subjective. In academics there is generally at least the threshold qualification of a particular degree.[70]

The notion that African-Americans are not qualified is quickly dispelled at all levels in sports by looking at the qualifications of the whites who hold or have held the power positions. On the field, Pete Rose, Lou Piniella, and Larry Bowa are just a few examples of whites who went straight from the playing field to managing in Major League Baseball. Dan Duquette, Kevin Malone, Bill Bavasi, Jim Bowden, Ed Lynch, and Randy Smith are examples of the young white men, some just barely in their thirties, in general manager positions in the early 1990s.[71] David Shula, the youthful Cincinnati Bengals head coach, is another example of a white fast-tracker. At a higher level, there are plenty of African-American lawyers who could have followed the paths of league commissioners David Stern and Paul Tagliabue. Both men have proven to be outstanding commissioners, but their opportunities began when they were attorneys for their respective leagues at major law firms, and law firms are notoriously poor performers in their own right in hiring and retaining minorities.[72]

The Duke University scenario is an example of the power a commissioner might exert. Under the various forms of the "best interests" powers granted to commissioners they may deliver edicts mandating minority hiring. The best interests clause in its broadest interpretation both mandates and allows a commissioner to take unilateral action in the best interests of the sport.[73] This right in baseball grew out of the Black Sox scandal, which immortalized "Shoeless" Joe Jackson in the 1919 World Series. When the commissioner's office was formed to resurrect public confidence in the sport after the Chicago White Sox allegedly "threw" the World Series, the owners gave the commissioner the power to act unilaterally. Other sports have more specifically outlined the duties of the commissioner in their leagues. In football, for example, when the duties are not specifically outlined in the National Football League Constitution, approval for actions must be obtained from the executive committee.[74] Over the years commissioners have exercised broad authority, from banning Pete Rose from baseball for life, to preventing Charles Finley from trading away star players from his World Series champion Oakland Athletics for solely financial reasons, to the suspension of star athletes in all leagues for gambling and drug abuse.[75] Although this power has been revised and reformed by the various leagues over the years, an aggressive established or incoming commissioner could certainly assert the authority, particularly in negotiating his or her incoming contractual arrangement.[76]

Conclusion: Selling Affirmative Action to the Sports Industry and Public

Affirmative action is still necessary because appropriate standards of merit have not yet become the sole determinant in society of who gets the job. This is particularly the case in the business of sports. African-Americans also appear to be less likely to receive a meritocratic evaluation than are whites. For affirmative action in the sports industry or in any other sector of society to be successful, there must be evidence for the so-called innocent victims that such programs are for the good of all involved, that diversity is important to the business. An example of this kind of evidence is the effect of cutout curbs in our cities today, put in place to improve wheelchair accessibility. Society overall has benefited through easier access for bicycles, strollers, and for making deliveries on foot, as well as for wheelchairs.

In sports it is difficult to articulate what this overall societal benefit would be. The sense of diversity as the right thing to do has not been enough for all people in other segments of society. The convincing argument by those in the power positions in sports must be that diversity is good for the sport; there has been much racism in the past, and the strong medicine of corrective change is necessary. One commentator has written on the unique perspective African-Americans bring to a situation:

> The possibility of a special burden born of "the experience of being black in America" is anything but mysterious to blacks. Blacks fully understand that to be an African American is in many respects to be uniquely branded for failure. It is to grow up constantly being told, in the schools and in the streets, that blacks are not as bright as whites and are not academically inclined.[77]

Only an African-American can inject into an industry the lessons learned from carrying this burden. Further, the sports owners who desire greater profits should see the African-Americans who do not attend sporting events en masse as an untapped source of greater profits. African-Americans at the management level in sports may better be able to find ways to attract African-Americans, and visible on-the-field management personnel may attract more African-American fans. Much like Coca-Cola searching for a way to increase overall consumption by getting consumers to drink their beverage for breakfast (the one traditional American soft-drink-free time of day), greater employment of African-Americans may be a step in increasing attendance. This need increases in significance in light of a study released in 1994 that found that African-American spending power was growing faster than the spending power of the United States as a whole.[78]

The NBA has certainly seen continued success with increased racial diversity at all levels. At the same time, the public relations perception of which league is the fairest from a race-relations standpoint clearly singles out the NBA. The league has consistently received high marks from the Northeastern University's Center for the Study of Sport in

Society in its annual evaluation of the racial progress made by individual leagues.[79] The dollars-and-cents translation is that African-Americans attend NBA games, whereas they tend not to attend baseball games. Although 90 percent of all professional sports league competition tickets tend to be sold, even with the present low African-American attendance rate, the evidence of the NBA's success in increasing African-American attendance may be used by league commissioners as an incentive for individual team owners to review and revise their hiring policies. African-Americans may be the group to target to sell the 10 percent of tickets that tend to be available.[80]

It will take a strong administration to lead a league in the direction of greater diversity. This is the appropriate stand for an important business to take in society today.

Color-Blind Propositions: The Collegiate Ranks

> This report may be just another indication that opportunities are being taken away from youngsters, and many more black youngsters in particular. If you want to have a great graduation rate, just keep raising the standards.
> —John Chaney, Temple University basketball coach, discussing improved National Collegiate Athletic Association graduation rates

> When we read about a proposition, and we were not involved in discussing or writing the proposition, that is insulting.
> —The Reverend Jesse Jackson

The Issues: Initial Eligibility Rules and College Front Office Positions

Just as with professional sports, the college ranks have had their share of Al Campanis-type statements. In 1968 the athletic director at the University of Texas at El Paso told *Sports Illustrated*, "In general, the nigger athlete is a little hungrier, and we have been blessed with having some real outstanding ones. We think they've done a lot for us, and we think we've done a lot for them."[1] Although the statement was made nearly thirty years ago, the trail of racism runs as clearly through collegiate athletics as through the pros.[2]

There are two race issues of principal concern at the collegiate level. The first is the concept of the student-athlete experience as a route of academic opportunity for African-Americans. The important matter in

Table 7: Initial Eligibility Landmarks

1889 Harvard University President Charles W. Eliot proposes reforms that would ban freshmen from intercollegiate competition and would restrict student-athletes to three years of eligibility.

1903 Harvard bans freshmen from athletics competition; many other institutions follow in 1906.

1906 NCAA founded; "home rule" gives members the latitude to enforce their own eligibility standards.

1939 NCAA votes to make freshmen ineligible for its championships.

1947 Sanity code adopted.

1950 Sanity code abandoned.

1965 NCAA "1.6 rule" approved (requires the incoming student-athletes be able to predict a minimum college grade point average of 1.6 on a 4.0 scale).

1972 NCAA reinstates freshman eligibility in all sports.

1973 1.6 rule rescinded; replaced with an eligibility standard that requires a high school student-athlete to have graduated with at least a 2.0 grade point average (GPA).

1983 Proposition 48 approved (minimums of 2.0 GPA in eleven core courses and 700 SAT or 15 ACT).

1992 Proposition 16 approved (initial eligibility index keyed to 2.0 GPA/900 SAT and 2.5 GPA/700 SAT, thirteen core courses).

1995 Proposition 16 reaffirmed with sliding scale dipping to 2.5 GPA/700 SAT or 17 ACT. Partial qualifiers allowed to receive athletically related financial aid. (See Tables 8 and 9.) Partial qualifiers allowed to practice but not compete during first year in residence.

SOURCE: *NCAA News* (January 4, 1995): 21, as revised and updated by author.

this area—which is influenced significantly by the pre-college educational experiences of prospective student-athletes—is the initial eligibility or academic admission rules. The key question is whether the present rules, and the often-contemplated changes to them, provide a basis for maintaining high academic standards in our colleges and universities without negatively impacting on the number of African-Americans who are eligible to attend these institutions with athletic scholarships. As Table 7 illustrates, revising the initial eligibility standards is almost an annual topic at NCAA conventions. And as Table 8 sets forth, new standards are scheduled to go into effect yet again in August of 1996.[3] An NCAA study shows that since the implementation of Proposition 48 in 1986, the percentage of scholarships allocated to black freshmen has dropped from 27.6 percent to 23.2 percent.[4] The NCAA forecasts, however, that there will be a statistical upturn. The long-term impact on African-American enrollment must clearly be reviewed carefully.

The other major sports-race issue at the college level is much the same as that at the professional level: the absence of African-Americans in the power positions and how to increase the representation of African-Americans in these roles. In a pattern similar to the skewed statistics at the professional level, in 1994 approximately 64 percent of the starting players in college football were African-Americans.[5] Forty-nine percent of every football team was African-American.[6] But of the 107 Division I-A schools participating in what is considered to be big-time football, only four had African-American athletic directors, and only three had African-American head coaches in football.[7] In 1995 the number of coaches doubled to six.

Both the initial eligibility and the hiring issues were brought to the attention of the public by threatened boycotts of college basketball in the 1993–1994 season by the Black Coaches Association.[8] Although negotiations averted the threatened boycott, these problems remain unresolved. The disparities in employment, however, are being examined by the federal government; the Department of Labor is investigating the hiring practices of twelve major universities.[9] The investigation of the universities comes in response to a letter sent on behalf of the Rainbow Coalition for Fairness in Athletics (RCFA) by the Reverend Jesse Jackson to Attorney General Janet Reno and Education Secretary Richard W. Riley, citing "a legacy of racism and sexism in intercollegiate athletics."[10] The letter, which specifically identified the universities of Arizona, Arkansas, Florida, and Duke—basketball's "Final Four" teams in 1994—and eight other schools, was referred to the Labor Department's Office of Federal Contract Compliance Programs. In a letter to Jackson, the Department of Labor wrote that compliance reviews would be conducted at the colleges over the next year.[11]

Initial Eligibility Rules

For those who attain the power positions in professional sports, a substantial amount of the training generally took place in the National

Collegiate Athletic Association. Playing at the college level may lead to the pros and opportunities to progress up the sports-business administrative ladder. It also often leads to graduate assistant positions, which in turn may lead to college coaching positions and eventually to positions in the pros. The latter path is certainly the exception, but it is more often available only to those who have participated in college sports. As few as the opportunities for advancement into professional sports administrative positions may be, they are almost nonexistent without collegiate experience.

Some student-athletes have used the opportunity that athletic scholarships have provided to obtain a quality education and excel in non-sports-related fields. But for the athletic scholarship, a university education and the student-athlete experience may not have been possible for some of these individuals.

Since the beginning of college sports there has been friction between the role of athletics and academic study in colleges and universities. In a Carnegie Foundation study of intercollegiate athletics in 1929, the threshold questions were "What relation has this astonishing athletic display to the work of an intellectual agency like a university? How do students, devoted to study, find either the time or the money to stage so costly a performance?"[12] There are still no satisfactory responses to these queries. In the past two decades some dramatic steps have been taken to define more clearly the role of athletics in American institutions of higher learning. Many of the changes flow from the reform-minded Knight Commission recommendations.[13] Historically, as Table 7 indicates, a number of attempts at reform have been made.

In the early 1900s there were "tramp" athletes who went from school to school over several seasons, taking the best offer to play in various sports—one year at Yale and the next at Harvard.[14] Athletes were lured from schools with such enticements as all-expenses-paid vacations to the vacation paradise of the time, Havana, Cuba.[15] A college degree was not always on the agenda of the athlete of that era. Initial NCAA reforms fought to eliminate the student who had no academic record whatsoever, to prevent participation in collegiate sports without progress toward a degree.

Later years saw reform attempts as extreme as eliminating all but need-based scholarships in 1947.[16] If the athlete and his family had no financial need, then no athletic scholarship could be offered, no matter the level of talent. During the brief era of this "sanity code," athletic scholarships were actually eliminated and monetary awards were based on financial need alone. This led many schools to cheat by giving under-the-table scholarships or other payments based on athletic abilities.[17] The sanity code was short-lived. Once it was clear that the winning schools were those that could beat the system by finding ways to pay athletes based on talent, regardless of the rules, athletic scholarships were reinstated.[18]

In 1965 the NCAA shifted away from its traditional "home rule" policy of admissions and adopted minimum eligibility standards for all NCAA student athletes.[19] The home rule policy had allowed schools to determine a student-athlete's eligibility based solely on the eligibility rules for each individual institution. The 1965 rule required students to "predict," based on their high school records, a college grade point average of 1.6, a grade in the traditional C − /D + range.[20] The prediction was made by a formula using high school grades or high school rank and the student's score on either the Scholastic Aptitude (later "Assessment") Test (SAT) or the American College Test (ACT).[21]

The 1.6 rule was repealed in 1973, and student athletes were required only to attain a minimum of a 2.0 grade point average from high school for eligibility.[22] A concern during that time was the variation in grading policies across the country. Was an A in rural Oklahoma the same as an A in a New York public high school? Had the star athlete in Tucson been given a passing grade by a basketball-fan faculty member? The standardized tests, SAT and ACT, loomed as the means to establish a uniform measure of academic capabilities.

It was not until the NCAA rule changes in 1983 that questions of racism consistently began to be raised in connection with these eligibility rules. The questions of whether the rules have a harsher impact on African-Americans and whether there is some intent to discriminate against African-Americans student-athletes, have only intensified over the years.[23]

Proposition 48

Proposition 48, officially NCAA Bylaw 14.3, initially required student-athletes to attain a minimum grade point average (GPA) in an eleven-course core curriculum that mandated courses in math, English, natural sciences, and social sciences.[24] Additionally, students were required to achieve a minimum combined score of 700 out of 1600 on the Scholastic Aptitude (Assessment) Test or a score of 15 on the American College Test.[25] Star college players such as Chris Washburn and John "Hot Rod" Williams were the types of athletes who caused the NCAA to change to this rule. Both had a combined score of 470 on the SAT, but both were recruited by over one hundred schools. The average combined SAT score at North Carolina State University, where Washburn ultimately enrolled, was 1020, and at Tulane University, where Williams enrolled, it was 1120.[26]

Proposition 48 has been strongly criticized by members of the African-American community from its inception in 1983. The criticism is not only for the projected negative impact on African-American enrollment but also for the lack of inclusion of African-Americans in the original creation of the rule, as the epigraph quotation from the Reverend Jesse Jackson at the beginning of this chapter indicates. The absence of African-Americans, as well as the absence of representation from historically black colleges and universities, on the ad hoc NCAA committee that first proposed the rule led Jesse Stone, a former Louisiana Supreme Court judge and dean of the Southern University Law School in Baton Rouge, Louisiana, to call the new standards "patently racist."[27] This was the mood that surrounded the creation of rules which the NCAA stated were designed to "assert the supremacy of academic values" in college sports and to "preserve the integrity of the NCAA and of our [college] institutions."[28]

The freshman class of 1986–1987 was the first Proposition 48 class. The first-year student-athletes entered their respective colleges and universities by satisfying Proposition 48's eligibility requirements. The graduation rate of that class was 57 percent, an increase of 6 percent over the pre-Proposition 48 classes of 1983, 1984, and 1985. The average graduation rate for all students in the freshman class of 1986–1987 was 55 percent. Even more dramatic than the 6 percent overall increase in athlete graduation rates, supporters maintain, is a 9 percent increase in the graduation rate for black student athletes.[29]

It is this identified success in increased graduation rates that has made Proposition 48 in the past and will continue to make it in the future a prime candidate for further tinkering. The NCAA membership voted to make Proposition 48 standards even more restrictive at the NCAA convention in 1992.[30] The members voted to increase the number of core courses required, from eleven to thirteen. A sliding scale was also introduced, correlating GPA with SAT score. The standards should certainly be considered even more restrictive, as an athlete with a 2.0 GPA is required to have a combined score of 900 on the SAT to be eligible to play as a freshman, compared with the previous 700 SAT score.

The statistic that has not received as much attention as the declared increase in graduation rates under Proposition 48 is how many students the rule may have negatively affected, that is, how many students who do not meet the Proposition 48 standards might have graduated in spite of a low high school grade point average or standardized test score. According to Richard Lapchick of the Northeastern University's Center for the Study of Sport in Society, "If Proposition 48 had been in use in 1981, 69 percent of all black males would have been ineligible. But 54 percent of those athletes eventually graduated. Clearly they had the skills all along, they just needed to be developed."[31] Had it been in use at the time, Proposition 48 would have deprived that group of African-American males of an opportunity to earn a college degree. The missed opportunity is one not just of showcasing athletic talents but of exposure to the academic opportunities in which all college students share. Previously more relaxed rules gave students who might not have otherwise had the opportunity to excel the chance to do so. Today those 54 percent would be what are commonly referred to as "Proposition 48 casualties." Not meeting the requirements not only causes the athlete to be ineligible to compete (and in various past proposals to revise the rule, to be ineligible for financial aid)[32] but also stigmatizes the athlete with labels such as "casualty" or "Prop. 48 kid."

Problems associated with this casualty stigma were articulated by former Memphis State University basketball star and now Orlando Magic star Anfernee Hardaway just as he was coming off a year of sitting out as a Proposition 48 casualty:

People think I'm dumb. I get it from both sides. Some people here [at Memphis State University]—but brothers from the 'hood do it, too. I went over to this girl's house. A guy came in and said, "Oh yeah, you that dumb ballplayer." He's known for selling cocaine. But I'm the dumb one, right?[33]

Hardaway highlights an issue that is not raised often enough in the Proposition 48 debate: the lifetime blot on the record of the player who fails to qualify. It is not that society owes any sympathy to an athlete who is now a multimillionaire. But should anyone have to be stamped, at any time in his or her life, by what may be an invalid presumption of lack of academic ability? And in reality, most of these individuals will not end up being millionaire superstars.

The negative impact on the stigmatized athlete is even harsher because the college game was historically more accessible to the African-American athlete than were the professional leagues. There were a number of African-Americans who participated in early collegiate team sports.[34] Proposition 48 may be viewed as a rule that negatively affects the role of African-Americans in sports. The laws against race mixing and rules for licensing jockeys discussed in earlier chapters were more direct, but the impact of Proposition 48—even if not intentional—on African-American athletes is distinct. The rule decreases the number of African-Americans eligible to attend college with the aid of athletic scholarships.[35]

There are valid arguments in support of Proposition 48-type rules. The principles of academic value and integrity set forth by the NCAA are undeniably admirable and commendable. With ten thousand-to-one odds of a high school athlete becoming a professional athlete, something must be done to ensure that there is an appropriate focus by these individuals, and by the institutions they attend, on education.[36] Efforts must continually be made to ensure that the term *student-athlete* does not become the ultimate oxymoron of the next millennium.

In January 1990 a major rule change designed to strengthen Proposition 48 was proposed at the annual NCAA convention. This new rule, Proposition 42, which relied heavily on the SAT, was in theory designed to attain the goal of redefining the focus of high school and collegiate student-athletes. As the discussion that follows sets out, a barrier to entry into college, whether actual, through the denial of admission, or de facto, by not allowing financial aid awards, should not be based on a standardized examination. Any comprehensive analysis of Proposition 42 and other revisions of the initial eligibility rules cannot overlook the historical and existing problems that arise when standardized tests are used as a qualification for entry.[37] Only color-blind rule makers could give standardized tests such an important role in the future of young student athletes.

While much is made of these tighter initial eligibility standards increasing graduation rates, there has been other activity as well. With the greater scrutiny, many schools have improved their academic support programs. The NCAA has also instituted rules reducing the number of hours college athletes may practice per week.[38] But it is the SAT that is most often pointed to as the reason for increased graduation rates. According to Pamela Zappardino, the executive director of the National Center for Fair and Open Testing, the test receives so much credit because it "looks objective, looks scientific, but Prop 48 and all that followed from it is an abuse of standardized testing."[39] The Scholastic Assessment Test[40] itself and the manner in which it is used are key elements in the initial eligibility debate.

The Scholastic Assessment Test

The average SAT score for African-Americans in the 1980s and 1990s has hovered around 730, while the average for whites during the same period of time has remained about 200 points higher, at approximately 930.[41] There are allegations that the reason for this disparity in scores is cultural bias in the exam.[42] Others assert that the reason is racial bias.[43] Some point to the difference in the quality of schools between the black and white communities.[44] Still others point to African-American students not being aware of or not being able to afford courses that prepare students for the standardized exams. Experts have supported and disputed all sides of this debate. Whatever explanation is presented for this disparity, the average scores are fact. Only a color-blind analysis could completely ignore this factual racial disparity in exam scores.

In search of an explanation for these types of test-score disparities, Stanley Fish has synthesized a series of sources that point to the creator of the exam, Carl Campbell Brigham, as the root of the genuine or perceived cultural bias of the SAT. In Fish's words, Brigham "was an out-and-out racist."[45] Fish cites David Owen's *None of the Above: Behind the Myth of Scholastic Aptitude,* as the basis for his conclusion.

Owen noted that *A Study of American Intelligence,* written by Brigham, warns America of "a possibility of racial admixture . . . infinitely worse than that faced by any European country today, for we are incorporating the Negro into our racial stock, while all of Europe is comparatively free of this taint."[46] Prior to writing that study, Brigham analyzed the Army Mental Tests using Madison Grant's *The Passing of the Great Race,* which divided American society into four distinct racial groups. Nordic-featured whites were at the top and the American Negro was at the bottom. After his Army Mental Test work in 1925, Brigham went to work for the College Board and developed the SAT.[47]

In fairness to the Educational Testing Service, which prepares the exam, and to SAT supporters, the exam has been revised since 1925. But its foundation cannot be revised. Brigham's background is discomforting.

Despite the SAT's background, the member institutions of the NCAA pushed for Proposition 42, which maintained that if a student-athlete did not have a minimum of a 700 combined score on the SAT or a comparable score on the ACT and a 2.0 grade point average, he or she could not receive financial aid of any type from an NCAA member institution. The economically disadvantaged student, of course, would have been affected more harshly than a student with the resources to pay for his or her own education. The student with resources could enroll and pay for that first year while studying towards academic eligibility, while the poor student would have the choice of not going to college, attending junior college, or hoping to receive a scholarship from a lower-division school or a National Association of Intercollegiate Athletes (NAIA) school.[48] After extensive criticism, Proposition 42 was modified at the 1990 NCAA convention. Under the revamped version, partial qualifiers were able to receive nonathletic university financial aid.[49]

In 1993 and 1994 the NCAA undertook to review whether the SAT was an appropriate mechanism to use in its initial eligibility rules. Key members of the Data Analysis Working Group that was reviewing the exam were accused by a graduate research assistant of one of the group members of having their own racial insensitivities and possibly being affiliated with "Beyondism," whose views on eugenics and vision of a future world that improves itself through selective breeding have been described as racist and abhorrent. Both *USA Today* and U.S. Representative Cardiss Collins of Illinois brought the allegations forward to the public.[50] Those accused denied the connection, and an NCAA investigation found none. An independent group of academics, the Scientific Conference on Re-examination of the Academic Performance Study, reviewed the Data Analysis Working Group's statistics and found, contrary to the group's conclusions, that they did not "serve as a very reliable basis for judgment" that the SAT score and admission standards do not hurt African-Americans.[51] One member of the independent group said that the SAT helped "rotate out qualified blacks" while more whites were rotated in. At the end of their 1994 national convention, the NCAA resolved to examine the initial eligibility rules more thoroughly before going forward with the planned changes.[52]

In 1995 the NCAA membership voted to retain the SAT and ACT in their initial eligibility standards. Arguments to eliminate freshman eligibility were also ignored, and an action in that regard was defeated. Students with a 2.0 grade point average in core courses must score at least a 900 combined score on the SAT or 21 on the ACT. As Table 8 indicates, for each ten-point drop in SAT scores, students must have a corresponding .025 increase in grade point average.[53]

No matter what one hears about how many points a student gets for signing his or her name on the SAT, the average African-American student is only about 30 points above the minimum cut off for financial aid, while the average white is 230 points above. Further, assuming an average student has a grade point average of 2.0, he or she would have to score nearly 200 points above average on the SAT to qualify. One has to consider that only the rare student is going to excel in a composite of the arts, academics, and athletics. If it is assumed that the SAT does indicate academic promise or past performance, it may be expected that the star athlete could fall below the average on this exam, just as the virtuoso violinist may be a below-average test taker or tennis player. A test score should not be the single determining factor for financial aid or, in a more indirect way, for an opportunity for a college education.

Table 8: Initial Eligibility Standards, 1996 and Thereafter

Qualifier
•Graduation from high school.
•The following core grade point average in thirteen core courses with the corresponding ACT or SAT score:

Core Grade Point Average	SAT	ACT
2.500 and above	700	17
2.475	710	18
2.450	720	18
2.425	730	18
2.400	740	18
2.375	750	18
2.350	760	19
2.325	770	19
2.300	780	19
2.275	790	19
2.250	800	19
2.225	810	20
2.200	820	20
2.175	830	20
2.150	840	20
2.125	850	20
2.100	860	21
2.075	870	21
2.050	880	21
2.025	890	21
2.000	900	21

Partial Qualifier (does not meet standards for qualifier)
•Graduation from high school.
•The following core grade point average in thirteen core courses with the corresponding ACT or SAT score:

Core Grade Point Average	SAT	ACT
2.750 and above	600	15
2.725	610	15
2.700	620	15
2.675	630	16
2.650	640	16
2.625	650	16
2.600	660	16
2.575	670	16
2.550	680	16
2.525	690	16

● No competition during the first academic year in residence.
● Three seasons of competition in Division I.
● Eligible to practice at the institution's home facility during the first academic year in residence.
● May receive institutional financial aid (including athletic financial aid) during the first academic year in residence.

Nonqualifier (does not meet standards for qualifier or partial qualifier)
● No practice during the first academic year in residence.
● No competition during the first academic year in residence.
● Three seasons of competition in Division I.
● Whether recruited or not, may receive only institutional, need-based financial aid (which may not come from an athletics source) during the first academic year in residence.

SOURCE: *NCAA News,* (March 15, 1995): 1.

Standardized Test Litigation

New York State courts have agreed with the position that the SAT should not be the sole indicator used to determine which students receive scholarships. Those courts addressed the issue in *Sharif v. New York State Education Department,*[54] a case involving the state education department's use of SAT scores alone to determine the recipients of New York State Regents Scholarships and Empire State Scholarships. On average, girls were receiving lower SAT scores than boys and thus fewer scholarships. The case was settled with the New York State Education Department agreeing to use both the students' grades and their SAT scores to determine the recipients.[55] The American Civil Liberties Union (ACLU), which spearheaded the *Sharif* action, filed a new action against the Educational Testing Service on February 15, 1994, challenging the use of the test for students to qualify for National Merit Scholarship awards.[56]

Proposition 42 allowed the standardized test to be the sole factor that could bar the receipt of a scholarship. The athlete's entire application package, including grade point average, becomes irrelevant if the minimum score is not received. Unfortunately, *Sharif* is probably applicable against the NCAA only by analogy, as the NCAA is not subject to the same level of judicial scrutiny in discrimination matters as is a government entity such as the New York State Education Department.[57] The NCAA has been found by the Supreme Court of the United States not to be a state actor.[58]

A conclusion on the use of standardized tests similar to that of *Sharif* was reached in *Groves v. Alabama State Board of Education* in 1991.[59] The test involved in this case was the ACT. The Alabama State Board of Education required that college sophomores who desired to enter the state teacher-training programs have a minimum score on the American College Testing Program's ACT exam. The plaintiffs alleged that the requirement discriminated against African-Americans on the basis of race. They brought the action under Title VI of the Civil Rights Act of 1964,[60] asserting both disparate impact and disparate treatment. They were successful in their disparate impact claim.

The board of education in Alabama incorporated a standardized test into its qualification equation for much the same reason as the NCAA instituted the SAT and ACT minimum scores. The board was concerned that grades alone would not provide a uniform measure by which to evaluate applicants. The fear was that "the State Board did not oversee grading practices, and the committee [evaluating the system] shared a perception held by much of the public that certain institutions awarded passing marks to students regardless of ability or achievement."[61] The ACT was chosen without much deliberation because it was a nationally standardized test taken on a routine basis by Alabama college-bound students.

The score in *Groves* was used not as a predictor but more as a public relations vehicle. The committee that determined the appropriate minimum score ignored the data they possessed on the disparities in scores broken down by race. The committee decided that "the teacher ought to be as smart as at least half the students she's teaching."[62] As one committee member described the decision:

So [one of the steering committee members] was commissioned to go to his office and find out what the average ACT was for graduates, came back and said, I believe it's 16.4. So our big decision was whether to go to 17 or 16. And the only argument [I] think I recall them arguing for 16. Then we could go back out and say, looka here. Of course, this is also a fallacious argument because the student—the teacher never is as smart as half the students. . . . [But] that was the scientific basis of it gentlemen and lady. It was just that scientific.[63]

Groves was a class-action Title VI lawsuit that included all past, present, and future black students denied admission into teacher education programs in Alabama solely on the basis of failing to attain an ACT score of 16.[64] Title VI specifically provides that "no person in the United States shall, on the ground of race, . . . be excluded from participation in, be denied the benefits of, or be subjected to discrimination under any program or activity receiving Federal financial assistance."[65] Proof of discriminatory intent is not required for a successful private action.[66] A facially neutral rule cannot have "an unjustifiable disparate impact on minorities."[67] The elements of a Title VI disparate impact claim are similar to those of Title VII, described in Chapter 3.[68] A 1978 study showed that 85 percent of white Alabama students achieved an ACT score of 16 or above, while 21 percent of African-Americans scored at that level.[69] This test-score disparity remained substantially the same over the years.

The court in *Groves* noted that no rigid standard for finding a mathematically adverse impact exists. The court did state, however, that

the Supreme Court's "formulations . . . have consistently stressed that statistical disparities must be sufficiently substantial that they raise . . . an inference of causation"—in other words, adequate to "show that the practice in question has caused the exclusion of applicants for jobs or promotions because of their membership in a protected group." However, the Supreme Court and lower courts have adopted various formulas to measure the degree of disparate impact in a particular case. The Equal Employment Opportunity Commission generally infers adverse racial impact where the members of a particular racial group are selected at a rate that is less than four-fifths, or 80%, of the rate at which the group with the highest rate is selected.[70]

The court concluded that a substantial enough statistical disparity existed and that the test was not justified as a screening method for qualified teacher-training candidates. The court examined the selection of the test as the measure of ability as well as the selection of the cutoff point and found them to be "homemade methodologies" to sort out unqualified teacher candidates.[71]

Sharif, combined with *Groves*, illustrates the scrutiny that an institution's use of a standardized test should undergo. The disparity in average scores between African-Americans and whites makes this an area where "homemade methodolgies" for determining who will be the successful students are inappropriate and arguably illegal. The ultimate question is whether a standardized test should be used in the equation at all.

Needed Reforms regarding Initial Eligibility Standards

■ *Retain Partial Qualifier Opportunities.* The partial qualifier system may give the poor test taker the opportunity to show that he or she can handle the rigors of college academics in spite of a standardized test score below the qualifying minimum. Partial qualifiers are allowed to enroll in an NCAA member institution and receive both athletics- and nonathletics-based financial aid, and they may practice, but not play, with the athletic team for the first year.[72] If a student-athlete's test score and grade point average are not high enough, he or she is a nonqualifier. Where a partial qualifier may receive athletics-based financial aid, a nonqualifier may receive only nonathletic institutional financial aid, based on need and institutional guidelines.[73]

Richard Lapchick provides even more facts which indicate that the harsh consequences of a Proposition 42-type reform are not necessary. Of those students who failed to meet the minimum standards in the academic years 1986–1987 and 1987–1988, the partial qualifiers, a full 79 percent, were in good academic standing once given the opportunity to succeed. This percentage is equal to that reflecting the academic progress of students who met the initial Proposition 48 standard. As Lapchick phrases it, "The predictions of disaster for athletes who were asked to do more proved false. The players produced."[74]

What does the Educational Testing Service (ETS) say about its own exam? The organization that administers the exam expressed concern to the NCAA at the introduction of both Proposition 48 and Proposition 42. Regarding Proposition 42, Gregory R. Anrig, then president of ETS, wrote to Richard Schultz, the former executive director of the NCAA:

I want to express concern again, this time about the test use provisions of the recently enacted Rule [Proposition] 42. With this rule, as with its predecessor, admission test scores are used in a manner inconsistent with the way they properly are used in combination with other student information in reaching admissions decisions at colleges and universities.[75]

ETS argues against any bias in the exams but also recognizes the confines in which its exams should be used.

The NCAA has a duty to strive for higher academic success. A minimum grade point average should continue to be required. A standardized test, however, that even its creators question and which statistics show to be a questionable predictor for the academic performance of student-athletes should not be the determining factor for the rest of a student-athlete's life.[76] Incentives should be included that all student-athletes have the equal opportunity to attain. Future reforms of Proposition 48 should continue to place less value on the role of the SAT and ACT.

The initial Proposition 42 implementation was delayed when many protested the rule as in the highly visible walk off the court by Georgetown basketball coach John Thompson. There were also boycotts discussed by the Black Coaches Association.[77]

■ *Eliminate Freshman Eligibility.* Freshmen should be ineligible to participate in the major revenue sports. The freshman eligibility change serves two purposes. First, it gives our institutions of higher learning the opportunity to assist students with any academic deficiencies they might have. At the same time, it requires all academic institutions to invest in the academic career of student-athletes. Maybe more important is the serious message sent to entering students: universities are, first and foremost, places for learning. One of the major collegiate sports errors of the 1990s was the return of freshman eligibility to Ivy League football. Instead of serving as an example of the model relationship between athletics and academics, the Ivies have taken a huge step backward.[78]

The issue of eliminating freshman eligibility was introduced in the 1995 NCAA convention. After one of the most heated debates of the convention, the proposal to eliminate was voted down.

■ *Add a Fifth Year of Eligibility.*   The five-year scholarship would provide student-athletes with adequate time and funds to receive their undergraduate degrees. The fifth year could be used at any time, even after the completion of a pro sports career. This additional year of eligibility was also raised at the 1995 NCAA convention. After much debate and a call for reconsideration of the matter after it was first voted down, the proposal to reinstate an additional year of eligibility failed.

In the case of both the elimination of freshman eligibility and the addition of a fifth year to athletic scholarships, altruism certainly clashes with financial considerations. Institutions would have to pay for an additional year in order to receive four years of the student-athlete's talents in a sport. Under the current standard, the institution pays for four years and receives four years of performance in return.

■ *Drop the Use of Standardized Test Scores Completely.*   With success several institutions have dropped the use of standardized tests in their admissions decisions.[79] In *The Case against the SAT,* the authors cite cases where the SAT was optional at Bates and Bowdoin colleges.[80] They also cite the dropping of standardized admissions tests at Harvard Business School and Johns Hopkins Medical School. Both Bates and Bowdoin studied the academic performance of students after the optional use of the exam and found no negative impact. According to Paul Shaffner, a psychology professor at Bowdoin who analyzed his institution's results:

The feasibility of the policy has been demonstrated. Administrative aspects have worked smoothly; virtually all matriculants were aware of the option to submit or withhold their SAT scores and knew their scores in advance so as to have been able to make informed choices. . . . The policy was overwhelmingly endorsed by students. More important than administrative considerations, though, is that virtually all students in both groups have proved capable of meeting the college's educational requirements. Of the dozen students permanently dismissed for academic and/or disciplinary reasons in the four academic years since fall 1979, only two had withheld SAT scores upon application.[81]

■ *Improve Education prior to College.* The primary culprit is the pivotal role of the SAT and ACT. Donald Stewart, president of the College Board, presents a realistic reason for the black-white score differentiation. "Score differences among [racial and ethnic] groups are not the result of bias on the SAT but reflect in large part the unequal educational opportunities that still exist in our country."[82] This may be the case, and bias may be fully removed from the exam; but the complete absence of any bias remains doubtful.

Stewart's comments are probably the most significant in relation to Proposition 48. It is before the student reaches college, before the student takes the aptitude test, before the college GPA is acquired that academic deficiencies develop. It is primarily public education that has the responsibility to form academic standards. That is where the great minds should focus their efforts, not on screening out those without a particular minimum grade point average or test score. The theory of those who advocate tightening the eligibility rules is that to do so will force the public schools to improve their effort. A direct focus on the schools, rather than the imposition of a questionable rule that relies on a controversial exam, would be a wiser allocation of resources.

Power Positions in Collegiate Sports

The other significant problem in college sports, just as at the professional level, is the absence of African-Americans in positions of power. The small number of head football coaches and athletic directors was noted earlier. The racial composition of the 1994 NCAA Final Four basketball teams in comparison to that of their athletic departments further illustrates this. According to a study conducted by the Rainbow Commission for Fairness in Athletics, the college front-office numbers resembled those of their professional counterparts.[83] Of 55 players, 36 (or 65 percent) were black, and 19 (35 percent) were white. On the coaching staffs (including assistants, coaches responsible for strength and conditioning, and trainers), of 119 coaches, 103 (86 percent) were white, 14 (12 percent) were black, and 1 (6 percent) was Latino. Again, an absolute correlation between those that play on the court and those in management is not necessarily expected. But the disparity is simply too large.

The same holds true for African-American women. According to sports analyst and former University of Southern California basketball coach George Raveling, "More white males are coaching women's sports than black females."[84] Not only are African-American women confronted with the gender issue of primarily white men coaching women's athletics, they also suffer from discrimination against African-Americans in sports.

A broader study from 1990 that assessed the racial makeup of Division I-A athletic directors and football coaching staffs found that of 105 institutions, 3.7 percent of the athletic directors, 3.5 percent of the head coaches, and 7.2 percent of the offensive coordinators were black, as were 21.4 percent of the assistant coaches.[85] One college official noted to me that even when African-Americans did get head coaching positions in college football, the teams have tended to be bad. Dennis Green has been the only African-American college football head coach to take a team to a major postseason bowl game.[86]

An African-American college sports administrator had the opportunity to assault some of these issues in the courtroom. Marvin Cobb, a former assistant athletic director at the University of Southern California (USC), asserted in a lawsuit against the university that discrimination was the reason for his not getting a promotion to associate athletic director, as had been promised to him when he was hired. Cobb provided as support of the racism present on the campus a memorandum that was written by the baseball coach, Mike Gillespie, to Athletic Director Mike McGee. The letter was written after the initial lawsuit had been filed:

Please be informed that you have at least the moral support of your loyal baseball staff in your pending litigation with the Assistant Athletic Director. If it will help, Detective Klein [a volunteer assistant coach of the baseball team] is willing to bury him with a phony drug bust. P.S. Promote me to head football coach with a guaranteed L.A. Gear shoe contract or the Association of Americans of Scotch-Irish Descent will have you in court also.[87]

Cobb told *Sports Illustrated* that his concern was not with his position alone but with black athletes in general at USC: "USC and a lot of schools like it aren't holding up their end of the bargain to a lot of black athletes. The issue to look at is not whether USC kept its promise to me about a promotion. It's whether universities are keeping their promise to black athletes about an education."[88] The decision by a lower court found that the university had breached its promise to Cobb regarding a promotion. For that breach of contract and the accompanying emotional damages, the trial jury awarded Cobb $2.1 million.[89] The jury, however, was undecided on the charges of racial discrimination. The vote was eight to four by the jury on the discrimination issue.[90]

The plaintiff's discrimination theory was unique and, depending on the final outcome on appeal, could have far-reaching implications. The allegation by Cobb was that there was discrimination not against him but against programs he was intending to implement to improve the academic status of African-American athletes.[91] He maintains that he was not promoted because he was attempting to push forward these academic enhancement plans. Cobb cites the action against him as being also an action against African-American athletes. The theory is that colleges should be supportive of such plans and, at a minimum, not work against those employees seeking to implement them.[92]

Racism remains an extremely difficult matter to prove. Regarding head coaching positions, however, Rudy Washington, the president of the Black Coaches Association, believes that "[school] presidents aren't comfortable having an African-American run a program."[93] The reaction by the public also can be harsh when African-Americans are hired at the college level. When Stanford University hired its second African-American head coach, some alumni and others were not pleased. According to Athletic Director Ted Leland, "We did have an unbelievable reaction from a small group of alums when Tyrone's hiring was announced. [It was] unbelievable that anyone would think that we'd be so narrow in our thinking to hire someone solely on their race."[94] Leland and those who made the decision at Stanford felt that Tyrone Willingham was the best qualified for the job.

Needed Reforms in Collegiate Athletic Administration

The lack of diversity in college sports administration certainly parallels the problems at the professional level. (In loose correlations, the college president can be equated with the owner and the athletic director with the general manager.) The problem may even be greater in colleges for they also have the unpaid student athlete about which Cobb expressed concern. Academic institutions without question conduct business in a manner distinct from that of private enterprise. Where the owner of a team, such as Ralph Wilson, Peter O'Malley, or Jerry Buss, might be able to make a unilateral decision regarding a general manager, a college president will at least receive the advice of a specially formed search committee regarding the hiring of an athletic director. Generally, however, a president has a strong influence on decisions regarding athletic hirings. This was a significant consideration in the major reform recommendation of the Knight Commission on Intercollegiate Athletics. The Knight Commission urged that university presidents take charge of their athletic programs.[95]

Similarly, athletic directors, like general managers, may have varying degrees of independence in their decision-making powers—particularly with regard to the selection of coaching staffs. It may, in fact, be the head coach who has complete discretion as to who his or her assistants will be.

Ted Leland observes that unless there are changes, "the athletic director position will continue to lag behind coaching. Something will need to happen at the assistant and associate level."[96] A stream of minority talent needs to be piped into the college network just as much as at the professional level.

It is difficult at this level for the athletes themselves to take any action to bring about change. They are in college only for a short period of time and have little leverage and no income. It is up to the leaders of these institutions to bring about change. Student-athletes could be better educated by their parents and others to ask appropriate questions as they are being recruited out of high school: "How many African-American coaches do you have? Do you plan to hire any?" This subtle pressure can convey to universities and colleges the importance of this issue to the most essential component of college athletics—the athlete.

The Law

A number of cases have developed the law as it applies to private associations.[97] Essentially, the voluntary members of a private association may establish rules with wide latitude. Just like a commissioner acting in the best interests of a sports league, members of a private association such as the NCAA may establish rules to improve the racial situation in their organization. The guidelines established for collegiate institutions could closely resemble those proposed at the professional level.

As has been noted, Title VII is applicable to both public and private institutions. In addition, institutions receiving federal funding, particularly educational institutions, are subject to both Title VI and the equal protection clause of the Fourteenth Amendment of the U.S. Constitution.[98] Noncompliance with federal guidelines for affirmative action could cause a college or university to lose federal funding. This governmental nexus allows for the compliance investigations being conducted by the Department of Labor, cited earlier. Although the individual institutions are subject to this governmental Title VI scrutiny, the NCAA as a single entity probably is not.[99]

Conclusion

The initial eligibility rules should avoid reliance on standardized examinations. Both the unanswered question of the racial bias of the exams and their true value as a predictor must be taken under consideration regarding their impact on African-Americans. While academic integrity needs to remain a high priority, the standardized exam is not

Table 9: Four-Year Average Graduation Rates for 1995—Final
Associated Press Top Twenty-five Football Teams*

AP Rank		Black (%)	White (%)
1.	Nebraska	26	66
2.	Penn State	76	71
3.	Colorado	43	64
4.	Florida State	31	50
5.	Alabama	41	40
6.	Miami	48	63
7.	Florida	29	60
8.	Texas A & M	23	56
9.	Auburn	23	52
10.	Utah	36	41
11.	Oregon	48	61
12.	Michigan	63	70
13.	So. California	54	51
14.	Ohio State	29	63
15.	Virginia	69	78
16.	Colorado	40	65
17.	No. Carolina St.	24	67
18.	Brigham Young	38	45
19.	Kansas State	14	56
20.	Arizona	42	52
21.	Washington St.	28	61
22.	Tennessee	36	60
23.	Boston College	88	89
24.	Mississippi St.	47	67
25.	Texas	21	60

*Graduation rates are based on a four-year average and pertain only to members of the football team.
SOURCE: 1994 NCAA Division I Graduation-Rates Report

the determinant of its presence. Certainly the use of high school grade point averages alone is problematic as well. Grades tend to have different meanings in different school districts. The documented racism found in the SAT is not present in grade point averages. The problem is a difficult one to reconcile. The SAT, however, should not continue to hold its current lofty position.

As Table 9 illustrates, much work remains to be done. African-American athletes still generally have a lower graduation rate than whites from the major college sports powers.

Any concerns held by college administrators about liability for student-athletes that do not successfully obtain an education are unfounded. The institutions should use their many resources to ensure that those student-athletes they do admit receive an education. Yet if the school fails in that regard, there is little legal liability. A greater concern exists regarding those students admitted who bring breach-of-contract actions when, in the end, they do not get the education promised by the school.[100] *Ross v. Creighton University* is an example of this type of action, in which a United States appellate court upheld a ruling supporting the existence of a contractual relationship between student-athletes and private universities or colleges.[101] But a similar argument, also asserted by Kevin Ross, the plaintiff in *Ross v. Creighton University*, argued the existence of "educational malpractice."[102] The courts have not been supportive of those allegations. The obligation is moral.

In regard to the issue of college administrators and coaches, with all I knew about college sports I was still shocked at the lack of diversity in the room when I attended my first NCAA convention in 1994.[103] Although, unlike the professional ranks, African-Americans do not make up the majority of the athletes on the fields and in the arenas in college, the percentages of African-Americans in the power positions are still low and need dramatic improvement. There are African-Americans prepared to fill the roles, and affirmative action policies are the appropriate route. The large numbers of state and federal dollars that support these institutions establish a governmental nexus which should mandate that the appropriate agencies require and then monitor change. Actions such as the examination and follow-up letter by the RCFA, cited at the beginning of this chapter, will help encourage this type of change.

"The White Man's Ice Is Colder, His Sugar Sweeter, His Water Wetter, His Medicine Better": Sports Agents

> "You call yourself a role model for young blacks," one friend snapped at me not long ago, "but you have a white man handling your money?"
>
> "I don't call myself a role model," I replied. "And I don't have a white man handling my money. I have Donald Dell, who happens to be white."
>
> "There's no difference, Arthur. None at all."
>
> "Yes, there is!"
>
> "I'm surprised," he went on, "that you don't have a white wife!"
>
> "Well, if I had one, it would be my business and my business alone, wouldn't it? And she would be my wife, first and foremost, who happened to be white."   —Arthur Ashe, *Days of Grace*

The Myth: The Use of African-American Professionals by African-Americans

Should we be color-blind to the race of those we hire to provide professional services? This chapter examines the question by looking at the role of the African-American sports agent in representing African-American athletes. What role should race consciousness play in the agent-selection process?[1] Many outsiders see African-American sports agents representing successful members of their own race in contract negotiations as a natural occurrence. The reality is that until recently, such black-on-black representation was a rare event.[2]

The lack of patronization by African-Americans of African-American businesses is apocryphal. The business relationship between African-American athletes and sports agents is not unique in this regard. It is also a topic that has received little attention, except in instances where controversy arises. Recent focus on the issue has centered on the success of Korean-American shop owners in African-American communities where African-Americans have failed.[3] At various times this has been a major issue in the Los Angeles and New York media, sometimes resulting in civil unrest.[4]

A classic story, most often credited to Malcolm X, provides an insight into the black community's perception of the competence of our own professionals. The story has it that in a small southern town on some hot day, people stood in a long line wrapped around a corner to purchase ice. On the other side of town a black ice vendor sat with plenty of ice, doing very little business. When a black patron in the long line was asked why he would stand in the long line rather than purchase the ice in his own neighborhood, he responded, "Well everybody knows the white man's ice is colder."[5]

Different versions of the same story have been used to explain similar instances where African-Americans do not patronize African-American businesses or trust African-Americans in positions requiring good faith and expertise. In the Negro League of the late 1920s, a controversy arose over the preference and use of nonblack umpires and the implication of inadequacy on the part of black umpires. By August 1929 the situation had simmered to such a point that the usually supportive African-American newspaper *The Philadelphia Tribune* lashed out at manager Ed Bolden and the Hilldale club:

In order to maintain order and discipline it is necessary—according to the reasoning of Hilldale's management—to have a white man oversee the game. It is a reflection on the ability and intelligence of colored people. *Are we still slaves?* It is possible that colored baseball players are so dumb that they will resent one of their own race umpiring their game? Or is it that the management of Hilldale is so *steeped in racial inferiority that it has no faith in Negroes.* Aside from the economic unfairness of such a position the employment of white umpires at Negro ball games brands Negroes as inferior. It tells white people in a forceful manner that colored people are unable to even play a ball game without white leadership. It is a detestable mean attitude. There is no excuse for it. Hilldale depends on colored people for its existence. If the management lacks sufficient racial respect to employ Negro umpires the public should make it listen to reason.[6]

It is apparent that some vestiges of this negative race consciousness have carried over into the African-American athlete's selection of a sports agent.

When I was growing up in inner-city Los Angeles, my father was a surgeon. More than once I recall him telling a colleague or a friend about the longtime patients that came in for remedies to treat the common cold or to ease aches and pains. At some point they would have an ailment that required surgery. They would ask my father whom he could recommend, knowing his training but presuming that his race precluded him from being the "best." It seemed "a black doctor is fine unless you've got cancer." I remember the words.

I also recall various times during my childhood when the concepts of "buying black" or "recycling black dollars" in the "community" were the watchwords of the day. The issue of buying black was raised prominently again after the riots in Los Angeles in 1992. Bernard W. Kinsey, co-chairman and chief operating officer of the redevelopment organization Rebuild L.A., said, "To the extent that we spend our money outside of our community, we make someone else more productive than us. Ask yourself: Who is my lawyer? Who is my doctor? Where do I eat? Who does my tax returns? All of these services can be supplied by African-Americans."[7]

The debate over black-on-black representation is similar to the debate over whether African-Americans in Hollywood should direct motion pictures focusing on African-American subjects. At a panel discussion on the subject at New York University in 1994, renowned African-American director Spike Lee commented that just as Francis Ford Coppola and Martin Scorsese brought their backgrounds to films on Italian-Americans, African-Americans should be allowed to do the same. The discussion rages on both sides. Bill Duke, another African-American director said, "We should not be limited by ethnicity, only by our ability."[8] Similarly, Lee added, "There's no guarantee that just because it's black it's going to be great. A lot of the black programs on television are minstrel shows, and they are written by black writers. There's no guarantee."[9]

The Sports Agent Business

Like the director in the movie industry, the sports agent is a powerful player in the sports world. The sports agent may be in solo practice or in any size entity ranging up to the large sports marketing and management firm. No matter the type of entity, the sports agent not only negotiates player and marketing contracts for the athlete but also often guides the athlete in investment and personal life decisions.[10] The key distinction is that in Hollywood, African-American actors do not usually select their directors; in sports, however, African-Americans have the power to do so.

The sports-agent business is not one with a multitude of success stories, black or white. Although there are probably a few thousand individuals calling themselves sports agents, apart from employees at a few of the major sports management and marketing firms there are fewer than two dozen people who make a living exclusively at that job. Others combine their sports-agent business with careers that range from attorney, accountant, and insurance salesperson to recreation director.[11] Because sports agents confront no formal educational requirements and only the rare bona fide license requirement, the agent may come from any profession. Although there is no federal law regulating the field, several states have agent regulatory statutes.[12]

The competition among agents for athlete clients is vigorous. In the last available statistics published to break down the numbers of agents by race, there were 200 agents registered with the Major League Baseball Players Association in 1992.[13] Of those 200, 150 had active clients. Only 5 of those 150 agents, or a little over 3 percent, were African-Americans. In football the numbers were similar: in 1991 there were 675 agents registered as contract advisers with the players association; 320 had active clients and 45, or 14 percent, were African-Americans. Once again, we would not expect a direct percentage correlation between the race of players on the field and their agents. But a greater African-American presence in the agent business than the percentages noted would seem reasonable.

The reason for the fierce competition is the high income potential of the sports agent. For example, Emmitt Smith, the star running back for the Dallas Cowboys, has a player contract for a reported $13.6 million over four years.[14] Based on Smith's salary alone, his agent stands to earn $544,000, or 4 percent, over that four-year period, or $136,000 per year for a single client. This does not include any commissions from endorsements, where the rate to the agent is more likely to be 20 percent of the value of any contract. For a superstar client, endorsement fees are likely to exceed the value of the player contract.[15]

It should also be recognized, as Arthur Ashe alludes to in the quotation that forms the epigraph to this chapter, that the selection of an agent is a highly personal matter. It is the type of relationship that involves a great deal of personal interaction. Thus the sports agent-athlete relationship is an area where the law should not—and in fact, will not—compel a continuing relationship.[16] Athletes, regardless of their race, should simply select the best agent for their particular circumstances. As in many businesses, most often because of historical barriers, whites tend to have longer track records in the industry.

The African-American sports agent has, however, begun to have some success in the recruitment of clients, and although this progress has been slow, it is measurable. Ten years ago, as one writer phrased it, "high profile black sports agents were rare as snowballs in Miami."[17] None of the leagues or players associations currently track the race of players' agents.[18] Thus there are no official tabulations of the changing role of African-American agents. With that in mind, looking at the representatives of athletes taken in the first round of the National Basketball Association draft, of twenty-seven players drafted in 1992, five had African-American agents; of twenty-seven players drafted in 1993, nine had African-American agents; and, of the twenty-seven drafted in 1994, nine had African-American agents.[19] USA Today found that in the 1993 NFL draft, twenty of the first fifty-six athletes selected had hired African-American agents.[20] This number represented 36 percent of the players in the first two rounds.

There is not always a great deal of science incorporated into the agent selection process by student-athletes.[21] One of the major players in this decision-making process is the player's head coach. As was noted in chapter 5, in the National Collegiate Athletic Association's Division I-A, this person is probably white.[22] Arguably, a white coach is less likely to refer an athlete to an African-American agent. The life experiences and associations of a head coach are likely to be no different from the associations of anyone else, largely limited to one's own race. Thus there is probably no negative racial motivation in a "same-race" referral but just a reflection of American society.[23]

The Race Card

Is it wrong to include the race of the sports agent in the athlete's selection criteria? Is this race consciousness appropriate in this or any situation? Should the selection of an agent be made on a purely color-blind basis?[24]

Race As a Positive Factor

The father of NFL running back Barry Sanders accurately expressed to *Black Enterprise* part of the reason for the recent increase in the use of African-American agents by African-American athletes:

I wasn't going to raise my son his whole life and then turn him over to some white people and let them run his life. A lot of them called me and told me how well they knew all the owners, how they played golf with them, but to me that's the worst thing for a player if the agent and owner are that close. I was looking for somebody honest, somebody I could communicate with and go to church with. I just felt more comfortable with blacks. Some people might say that's prejudice, but it's not. Plus, their kids don't sign with black agents; why should ours sign with white agents?[25]

This is arguably a positive expression of race consciousness.

Similarly, Chris Webber, a premier basketball player for the University of Michigan, announced that he would hire a black agent after he decided to enter professional basketball. When asked if he was being racist, he responded, "It's not being racist, it's about giving your own a chance."[26] Webber's expression of consciousness, too, is not negative toward another race but positive toward his own.

According to C. Lamont Smith, a prominent African-American sports agent, "The sports and entertainment industry is to African-Americans what technology is to the Japanese and oil is the Arabs. It is incumbent upon us to work to control our natural resources."[27]

The Prevailing Negative Image

African-American sports agents are not only confronted with the historic allegiance of African-American athletes to white agents and a lack of positive race consciousness by these athletes but also with the negative commentary of the white sports agent. One of the pioneer African-American sports agents, Fred Slaughter of Los Angeles, told writer Phillip Hoose:

[White agents] just tell the kid, "Only a white man can make that deal for you." They have actually said that. And some kids, kids who are sitting in a well-furnished office with computers clicking and listening to a guy with gold teeth say that, they'll think, "Wait a minute: If he's sayin' that, he must be right." There are a lot of problems. It's been rough.[28]

Slaughter also recalls a black athlete he was trying to sign on as a client in 1975.[29] He was competing against a white agent for this athlete. The player, who was black, told Slaughter that the white agent said to him, "You know that Slaughter is qualified. He played basketball at UCLA, and he has a law degree. But, what you have to understand is that representing professional athletes is a white man's business. Only white men can sit down with other white men and get you the money you deserve."[30]

In a response to Slaughter's experience, agent George Andrews, who is white, said that he thinks no reputable sports agent feels that way today.[31] Andrews even touted his own efforts to include blacks on his negotiating team. It is, of course, impossible to know all the feelings of agents on this issue. But apparently, the use of the white-agent-is-better-than-black rhetoric has continued since Slaughter's cited encounter. And if the argument is not coming directly from the agents, the belief is still ingrained in some African-American athletes. Often the decision of all athletes in selecting an agent is not color-blind but one that gives a preference to white agents.

African-American sports agent Ray Anderson told *Black Enterprise,* "Unfortunately, some of the star black players have swallowed the line that you've got to have a white agent and maybe a white, Jewish agent to get the very best deal."[32] Anderson's beliefs are confirmed by African-American Hall of Fame football player and college All-American tight end Kellen Winslow. As a college senior at the University of Missouri destined to be a top first-round draft pick, Winslow reflects:

I needed someone white and preferably of the Jewish faith. My statements concerning the type of agent I wanted reflected the worst. It showed that I went beyond understanding and into the realm of believing that I and those like me, black people, were not only disadvantaged, but unable to handle my affairs with the NFL.[33]

Winslow considered further that much of the reason this white-agent-is-better-than-black mentality works results from the environment in which the African-American athlete's career is developed. More than likely, if the athlete plays at a major college program the coach is white. As was noted, there were only three African-American head coaches in the NCAA's Division I-A in 1994.[34] The coach understandably becomes one of the most controlling figures in the athlete's life. Outside of the sports culture, the typical media portrayal of the sports agent that a black athlete sees growing up is not likely to be of a black man or woman as the competent negotiator but of a white male.

The image of the sports agent as white also affects who will enter the business. In 1979 a young production assistant with WATL-TV in Atlanta, who also ushered at Hawks basketball games, was considering sports management as a career. He was told by then general manager of the Atlanta Hawks Lewis Schaffel, "You're bright and articulate, but there's one problem. You're black."[35] That young man was C. Lamont Smith, who is now the president of one of the largest sports management companies in the country, All-Pro Sports and Entertainment. Despite Schaffel's concerns, Smith has successfully fought to establish himself in the sports industry. He has not, however, been able to escape racism. Smith says, "Hundreds and hundreds of years of stereotypes are attached to you. This is not unique to the sports industry, if you work for Proctor & Gamble the same thing may happen to a salesperson. You have to convince the potential client that the myths are not the facts."[36]

Noted psychologist Kenneth Clark produced the most famous work on black people's negative view of themselves.[37] In a study of the impact of school desegregation in the American South, he found that to most of the black school-age children shown both black and white dolls, black dolls were "bad" and "a nigger" while white dolls were described with positive attributes such as "nice" and "better."[38] In 1985 a similar test was conducted and the same results of negative self-esteem and image among black children were found.[39]

In addition to the empirical statistics in 1993 that demonstrate greater patronage of black agents by black athletes, another former NFL All-Pro, African-American quarterback Doug Williams, reconsidered his decisions regarding agent selections he made in years past. After his retirement in 1993, Williams said that he would hire an African-American agent "if I was a number one draft pick coming out today."[40]

Williams recognizes a disparity that is present with most African-American agents. "What they don't have access to is the same type of clientele. Most black agents don't have resources or contacts to fly in players, advance them money or get them a loan for the car of their dreams like a lot of white agents can." Williams further recognized that a top-round draft pick "can do more for black agents than the law allows."[41] In the sports-agent business, an agent's success lies largely in his or her client pool. "Who else do you represent?" is the first question asked by most athletes.

Race Consciousness and the Sports Agent Selection

Economics is unquestionably one reason a greater role for African-American agents is desirable. The more investment there is in a specific community, the greater the general welfare of that community will be: Starting with an increase in the number of businesses, leading to greater employment, leading—the long-range logic goes—to less crime.

Beyond direct and indirect economic benefits, there are also role-model issues. An African-American agent, with some of the same experiences and background that the athlete may have, may be better qualified to render services to the black athlete than the white agent. The African-American agent will probably also be more successful in preparing the African-American athlete for the transition into a world where he is no longer the coddled superstar and must face the same issues of racism impacting on all African-American males. Certainly, a white agent can help in this transition, and many have done so successfully. Similarly, there are African-American agents who have not aided in this transition. But the African-American agent is better positioned to serve as this transitional role model.[42]

This positioning is the outcome of the closer sociological relationship between two African-Americans.[43] The similar life experiences of two African-American men is a bond that is unique. This bond is certainly difficult to explain but was reflected visually in the 1995 Million Man March on Washington, D.C. The potential for an older African-American man to prepare the athlete for the issues he will confront when he is no longer the revered athlete are difficult for those who have not suffered to understand.

A final argument for the use of African-American agents by African-American athletes is an extension of the role-model issue raised in this chapter's opening epigraph.[44] If African-American athletes patronize their own businesses, then young African-Americans and others who admire them will follow this lead. That is the optimistic implication.

In this arena the race factor should be recognized as an asset. However, there are white and black athletes who will benefit in a greater way from the decision to hire a particular white sports agent.[45] It is sufficient that athletes grow to view the race of any sports-agent candidate not as negative but as potentially positive.[46] In other words, in the bundle of qualifications to consider in a prospective sports agent, race should be one of them. No one is capable of making these decisions in a color-blind manner. Race has always been a factor, but one in which being white was positive and black negative. Given the presumption that agent and athlete, both African-Americans, may have some shared experiences, an otherwise equally qualified white agent may not be the person who should be hired for the job.[47]

This chapter's opening epigraph, quoting Arthur Ashe, shows that the presumption of shared experience on the basis of shared race is not always present. Race should, however, represent a positive factor in the African-American athlete's agent-selection process and certainly not a negative in evaluating the African-American agent.[48]

Reforms and the Law

Reforms

The ultimate route to increase the role of African-American agents has three stages. The first step of the process, which is already in place, is to have a qualified pool of African-American agents in existence. Second, African-American athletes and also non-African-American athletes must use the services of these agents. Third, there is arguably a moral obligation for the large, established, white-owned sports agencies to provide African-Americans with meaningful roles within their firms. Many African-American athletes are represented by large sports marketing concerns.

International Management Group, Advantage International, and ProServ are the three largest firms in the business, all with offices around the world. These firms, much like the leagues and teams, have lagged behind in terms of hiring and retaining African-Americans at the highest levels in relation to the racial percentages on the field.[49] Traditionally, where the major white firms have employed African-Americans, it has been in the capacity of "runners" or "bird dogs"—the individuals who recruit the African-American clients for firms.[50] The key for these firms is to present opportunities for African-Americans to obtain an equity interest in the business and provide the sensitivity that only an African-American can bring, as in the case of directors of African-American-based motion pictures.[51]

In some instances the athlete may have a preference to be represented by an African-American agent. The athlete may develop a personal relationship with the African-American employee of the white agent. The role of the African-American "runner" is intentionally kept vague, leading the athlete to believe that the runner is, in fact, in charge, not the white men back at the home office.

Role of the Law

It is possible that individual African-Americans seeking employment at these large sports marketing and management firms could bring discrimination actions if the facts allowed. But just as with other businesses, courts are reluctant to compel sports business owners to take on new employees and/or promote current associates to partners with an equity interest in the business. If the reason for an existing or prospective employee's rejection is not illegal, courts are not likely to intervene.[52]

The introduction of race into the equation does not improve the plaintiff's position either. Similar to the issues raised in franchise-ownership discussion in chapter 2, barring African-Americans from an equity interest in a sports management firm resembles those cases where a person is denied partnership in a law firm based on race.[53] As was noted there, the law most applicable in firm partnership cases is Title VII of the Civil Rights Act of 1964.[54] But Title VII is applicable only to employer-employee relationships, that is, only where there is the preexisting relationship, not where a relationship is being sought.[55] Like an associate at a law firm, the appropriate plaintiff in such a case would be a current "associate-level" employee denied "partnership" status.

The Civil Rights Act of 1870 may similarly be applicable here.[56] As we saw in chapter 2, Section 1981 may provide relief whenever an individual is denied admission to a partnership based on his or her race, since a partnership is a contractual agreement.[57] If an individual is denied the opportunity to become a partner of a sports management firm due to race, he or she is denied the opportunity to make a contract, in violation of Section 1981.[58] However, to successfully bring this type of action, a plaintiff would have to establish racial motivation, not just the absence of African-American equity ownership at the firm or other, comparable statistics.[59] Absent the unlikely event of a management firm's owners publicizing that they have denied a party an equity or even an executive or management-level position in the firm on the basis of his or her race, the use of Section 1981 will not bring about change. And again, just as with franchise ownership, although under both Title VII and Section 1981 a court of equity can mandate the adoption of an affirmative action program[60] in a firm's hiring process, courts probably will not mandate that a management firm admit partners it does not desire.[61]

Finally, as was illustrated in *Hishon v. King & Spalding*,[62] compelling admission of partners or equity owners may interfere with the present partners' freedom of association. In short, although freedom of association is not a defense in the employer-employee context,[63] it may be outside the employer-employee context, for instance, in the selection of partners from without.

Conclusion

In the end, apart from competence in contract negotiations and the other services a sports agent provides, what is important regarding any sports agent who represents an athlete is aiding in the defeat of what one former professional athlete calls the "meet the bus at 8 A.M. syndrome."[64] An athlete pampered and taken care of from the youth leagues on through the pros may have had no other obligation than to meet the bus, driver, or other escort at an appointed time. He or she is then whisked through the airport, handed a ticket, picked up at the destination, handed a key in the hotel lobby at a specially designated table, and finally the athlete receives a wake-up call—to meet the bus at 8 A.M. Once the athlete's career is over, there is no one to perform these or the more complex day-to-day financial and other matters that someone else handled so long as he or she was a star. Whoever represents the athlete has to prepare him, regardless of the difficulty in convincing him of the necessity, for life after the playing days come to an end.

Major changes could be made in this area, provided athletes—African-American and otherwise—begin to choose their agents based on the agent's qualifications alone, with race viewed as a potentially positive factor.[65] The star African-American athlete has unique power not only in hiring an individual agent but to stress the importance of African-American representation in dealing with one of the major firms. A first-round draft pick has more leverage than he realizes in affecting the hiring of prospective agents. The athlete's stake in improving this business is both personal and societal.

The Next Millennium

It's not my place to fight it, that's why we have a Jesse Jackson. I don't agree with discrimination or racism, but I'm not in the front office. I'm on the front line. I'm a black athlete who has been well taken care of.
— Barry Bonds, quoted in *Sports Illustrated*, April 5, 1993

Mention race relations to people in sports in any capacity, and the likely response is a shrug. Few volunteer to discuss the subject, and when it does come up, it's quickly brushed off.
— Frederick C. Klein, Wall Street Journal sports columnist,
October 13, 1995

Would the Yankees hire a minority manager and general manager in the same year?   — *New York Times*, October 28, 1995

The Ideal Industry

In the movie *Mondo Cane,* New Guinean Aborigines built an airstrip, hoping to attract the planes that frequently passed overhead. They hoped to change the behavior of something they had no control over by putting all of the elements in place for the desired result—the landing of an aircraft. Antidiscrimination laws in the United States are often much like that airstrip. This is particularly true when the laws are interpreted to mean that color may not be a consideration in repairing racial inequities. A team, league, university, or sports management firm may not be violating any existing laws. Yet legislators put the present legal framework in place in the hope that equal rights and opportunity would come about for all races in all businesses. In some areas the planes still refuse to land; those at the controls have no desire to do so. A more positive characterization may be that those in the power positions in sports do not know how to bring about change or believe that enough is being done. The passage of antidiscrimination laws is unfortunately sometimes viewed as accomplishing equality because most formerly legal discrimination has been outlawed. As John Hope Franklin has written:

Neither the courts nor the Congress nor the president can declare by fiat, resolution, or executive order that the United States is a colorblind society. They can only facilitate a movement in that direction by discharging their duties in a way that reflects their commitment to such a goal. From that point on, it is the people of all colors who must work in every way possible to attain that goal. Those who insist that we should conduct ourselves as if such a utopian state already existed have no interest in achieving it and, indeed, would be horrified if we even approached it.[1]

Along similar lines, some Supreme Court opinions have begun to point to the concept of choice as the explanation for why a statistical racial disparity exists in a particular industry.[2] The argument is that although more African-Americans could be employed in a given industry, they are not because African-Americans have chosen a different industry for employment, exercising their right of choice. That may be the case in some industries, but there are many qualified African-Americans who have chosen to work in sports and are not even being considered for positions.

In broad terms, there is a three-step progression to reaching the ideal of diverse management in the sports industry. Initially, there must be a recognition of the existence of racism, discrimination, and limited-access networks. Next, there must be a successful transition into a period where racial diversity is the standard. Diversity can be attained through affirmative action—affirmative action that focuses on opportunities for those with merit who have been ignored due to their race—affirmative action that focuses on breaking down the sports old boy network. The value of diversity must evolve to be appreciated. As this transition is completed, the accomplished goal would be multiculturalism—an industry with representation from across American society without racism, discrimination, or affirmative action programs.[3] With that as the ultimate goal, one can see why the transition period of affirmative action programs as a means of striving for diversity may be with us for a while—if we can ever get there.

Former NFL commissioner Pete Rozelle tried to explain the lack of African-American head coaches by saying that picking a head coach is "like choosing a wife."[4] The social impact of the phrase and the reasons for Rozelle's selection of it are almost haunting. Even though marriage between the races is now legal and accepted by most, some people still whisper when an interracial couple passes. In the case of Wedowee, Alabama, a high school principal attempted to cancel the school's 1994 prom because some interracial couples planned to attend.[5] It is a permanent part of our consciousness. As John Hope Franklin has written, "The color line is alive, well, and flourishing in the final decade of the twentieth century."[6]

How to Get There

Concerted Effort

It will take a concerted effort by many to bring about change in sports. Obviously, owners, commissioners, and anyone in the position to hire has the power to make an immediate impact in isolated situations. As one franchise executive maintained, the owner or chief executive officer has to believe in diversity: "That makes my job easier, when you have support from the top, and people realize that it's an area of importance and it's something we want to concentrate and focus our efforts on."[7] Others, including the leaders of the NCAA, college presidents, athletic directors, and major sports management firms, must act as well. These people in power can hire or admit an African-American with no plan, program, or person compelling them.

To combat racism in sports, we must deal with both what America and sports in reality look and act like and the paragon of what they *should* look and act like in that ideal moment in the future. To get there, an intermediate period of transition is necessary. This transition period may well become permanent. The concept of permanence is not highly regarded by the courts in the current state of antidiscrimination jurisprudence as it relates to affirmative action programs.[8] The law will continue to wrestle with this problem, but currently, to be upheld, the plans must in all likelihood have a termination date in order to pass judicial scrutiny. Alex Johnson has written appropriately:

My ideal society is one in which race is, during a transition period, viewed and thought of in much the same way as we view religion; at worst, as a matter to be tolerated, at best, as one to be prized as a product of our diversity. In this ideal society, race is taken into account not in awarding entitlements, but as an important characteristic that is acknowledged and that mandates limited differential treatment. This recharacterization of race is accomplished through the adoption of a multichromatic conception of race that respects racial diversity rather than condemning it. Similarly, diversity is viewed as part of society's strength rather than as part of its weakness. It is only through this transitory stage in which diversity is prized or simply tolerated that the ideal society can ultimately be achieved.[9]

How can the sports industry move into this transition phase?

Changing the Focus of Youth

The saddest side of sports is that it serves as a magnet for young African-American males but rejects them when their playing days are over. One portion of an ideal solution would be to remove sports as the brass ring in depressed communities and immediately replace the goal of athletic success with that of becoming something more attainable, such as a businessperson, physician, engineer, attorney, or architect. In 1968 a Louisiana high school coach said, "A white kid tries to become president of the United States, and all the skills and knowledge he picks up on the way can be used in a thousand different jobs. A black kid tries to become Willie Mays, and all the tools he picks up on the way are useless to him if he doesn't become Willie Mays."[10] As the longest of long-term goals, this transition to a change in priorities is mandatory. To reach this point would require corporate advertisers, moviemakers, team owners, and fans to stop idolizing the athlete. Achieving this goal approaches the difficulty of eliminating racism itself. To suppress somehow the public knowledge of the salaries that the athletes receive is next to impossible. This would have to be done, at the same time making other routes to success more palatable. The task of deflating the fantastic status of sports in society is formidable. In short, it is not going to happen in the foreseeable future.

Assuming we find ourselves well into the next century with sports as an industry that increasingly employs minorities to play the games, the disparity between on-the-field and off-the-field representation could become even wider unless significant strides are made in bringing about change. If the role of sports in the African-American community retains its level of importance, and if racism is permanent, then there should be a permanent struggle to correct the inequities that are and will continue to be present. Sport is one segment of society where, although racism may never be overcome, at least a more representative role and improved status for African-Americans can be achieved.

The strangest irony is that even as the skewed role of sports in the African-American community is probably permanent, so too is racism. The focus on sports by African-Americans continues because of the good that sports can do. Not to be denied, there are the few financial success stories. There are also the stories of sports "keeping kids out of trouble." Midnight Basketball leagues are springing up in a number of cities as a late-night alternative activity to gang-banging. With all good intentions and probably little or no thought to invigorate professional contract dreams, Senator Carol Moseley Braun proposed a bill to provide 6 million dollars in federal funding for basketball leagues that begin play at 10 p.m. and later.[11] Second to the ban on assault weapons, funding for Midnight Basketball, may have been the most talked-about line item in the 1994 federal crime legislation.[12] However, with all the good sports can do, athletics should not be held up as the ultimate way out for African-Americans.

Athlete and Union Action

The individuals with the most distinctive power, although not direct hiring power, are the athletes themselves. They are the key stakeholders in the sports business. They must take the risk and act. The athlete activists have historically been individuals who transcended sports in their actions. Muhammad Ali's stance against the Vietnam War and Arthur Ashe's battles against apartheid in South Africa and AIDS worldwide are prominent examples. Change will not come about, however, without a unified effort.

The unified effort can be conducted in a wide range of ways. Union activity would probably be the "safest" and most respected route for a combined effort by athletes. Any players union could avoid the problems which an isolated group of athletes face. But even unions have limitations on how far they can go to bring about more appropriate racial representation in sports.[13] Unions or other groups of athletes or teams might threaten to strike all-star games or to boycott the Super Bowl. Progress will not come without risk. African-American athletes might declare a "Black Saturday" to boycott a particular college sport.

The use of leverage is a relatively simple, if risky, concept.[14] Some of the actions by athletes would not have to be complex. Imagine the following scenario: A college recruiter is sitting in the home of a highly touted African-American student-athlete. During the discussion the young man says, "Coach, one thing that my parents and I feel is important for me to consider is the number of persons in positions of authority within your athletic department who are African-Americans. It is important to me because it reflects what the university thinks of me as an African-American and gives me some understanding of what my opportunities may be once I finish playing and may wish to coach or become involved in athletic administration."

An even greater opportunity for this type of action exists at the professional level. With free agency in its current state, imagine a highly sought-after free agent who is African-American speaking to the press about the teams he will consider joining. He says, "One thing that is important to me in selecting a team is the number of African-Americans in positions of authority with the team. It is important to me because it helps me define what my opportunities may be with that team after my playing days have ended." The short career of the athlete, as well as the subjectivity that is involved in determining careers, makes it that much more difficult to take the steps that may bring about change. Any action off the field may be cause for reduced playing time on the field, from management's viewpoint.

The epigraph quoting Barry Bonds at the beginning of this chapter indicates the attitude of those athletes who either do not care to follow history or are not aware of it. It is only fair to note that Bonds did make a public statement on discrimination when he believed race had something to do with the smaller salaries he and other black super-stars were being paid relative to their white counterparts. Bonds told *Jet* magazine, "Do you think Bobby Bonilla is worth more or less than Andy Van Slyke [a white ballplayer who received a larger contract than Bonds and Bonilla]? You know why. Let's leave it at that. He's [Van Slyke's] the Great White Hope here."[15]

Bonds and baseball are not alone in addressing inequality only as it pertains to individual matters like salaries and playing time. According to one NBA franchise executive, regarding athletes, "I really don't think they care. I'm not trying to make our players look bad by any means, but they're very self-focused."[16] And athletes are not the only African-Americans failing to step to the plate on overall race issues. Jesse Jackson proclaimed in 1994 that "many of our youth have not won anything. They've not won a boycott. They are not tough political fighters. And now they have a low confidence level."[17]

One executive placement specialist in the sports business indicated that an additional problem exists:

I'll assist an African-American to get a position, and they are not pro-active in looking to bring other minorities in. There are much fewer pro-actives. The sports world has never been pro-active. It's difficult to get those in power to even meet people. The whole sports world is a good-old-boy network.[18]

Once African-Americans are in positions of power, networking with African-American contacts can only improve the system. An example where this worked was the hiring of Tyrone Willingham, an African-American, as the head football coach at Stanford University. One of his major supporters was Minnesota Vikings and former Stanford head coach Dennis Green, who also happens to be an African-American. No major protest was required, simply participation in existing networks.

There are a few stars of the 1990s, in addition to Bonds, who have taken solo stances on race issues. David Justice of the Atlanta Braves told a reporter, "There are a lot of good guys on this team, but there are a few who I know use the 'N' word when I'm not around. . . . How many white players do you see get abused in the paper? We see it happen all the time with black players. No matter what you do, you're still a nigger. Baseball is just an extension of life."[19] *Sports Illustrated* reported that one of Justice's black teammates told him, "I'm glad you said that, but I never could have."[20]

Also supportive of this sort of speaking out is the coauthor of the Episcopalian pastoral letter condemning racism, the Reverend Arthur Williams. Williams told National Public Radio:

African-Americans, as they move ahead in society . . . often will find themselves not speaking clearly and sharply, confronting racism, enjoying the benefits of the system if they can kind of move into that without being noticed. . . . Call people on their racism. Just don't sit back and melt in.[21]

Individuals with the success and income of the superstar athlete have much to lose by being involved in political action. In fact, when they are riding high, they may not receive any of the negative treatment the average African-American in society might encounter. Occasionally a star or former star finds out otherwise. Baseball Hall of Famer Joe Morgan was harassed by police at the Los Angeles International airport, Boston Celtic Dee Brown was stopped and thrown to the ground by Boston police, and NFL star linebacker Bryan Cox of the Miami Dolphins was called racial epithets by Buffalo Bills fans as he entered Rich Stadium in Buffalo.[22]

An awareness of the history of struggle in sport is certainly not too much to ask of our athletes. When writer-broadcaster Bryan Burwell was a sports columnist with the *Detroit News*, a quote from a 1991 interview he conducted was cited quite frequently. Burwell was asking a nineteen-year-old African-American Major League Baseball prospect, Eddie Williams, about his plans for the future. Williams was a catcher, so Burwell asked him if he could imagine what it must have been like for Josh Gibson in the Negro Leagues. When Burwell informed Williams that the Hall of Fame catcher was barred from the opportunity Williams was getting, the young catcher responded,

"Never have a chance to play in the majors? Wow, I could never imagine that. Never in a million years."[23] This lack of knowledge about past struggles and successes isolates today's athletes from the larger role they play in society.

Whatever the strategy, the goal should be for those who have not historically had the opportunities in the power positions in sports to gain power—that is, to have the opportunity to show they can excel at the task. Dusty Baker, Cito Gaston, Nolan Richardson, Denny Green, Wayne Embry, Bill White, Frank Robinson, John Lucas, and John Thompson are examples of those who have made the most of their opportunities. If one speaks with people in sports—particularly athletes—one hears them say, "thanks for the opportunity," or, "Just give me the opportunity." The title of golfer Charlie Sifford's autobiography, *Just Let Me Play*, bespeaks the on-the-field attitude. The same applies to many desiring the front-office posts.

Voluntary League Action

Leaguewide action is imperative. Some of the actions already taken have been noted, and others are on the way. According to the NFL's executive vice-president Harold Henderson:

We're putting together a diversity program. We two years ago introduced the subject to the owners and got authorization to move forward, and we're still in the developmental stages, but it will entail an education program and sensitivity training and specific advice on how to go about identifying qualified minorities for your position. You can't do it in the traditional way all the time of having existing people look back in their own backgrounds and pull up the people they encounter, which is the way it's usually done.[24]

But leaguewide affirmative action plans, with great specificity, are difficult to have implemented.

Published plans to fight racism formally and to provide these opportunities in sports are not an everyday occurrence. In 1987 the *New York Times* reported that Ueberroth had an affirmative action plan forthcoming. On July 5, 1987, the *New York Times* reported, "On June 10 [, 1987, Baseball Commissioner Peter] Ueberroth set a 30-day deadline to put an affirmative-action plan in place."[25] That plan was never presented, at least not publicly. There is nothing illegal about this nonpublic presentation; the Supreme Court in fact discourages full disclosure of affirmative acton plans.[26] This prevents the full public discussion of these plans and their value. In this vein, Solicitor General Drew Days observed:

[Many affirmative action programs] have not been openly adopted and administered. Consequently, they have not benefited from the scrutiny and testing of means to ends assured by public deliberation. Programs that cannot survive the light of explicit consideration are highly susceptible to abuse and unlikely to have a stable existence. In a society in which we place such importance upon "uninhibited, robust, and wide-open" debate of public issues, it is difficult to justify the idea of privately adopted programs using racial criteria to allocate resources.[27]

In 1993 the rare event occurred of three different types of plans being proposed within weeks of one another. All of the plans were directed at baseball. Two of the plans, Jesse Jackson's and Major League Baseball's, were set forth in chapter 3. The third plan, presented by former director of outreach activities for the Oakland Athletics, Sharon Richardson Jones, is presented in Table 10.

One of the greatest difficulties I had discussing solutions with people inside and out of the sports industry was finding a way to indicate that the desire is to ensure that African-American candidates receive opportunities. As clear-cut as the concept may be, if a proposal is labeled "affirmative action," a nervousness settles into the discussion. If the phrase "affirmative action" was not used, then some argued I was practicing deception.

The long history and success of African-Americans at non-power-position levels in the industry are evidence that a huge qualified pool exists. Athletes have traditionally moved from the playing field to coaching and other front-office positions. How can owners be compelled consistently to consider this pool? In addition to the routes already discussed, another is financial sanctions by the relevant league or by the NCAA. Some type of reporting system would have to be in place to determine when an owner or university breached the established standards. At both the pro and collegiate level, the financial sanction would come from the violator's share of television or licens-

Table 10: Jones Plan

---

1. As the governing body of baseball, take immediate action to adopt, as inherent to your mission, the responsibility to model "respect and value of diversity" in all employee policies and practices.
2. Initiate a system-wide planning process to eliminate racism, sexism, anti-semitism and other forms of discrimination within Major League Baseball. This should begin with the appointment of an independent fact finding committee including representatives from the NAACP, the National Urban League, and the Rainbow Coalition Committee on Fairness in Sport.
3. Revise all institutional policies and procedures in support of multicultural respect.
4. Require all executives and managers to engage in diversity training and planning. Every baseball team should develop their Multicultural Advancement Plan.
5. Develop guidelines for the recruitment, retention and promotion of people of color in management and executive positions. Every baseball team would identify benchmark hiring standards reflective of their geographical communities.
6. Engage managers and ball players to develop local plans or programs for promoting and modeling multicultural respect.
7. Involve local, regional, and national leadership of various people of color communities in developing plans and programs involving people of color in financial benefits inherent to baseball.

SOURCE: Sharon Richardson Jones, "Race and Baseball: Getting Beyond Business as Usual," *Journal of Sport and Social Issues* 17,1 (April 1993): 67, 70.

ing revenues. An appropriate percentage would have to be decided on. But as far as getting a majority of the members of the NCAA or a league to agree on such sanctions goes, the odds are not great. According to Lal Hennigan of the NFL Management Council, "Anything is difficult to get done on a leaguewide basis. You need twenty-three of the thirty owner votes to get anything done."[28]

Civil Rights Action

In addition to athletes, owners, and commissioners, others must remain involved and participate in the struggle as well. There are certainly nonathletes who have worked to change things from the outside—Richard Lapchick, Harry Edwards, Jack Scott and those who have had lesser but still important roles, including present California Supreme Court justice Stanley Mosk. As California attorney general, Mosk took an interest in the plight of the African-American golfer Charlie Sifford. According to Sifford, after Sifford told Mosk that he could not play in most PGA tour events simply because of his race, Mosk went into action in 1959:

He contacted the PGA and asked them to verify that they practiced open discrimination as a matter of policy. He presented me as a resident of California whose civil rights were being violated and asked them to show reasons other than race why I was being denied membership.[29]

As a result of this action the PGA—after a couple of years of wrangling—granted Sifford full PGA membership.

The traditional civil rights organizations can play a greater role in the process as well. In one instance, the NAACP issued a press release comparing the hiring practices of the 1994 Super Bowl champion Dallas Cowboys with those of a "plantation."[30] At the time, nearly 75 percent of the Dallas players were African-American, and all eleven front-office positions were held by white males.[31] Some months later, Cowboys owner Jerry Jones announced that three African-Americans would shortly assume front-office vice president positions.[32] In another example, the Rainbow Coalition for Fairness in Athletics now holds an annual forum to examine the issues of racism in sports. The RCFA also is planning to rate the hiring performance of NCAA member institutions.[33]

Black fans historically have been successful in contributing to bringing about change as well. A 1961 boycott of the minor league Pelicans in New Orleans took place when the baseball team dropped its five black players.[34] The boycott spread to the entire Southern Association, leading to the league's folding that same year. The weakness of boycotts by African-Americans alone, however, was noted earlier. Such actions would probably require broader public support.

Racism and discrimination in sports can continue in many areas because the measurement of skill is so subjective. Front office positions, according to the strictly off-the-record comments of people inside, are not technically difficult. Meeting trade deadlines and ensuring that draft selections are made on time are often the most difficult tasks management personnel are called on to accomplish. At the very top levels, levying fines and presiding over ceremonies are the mindboggling tasks.

Legal Action: Involuntary Affirmative Action

Apart from the political course, legal action, as has been discussed throughout, is another method available to assist in bringing about change. But the same factors that tend to sedate political action work against whatever legal action might be brought as well. The athlete is focused on accomplishment in his or her respective sport. Further, for the marginal player, any action of either nature, political or legal, is disruptive and may brand him or her as a troublemaker, thereby providing a legacy as an unclaimed name off of the waiver wire. Many of the same issues hold true for the nonathlete potential sports industry employee. The prospective management employee, attorney or physician may be reluctant to alienate the few employers in the industry of his or her dreams by bringing a lawsuit, even where there exists merit.

One conceivable path for legal action would be through the Equal Employment Opportunity Commission. Such an action was brought by Tommy Harper in 1986 when he was a coach for the Boston Red Sox. The formal language of the Harper complaint to the Massachusetts Commission against Discrimination and the Equal Employment Opportunity Commission sought his reinstatement with the Red Sox and asserted that the team discriminated against blacks with "different terms and conditions of employment related to fringe benefits accorded only to Caucasian employees." He claimed that his firing was punitive and violated the Civil Rights Act of 1964.

The complaint alleged that while at their Florida training camp, all of the team members and coaches were given courtesy passes to the Elks Club in Winter Haven—all except the black coaches and players. To make the problem clear, Harper stated to the press, "After practices and games they go to a segregated place where I can't go and they call me 'teammate'." This was not a short-term problem, according to Harper. He became aware of it in 1972 when he was a player for the Red Sox, over a dozen years before he brought his EEOC action. Harper noticed that guest cards for one of the few places in Winter Haven that served meals were placed in the lockers of white players only. One of Harper's African-American teammates, Reggie Smith, explained to him that the club did not serve blacks. Former Sox pitcher Bill Lee amplified the realities by saying, "The only way they would serve George Scott [an African-American ballplayer] at the Elks Club was if he were on the menu."[35]

In 1984, Harper approached management, and the statement was issued that the passes were "wrong and had to stop." He told the story to local newspapers and, he alleged, was dismissed by the Red Sox.[36] The Red Sox countered that Harper's contract "was not renewed because of management's dissatisfaction with his performance of his assigned responsibilities."[37] The *Boston Globe* reported that the Equal Employment Opportunity Commission issued a two-page report finding reasonable cause to support Harper's allegations.[38] The two sides ended up reaching a settlement, the terms of which were kept confidential.

A single action may not have much broad impact. But it may cause an individual franchise to think twice before sanctioning some sort of discriminatory activity. A series of actions or a class action would have an even stronger impact. A series of actions may lead to a negotiated consent decree. If the right case or series of cases could be brought against any of the major sports leagues, or even against individual teams, a consent decree is a potential route for moving toward the elimination of racism, or at least of its numerical impacts. A consent decree combines the elements of both a contract and a court order. The parties reach a settlement agreement and the court enforces it. A consent decree could incorporate an appropriate affirmative action program.

Government Intervention

A final route alluded to previously is government intervention.[39] The government could intervene in the operations of an individual league in a number of ways. Some of the vehicles that could be used were brought to the public's attention during the Major League Baseball Strike of 1994–1995.[40] However, the key limitations of government action were displayed then as well. Although the federal government, in the person of President Bill Clinton, was fairly successful in inserting a mediator in the labor-management dispute, it was not successful in rapidly bringing about resolution.[41] There was also only limited public support for equally limited resources to focus on sports.[42]

The other governmental routes are the traditional Justice Department actions, noted earlier.[43] Although unlikely, if investigations were pursued, the end result could be consent decrees that incorporate goals and timetables.[44]

Conclusion

The comedian-activist Dick Gregory has explained the key element in any plan addressing America's race problems. Solving the problem, Gregory has said, is not in fact a race but a relay. Coupled with views of the permanence of racism, this view clarifies that it is a never-ending relay.

When Jackie Robinson and Larry Doby broke baseball's color barrier, the baton was passed to the next generation of African-American baseball players and athletes in other sports to make further progress and open more doors. Branch Rickey and other management personnel and owners who brought about integration in the other sports had the obligation to pass the baton as well. Although many athletes have carried the baton at least part of the way, few on the management side have. According to Cheryl Nauman, vice president of human resources for the Phoenix Suns basketball team, "Personal effort on the teams makes it happen."[45] Similarly, the owner of the NBA's Houston Rockets, Leslie Alexander, said, "I'm for individuals like myself to go out and do things."[46] Rob Moor, the president of the Minnesota Timberwolves, views the effort to employ more minorities as

a kick in the pants to our staff to try a little harder. Don't just sit there and wait for people to knock on our door, let's go out and look for it, let's go out and be proactive. At the levels where I know we can compete salary-wise, my mandate to this company is we will hire the best person for the job, but we will not make a decision based on that we only found four white candidates.[47]

Earlier I cited Reggie Jackson's view that this change must come about by all parties, particularly all races, working *together*. The blame cannot be placed on the white owners of sport alone; nor can it be placed solely on college presidents or powerful African-American athletes. "Together" includes the participation of many, including the white athletes, to bring about parity.

At the 1968 Olympics, probably the most dramatic and powerful demonstration by athletes was led on the field by two-hundred-meter sprinters John Carlos and Tommie Smith. On October 16, minutes after the two-hundred-meter dash, gold medalist Smith and bronze medalist Carlos stood in stocking feet on the victory platform, bowed their heads, listened to the U.S. national anthem, and raised black-gloved fists to the sky. As recounted by writer Kenny Moore:

They meant their unshod feet to represent black poverty, Smith's black scarf and Carlos's beads to signify black lynchings, their fists to mean black unity and power. Any resemblance to Lady Liberty lifting her torch was ironic, for Smith and Carlos were taking U.S. society to task for having failed to extend liberty and justice to all.[48]

The protest grew out of months of discussions through the Olympic Project for Human Rights. The demonstration was not just sports-related but focused on the condition of blacks worldwide. Carlos and Smith were truly on the "front line."[49]

A number of whites competing at the 1968 Olympics wore buttons and spoke in support of the protest. Prominent among the supporters was the white second-place finisher in the two-hundred-meter sprint, Australian Peter Norman. He wore an Olympic Project for Human Rights button on his sweatsuit on the victory stand. Norman was later reprimanded by the Australian Olympic Committee.

In a strange way, Carlos and Smith latched onto the idea later expressed in the words of African-American conservative Shelby Steele:

Black Americans will never be saved or even assisted terribly much by others, never be repaid for our suffering, and never find that symmetrical, historical justice that we cannot help but long for. These things will never happen. Jean-Paul Sartre once said that we were the true "existential people," and certainly we have always had to create ourselves out of whole cloth and find our own means for survival. Nothing has really changed.[50]

Those who feel strongly enough that something is wrong must take the same risks as have the athletes of the past. The legal rights that have been won for equal opportunity are important but are not the needed end result. According to law professor Kimberlé Crenshaw:

Society's adoption of the ambivalent rhetoric of equal opportunity law has made it that much more difficult for Black people to name their reality. There is no longer a perpetrator, a clearly identifiable discriminator. Company X can be an equal opportunity employer even though Company X has no Blacks or any other minorities in its employ. Practically speaking, all companies can now be equal opportunity employers by proclamation alone. Society has embraced the rhetoric of equal opportunity without fulfilling its promise; creating a break with the past has formed the basis for the neoconservative claim that present inequities cannot be the result of discriminatory practices because this society no longer discriminates against Blacks.[51]

The ideal is empowerment at representative levels for African-Americans. The creation of and compliance with antidiscrimination laws is not enough. Claims by the leagues or by our colleges and others that equal opportunity exists are not enough. Claims of color blindness must be recognized as rhetorical camouflage. The hearts, minds, ideas, and beliefs of sports leadership may change, but that will take time. Compared to simply changing the laws, bringing about real change is a longer, if not never-ending, process. But the power that African-Americans rightfully deserve can be transferred in a much shorter time frame.[52] Management, NCAA officials, and college presidents—the risks and sacrifices may vary among these entities, but they must be taken or the inequitable position of the African-American in sport will not change. In the words of Frederick Douglass, "Power concedes nothing without a demand. It never did and it never will."[53]

Glass ceilings blocking African-American progression to top-level positions are present in much of American society. Part of the reason for the existence of such ceilings is the discomfort of many white Americans with African-Americans in positions of power. African Americans may not be treated dramatically differently by whites in the business setting until they seek a position of power—until they seek to break through the glass ceiling. This has been referred to as a form of *differential racism*. The best current example of America's glass ceilings may be Colin Powell's contemplation of running for President of the United States. While Powell would undoubtedly have been a candidate with many of the traditional qualifications for the office, he hesitated to run. Part of his thought process in deciding whether or not to run probably included the role that his race would have played in how people viewed him. The question Powell apparently saw many asking was whether a black man could really hold the top job in the world. While in the traditional sense nothing is lacking in Powell's qualifications, he is viewed differently when it comes to considering him for an even higher position because he is an African-American.

The difficulty in realistically discussing and bringing about change struck me in casual discussions after a presentation I gave to 350 sports lawyers, including sports executives. My topic was "Affirmative Action in Sports Franchise Front Offices." I asked if we accept that there is a problem, then what do we do? I emphasized that the sports industry today is what America will be in the future. The merit of African-Americans is not an issue in sports today. In other sectors of society, one can argue that the number of African-Americans with appropriate degrees, experience, or test scores is limited. Merit can be pointed to as an outstanding issue. But not in sports. So how can we deal with the problem unless we all take affirmative steps? At some point in the talk I said, quite a distance from my planned script, "Look around you, the composition of this audience is completely the opposite of those that play the game." I did see many members of the audience literally look around. I also saw a few nonchalant shoulder shrugs.

The shrugs, and the conversations I had with many in the hallway after the presentation, were indicative of the general reaction: "You couldn't possibly be talking about me." The reality is that I am. Anyone who can have an impact on the business of sports has a responsibility to act, because the way sports addressees the issues says much about how other sectors will address inequality in the future.

■ **N O T E S**

Preface

1. Ironically, as the former general counsel of the organization, I received a telephone call from a representative of Major League Baseball in 1993 about their using the name Baseball Network for their new joint broadcasting venture with NBC. The representative asked what the organization was; I explained and asked them to put their request in writing. I never heard from them again. They are now using the name. Please excuse any confusion, but the group of African-American ballplayers were using the name first.

2. See chapter 1, note 5 and accompanying text, for Campanis's entire statement.

3. Since 1987, the owners in baseball have stripped the commissioner of these broad "best interests" powers. See, e.g., Mark T. Gould, "In Whose 'Best Interests'? The Narrowing Role of Baseball's Commissioner," *Entertainment and Sports Lawyer* 12 (spring 1994): 1; and Matthew B. Pachman, "Limits on the Discretionary Powers of Sports Commissioners: A Historical and Legal Analysis of Issues Raised by the Pete Rose Controversy," *Virginia Law Review* 76 (1990): 1409.

4. Illustrative of this, a reporter was told by a veteran major-league baseball scout that "a lot of Mexicans have bad foot speed. It's a genetic-type thing. They have a different body type. Most all have good hands and good rhythm. That's why they dance so well. Rhythm is important in baseball; it means agility." See Rod Beaton and Jim Myers, "Stacked Deck: Stereotypes and the System Keep Mexicans Out of Major Leagues, Scouts Say Players Lack Speed, Power," *USA Today,* February 25, 1993, 1C. Also see Michael Oleksask, *BEISBOL: Latin Americans and the Grand Old Game* (Grand Rapids, Mich.: Masters Press, 1991), for a general discussion of baseball in Latin America.

5. For an examination of salary discrimination in hockey, see Lawrence M. Kahn, "Discrimination in Professional Sports: A Survey of the Literature," *Industrial Labor Relations Review* 44, 3 (April 1991): 395–419, esp. 406.

6. For an excellent examination of the Jewish athlete, see Peter Levine, *Ellis Island to Ebbets Field: Sport and the American Jewish Experience* (New York: Oxford University Press, 1992).

7. See "In Japan, a Weighty Charge of Racism," *Newsweek,* May 4, 1992, 57.

8. See Geoffrey C. Ward and Ken Burns, *Baseball: An Illustrated History* (New York: Alfred A. Knopf, 1994), 40, 41.

9. See Stanley Fish, "Reverse Racism or How the Pot Got to Call the Kettle Black," *Atlantic Monthly,* November 1993, 128, 136.

10. See Mike Capuzzo, "Spreading a Wider Oar," *Philadelphia Inquirer,* July 28, 1994, F1 (noting changes in Philadelphia rowing programs after the lack of diversity on the city's Schuylkill River was brought to light).

11. It is, however, somewhat curious that the residents of the predominantly black neighborhood where the Montreal Canadiens play rarely attend games. See Dave Sell, "Blacks and Hockey Maintain a Tenuous Relationship," *Los Angeles Times,* April 1, 1990, C6. The first black to play professional hockey was Willie O'Ree in 1958. There has been one black coach of a semipro team, John Paris of the Atlanta Flames. See Kevin Allen, "New Heights for Black Coach: Atlanta's Hiring of Paris Draws Positive Response," *USA Today,* April 8, 1994, 7C. See also William N. Wallace, "To Be Young, Black and Gifted on Ice," *New York Times,* February 7, 1995, B14 (discussing Mike Grier, the best African-American to play Division I collegiate-level hockey).

Introduction

1. See, generally, Adeno Addis, "Recycling in Hell," *Tulane Law Review* 67 (1993): 2253, 2256, and citations contained therein; and Frederick A. Morton, Jr., "Class-Based Affirmative Action: Another Illustration of America Denying the Impact of Race," *Rutgers Law Review* 45 (1993): 1089 and citations contained therein. See also Ian Ayres, "Fair Driving: Gender and Race Discrimination in Retail Car Negotiations," *Harvard Law Review* 104 (1991): 817; and Regina Austin, " 'A Nation of Thieves': Securing Black People's Right to Shop and Sell in White America," *Utah Law Review* 1 (1994): 147.

2. *Director, Division on Civil Rights v Slumber, Inc.,* 42 N.J. 412 (1980).

3. *Phiffer v Proud Parrot Motor Hotel, Inc.,* 648 F2d 548 (9th Cir 1980).

4. *King v Greyhound Lines, Inc.,* 61 Ord. App. 197 (1982). For an extensive list of incidents, see Derrick Bell, *Race, Racism and American Law,* 3d ed. (Boston: Little, Brown & Co., 1992), 128, sec. 3.6.1.

5. See Patricia A. Turner, *Ceramic Uncles and Celluloid Mammies: Black Images and Their Influence on Culture* (New York: Anchor Books, 1994), xvi. Some lessons were obviously learned when five years later, a Union, South Carolina, woman accused a black man of carjacking her vehicle and driving off with her two young children, when in fact she had driven the car into a lake and killed the two boys. In that instance skepticism was expressed by many, unlike in the Stuart case. See Mark Bowden, "Blaming 'Evil Black Man with a Gun'," *Philadelphia Inquirer,* November 6, 1994, D1.

6. See Janet L. Fix, "Reno to Banks: Push Services in Minority Areas," *USA Today,* August 23, 1994, B1. The bank and its Saul Mortgage Unit agreed to

invest the money in neighborhoods that the Justice Department had found the bank had refused to serve. But cf. Jonathan R. Macey, "Banking by Quota," *Wall Street Journal*, September 7, 1994, A14: "Banks . . . feel compelled to sign lopsided consent decrees in cases like this one because the government's leverage over banks is high."

7. See Don Terry, "Jeffrey Dahmer, Multiple Killer, Is Bludgeoned to Death in Prison," *New York Times*, November 29, 1994, A1.

8. See Stephen Labaton, "Denny's Restaurants to Pay $54 Million in Race Bias Suits," *New York Times*, May 25, 1994, A1.

9. See Frank Greve, "Black Federal Workers Are Fired at Twice Rate of Whites," *Philadelphia Inquirer*, October 20, 1994, A1.

10. Ibid.

11. Ibid.

12. See, e.g., Morton, "Class-Based Affirmative Action," 1089.

13. Donald E. Lively, "Reformist Myopia and Imperative of Progress: Lessons for the Post-Brown Era," *Vanderbilt Law Review* 46 (1993): 865, 866.

14. See Richard E. Lapchick, ed., *1995 Racial Report Card* (Boston: Northeastern University, Center for the Study of Sports in Society, 1995), 6–16. See also Mike Dodd, "Survey Finds Minorities in 'Power' Positions," *USA Today*, January 11, 1993, noting that ethnic minorities filled less than 5 percent of the key management positions in professional sports. (Ethnic minorities were defined in the survey as African-Americans, Latinos, and Asians. The management positions considered were president, general manager, finance director, scouting director, and manager or head coach.) One indicator of the progress of African-Americans in corporate America in general is the number of blacks on corporate boards, which has remained at 2.3 percent over the past several years. See Brett Pulley and Jeff Bailey, "Pool of Qualified Blacks Expands, but Very Few Sit on Corporate Boards," *Wall Street Journal*, June 28, 1994, B1.

15. Lapchick, *1995 Racial Report Card*, 1–6.

16. For a discussion of the concept of "equal achievement," see Owen Fiss, "A Theory of Fair Employment Laws," *University of Chicago Law Review* 38 (1971): 235, 237–38; and Bell, *Race, Racism and American Law*, 816–17, sec 9.2.3.

17. See, e.g., Robert K. Robinson, John Seydel, and Hugh J. Sloan, "Reverse Discrimination Employment Litigation: Defining the Limits of Preferential Promotion," *Labor Law Journal* 46, 3 (March 1995): 131, esp. 133.

18. See Kenneth L. Shropshire, "Eagles Hiring of Blacks Is Laudatory, but League Lags," *Philadelphia Inquirer*, February 8, 1995, A5.

19. Letter on file with author, February 8, 1995.

20. *Sheet Metal Workers v. EEOC*, 478 U.S. 421, 494 (1986), O'Connor, J., concurring in part and dissenting in part; quoted in *United States v. Paradise*, 480 U.S. 149, 197 (1987), O'Connor, J., dissenting.

21. But cf. Kingsley R. Browne ("Statistical Proof of Discrimination: Be-

yond 'Damned Lies'," *Washington Law Review* 68 [1993]: 477), who states that "statistical evidence of intentional discrimination should be abandoned as a primary method of proof and should become, at most, merely an adjunct to evidence that specific persons have been subjected to discrimination."

22. Barry R. Gross, "The Intolerable Costs of Affirmative Action," *Reconstruction* 2 (1994): 58, 61.

23. For a comprehensive bibliography of work in the area, see Richard Delgado and Jean Stefanic, "Critical Race Theory: An Annotated Bibliography, a Year of Transition," *University of Colorado Law Review* 66 (1995): 159.

24. See discussion in the section "Race Consciousness and Permanence," below, for elaboration of both these themes.

25. See chapter 2, notes 6 to 8 and accompanying text.

26. 163 U.S. 537, 559 (1896), Harlan, J., dissenting. See also Charles A. Lofgren, *The Plessy Case: A Legal-Historical Interpretation* (New York: Oxford University Press, 1987).

27. Gwen Knapp, "His Quiet Demeanor Isn't Biggest Hurdle Dungy Must Face," *Philadelphia Inquirer,* January 1, 1995, C10.

28. T. Alexander Aleinikoff, "A Case for Race-Consciousness," *Columbia Law Review* 91 (1990): 1060, esp. 1068–69.

29. "Vow from Orioles Owner," *New York Times,* April 14, 1987, A26.

30. Jerry Reinsdorf, owner, Chicago White Sox and Chicago Bulls, telephone interview with the author, June 12, 1995.

31. See Dungy's remarks *supra,* note 27.

32. See Fiss, "A Theory of Fair Employment Laws," 235, 236.

33. Ibid., 314.

34. See Andrew Hacker, *Two Nations: Black and White, Separate, Hostile, Unequal* (New York: Ballantine, 1992).

35. Charles R. Lawrence III, "The Id, the Ego and Equal Protection: Reckoning with Unconscious Racism," *Stanford Law Review* 39 (1987): 317, 322.

36. For an interesting discussion on why color does not determine race, see John Edgar Wideman, *Fatheralong: A Meditation on Fathers and Sons, Race and Society* (New York: Pantheon Books, 1994), xv–xxv.

37. These and other "reaction" qualifications are discussed in chapter 3.

38. Interview with the Reverend Arthur Williams, "Episcopalian Pastoral Letter Condemns Racism," transcript 1071–12, National Public Radio's *Weekend Edition:* May 14, 1994. When asked whether people without power could be racist, Williams responded, "It's not to say that black persons cannot be racist. I mean, if one is in a black-dominated country like Haiti or many of the African countries, certainly you can talk about black racism, but we really do feel that prejudice, coupled with the power to enact those prejudices, equals racism. That's the definition we're working with."

39. Derrick Bell, "Racial Realism," *Connecticut Law Review* 24 (1992): 363, 373.

40. Cited in Howard Schumon, Charlotte Steeh, and Lawrence Bobo, *Racial Attitudes in America: Trends and Interpretations* (Cambridge, Mass.: Harvard University Press, 1985), 2.

41. John Hope Franklin, *The Color Line: Legacy for the Twenty-first Century* (Columbia: University of Missouri Press, 1993), 5.

42. Rainbow Coalition for Fairness in Athletics, correspondence with the author, October 5, 1993.

43. Ibid.

44. For a discussion of white race consciousness, see Barbara J. Flagg, " 'Was Blind, but Now I See': White Race Consciousness and the Requirement of Discriminatory Intent," *Michigan Law Review* 91 (March 1993): 953.

45. Ibid., 953, 970, citing bell hooks, *Yearning: Race, Gender and Cultural Politics* (Boston: Southend Press, 1990), 54. For a further discussion of whites and colorlessness see Wideman, *Fatheralong*, ix–xxv.

46. Letter to the Editor, "Gibson Must Go," *Philadelphia Inquirer*, April 22, 1994, A26.

47. See, e.g., Elizabeth Comte and Chuck Stogel, "Sports: A $63 Billion Industry," *Sporting News*, January 1, 1990, 60 (estimating the 1989 sports gross national product at $63.1 billion).

48. See Stan Grossfeld, "Savannah's President One of Kind," *Washington Post*, May 3, 1987, C9.

49. The show aired on July 28, 1988 on New Jersey Public Television. The host was Renée Chenault. The other two panelists were Patrick Forte, then an executive with the Philadelphia Eagles, and W. David Cornwell, then an executive and attorney with the National Football League.

50. Rick Telander, "Shamefully Lily-White," *Sports Illustrated*, February 23, 1987, 80.

51. A. Bartlett Giamatti, *Take Time for Paradise: Americans and Their Games*, (New York: Summit Books, 1989), 13.

52. C. L. R. James, *Beyond a Boundary* (New York: Pantheon Books, 1963), 217.

53. See, e.g., Lapchick and Benedict, eds., *1994 Racial Report Card.*

54. 347 U.S. 483 (1954).

55. Quoted in Bob Herbert, "In America, Blacks' Problems, Seen Plain," *New York Times*, July 27, 1994, A21. Price states further that "the global realignment of work and wealth is, if anything, the bigger culprit." Arguably, however, the global realignment has only served to expand opportunities in sports.

Chapter One

1. See "Position Statement for Jesse Helms," *Washington Post*, September 24, 1992, T5. See also Patricia A. Turner, *Ceramic Uncles and Celluloid Mammies:*

Black Images and Their Influence on Culture (New York: Anchor Books, 1994), 9–11, 25 (discussing an exchange of letters in an Ann Landers column in 1982 that engaged in a heated debate over the appropriateness of these lawn ornaments); and Kenneth W. Goings, *Mammy and Uncle Mose: Black Collectibles and American Stereotyping* (Bloomington: Indiana University Press, 1994), 52 (delineating that Washington's slave's name was Tom Graves and that he was holding a lantern to aid Washington's troops in finding their way back across the Delaware).

2. As one commentator describes it, "The weirdest form of folk art is the lawn jockey. I have no idea when or where the lawn jockey originated, but there is nary a be-lawned home in the vast suburban encampments that didn't sport the lawn jockey at one time or another. Most of these grotesque statuettes of legless, horse-riding midgets were racist sculpturettes of black folk. Since such objects became subjects of some controversy in the past two decades, many lawn jockeys were removed to the safety of suburban garages, where secret rituals can be conducted around them out of the public eye" (poet Andrei Codrescu on lawn jockey art, on National Public Radio's *All Things Considered*, June 8, 1993).

3. See, e.g., Cable News Network (CNN) transcript 846–4 of a debate over the presence of lawn jockeys in front of businesses in Tiburon, California, August 14, 1994.

4. Two prominent African-Americans have made statements that have been labeled racist as well. Isiah Thomas made a comment about the popularity of Larry Bird being related to his race (see "Detroit's Thomas Sees Bird in Black and White," *Jet*, June 22, 1987, 50), and Los Angeles Raiders coach Art Shell, according to ESPN's Chris Mortensen, called his quarterback Jeff Hostetler a "dumb white mother[fucker]"; Shell denied the allegation and Hostetler agreed with Shell (see Mike Lupica, *Newsday*, October 27, 1994, A94).

5. Thomas Rogers, "Some Answers No One Expected," *New York Times*, April 8, 1987, B10.

6. One former Dodgers player told me, "The sad thing is Campanis was one of the best. He was the only one upstairs brothers thought they could talk to."

7. Rogers, "Some Answers," B10.

8. See Michael Goodwin, "Snyder Dismissed over Racial Remarks," *New York Times*, January 17, 1988, Sec. 5, 1.

9. The views are mixed and largely anecdotal as to whether breeding actually took place during the years of slavery in the United States. Historian Eugene Genovese terms the thought of sophisticated breeding "utter nonsense. . . . [The slaveholder's] biggest headache was that slaves ran away. The last thing they'd want to breed for was running faster" ("Experts Dispute Greek's Theory," *USA Today*, December 16, 1991, 4C). Others point out that

certainly breeding took place but was intended to increase the numbers of slaves, not to breed in or out any particular characteristics. See Jonathan Rowe, "The Greek Chorus, Jimmy the Greek Got It Wrong but So Did His Critics; Jimmy Snyder and His Views on Pro Sports and Race," *Washington Monthly* 20, 3 (April 1988): 31. (citing Michael Blakey, an anthropologist at Howard University and the Smithsonian Institute).

10. See "Winking at Baseball's Racism," *New York Times*, February 5, 1993, A26. See also "Remark Has Schott in Hot Water Again; Reds Owner May Be Suspended," *Washington Post*, May 20, 1994, B4.

11. "Around the Majors," *Washington Post*, November 1, 1993, C5.

12. Ibid. For a case where dismissing a coach for using the word *nigger* was found to be a violation of the coach's First Amendment rights see *Dambrot v. Central Michigan University*, 55 F3d 1177 (6th Cir 1995). No public action was taken against her comment regarding "fruits." See "An Apology for Latest Schott," *Washington Post*, May 21, 1994, C6. See also Victor Lee, "Baseball's Top-Level Minority Hiring a Slow Curve," *Palm Beach Post*, June 10, 1994 1C.

13. Ira Berkow, "A Black Star Long, Long Ago," *New York Times*, November 24, 1990, 39.

14. See John M. Carrol and Fritz Pollard, *Pioneer in Racial Advancement* (Urbana: University of Illinois Press, 1992), 37.

15. See Stephen Fox, *Big Leagues: Professional Baseball, Football, and Basketball in National Memory* (New York: William Morrow & Co., 1994), 317.

16. Geoffrey C. Ward and Ken Burns, *Baseball: An Illustrated History* (New York: Alfred A. Knopf, 1994), 43.

17. Ibid.

18. See Robert Peterson, *Only the Ball Was White* (New York: Oxford University Press, 1970), 18.

19. See Jules Tygiel, *Baseball's Great Experiment* (New York: Oxford University Press, 1983), 10.

20. See Peterson, *Only the Ball Was White*, 21.

21. Ibid., 23, quoting the periodical *Sporting Life*.

22. See Ward and Burns, *Baseball*, 44.

23. Ibid.

24. See, generally, Arthur Ashe, *A Hard Road to Glory* (New York: Amistad, 1988), esp. 1.

25. See Carolyn White, "Stereotype Grew to Doom Black Jockeys," *USA Today*, December 19, 1991, 10C.

26. Ashe, *Hard Road to Glory*, 50.

27. White, "Stereotype Grew to Doom Black Jockeys," 10C.

28. Ibid., quoting Lynn Renau, curator of the Kentucky Derby Museum in Louisville, Kentucky.

29. Ashe, *Hard Road to Glory*, 11.

30. Ibid.

31. Ibid.

32. See, e.g., Texas Penal Code (1933), art. 614–11(f), which prohibited "boxing, sparring or wrestling contest or exhibition between any person of the caucasian or 'White' race and one of the African or 'Negro' race." Similarly, a 1932 Atlanta, Georgia, ordinance barred African-American and white amateur baseball clubs from playing within two blocks of each other. For an exhaustive review of other statutes, see Timothy Davis, "The Myth of the Superspade: The Persistence of Racism in College Athletics," *Fordham Urban Law Journal* 22 (1995), citing C. Vann Woodward, *The Strange Career of Jim Crow*, 3d ed. (New York: Oxford University Press, 1974), 117.

33. Ashe, *Hard Road to Glory*, 69.

34. See Michael Santa Maria, "One Strike and You're Out," *American Visions* (April 1990): 16, 18.

35. See Paul C. Weiler and Gary R. Roberts, *Cases, Materials and Problems on Sports and the Law* (St. Paul, Minn.: West Publishing, 1993), 39.

36. See Peterson, *Only the Ball Was White*, 180.

37. See Ashe, *Hard Road to Glory*, 99.

38. See Alexander Wolff and Richard O'Brien, eds., "Forgotten Pioneer," "Scorecard," in *Sports Illustrated*, January 16, 1995, 9–10.

39. Fox, *Big Leagues*, 322.

40. See John Jeansonne, "King's Legacy: Sports Moves to Prime Time," *Newsday*, April 4, 1993, 18.

41. See Wolff and O'Brien, "Forgotten Pioneer," 9, 10.

42. See Nelson George, *Elevating the Game: The History and Aesthetics of Black Men in Basketball* (New York: Simon & Schuster, 1992), 16.

43. Ibid., 68.

44. Ibid.

45. See Richard Hoffer, "The Black Pioneers," *Los Angeles Times*, January 27, 1986, 20.

46. See Jeansonne, "King's Legacy," 18.

47. John Hope Franklin, *The Color Line: Legacy for the Twenty-first Century* (Columbia: University of Missouri Press, 1993), 6.

48. Julius Lester, *To Be a Slave* (New York: Dell, 1968), 84, 85, citing Thomas Jefferson's "Notes on the State of Virginia," in *Slavery in the South*, ed. Harvey Wish (New York: Farrar, Straus and Giroux/Noonday Press, 1964). Jefferson went on to proclaim:

> They are more ardent after their female; but love seems with them to be more an eager desire, than a tender delicate mixture of sentiment and sensation. Their griefs are transient. . . . In general, their existence ap-

pears to participate more of sensation than reflections. . . . Comparing them by their faculties of memory, reason, and imagination, it appears to me that in memory they are equal to the whites; in reason much inferior, as I think one could scarcely be found capable of tracing and comprehending the investigations of Euclid and that in imagination they are dull, tasteless and anomalous . . . never yet could I find that a black had uttered a thought above the level of plain narration; never saw even an elementary trait of painting or sculpture. In music they are more generally gifted than the whites with accurate ears for tune and time, and they have been found capable of imagining a small catch. Whether they will be equal to the composition of a more extensive run of melody, or of complicated harmony, is yet to be proved. . . . I advance it therefore as a suspicion only, that the blacks . . . are inferior to the whites in the endowments of both body and mind.

49. Quoted in Woodward, *Strange Career of Jim Crow*, 21.

50. Arthur R. Ashe, Jr., interview by Charlie Rose, *Charlie Rose*, Public Broadcasting System, October 28, 1992.

51. Jeansonne, "King's Legacy," 18.

52. Reggie Jackson, "We Have a Serious Problem That Isn't Going Away," *Sports Illustrated*, May 11, 1987, 40, 48.

53. It is not only jobs. One of the unique perks in sports is the giveaways, from caps, T-shirts, and cloisonné pins to golf clubs, bags, and sporting event tickets. There is a strange clamoring by those who could easily afford to buy these items outright to get them for free or to have the power to give them away.

54. Ralph Stringer, president, Ralph Stringer and Associates, telephone interview with the author, March 4, 1995.

55. See Ward and Burns, *Baseball*, 109.

56. Ibid.

Chapter Two

1. For analysis of the value of increased diversity of ownership in sports, see *infra*, notes 6 to 70 and accompanying text.

2. For an extensive work discussing the value of diversity, see Lawrence Foster and Patricia Herzog, eds., *Defending Diversity: Contemporary Philosophical Perspectives on Multiculturalism* (Amherst: University of Massachusetts Press, 1994).

3. For a specific breakdown of the 275 individuals with ownership interests, see Richard E. Lapchick and Jeffrey R. Benedict, *1994 Racial Report Card* (Boston: Northeastern University Center for the Study of Sport in Society, 1994), appendixes 1–3.

4. For a discussion of the concept of "equal achievement," see generally, Owen Fiss, "A Theory of Fair Employment Laws," *University of Chicago Law Review* 38 (1971): 235, 237–38.

5. The discussion below in the section on "Owner Revenues" with relation to financial diversity defines the role that race may play in the salaries paid to nonsuperstar athletes.

6. Professor Derrick Bell and others have argued persuasively that we should take symbolic events such as the successful civil rights effort to make Martin Luther King, Jr.'s birthday a federal holiday for what they are: not as the end of any struggle but as just one step along the way. They are not something to be pacified by, but a measured sign of success. See Derrick Bell, *Faces at the Bottom of the Well: The Permanence of Racism* (New York: HarperCollins/Basic Books, 1992), 12.

7. See Adam Clymer, "Daughter of Slavery Hushes Senate," *New York Times,* July 23, 1993, B6.

8. Ibid.

9. See Maureen Dowd, "Senate Approves a Four-Star Rank for Admiral in Tailhook Affair," *New York Times,* April 20, 1994, A1.

10. Ibid.

11. For a criticism of the cover, see Joseph Perkins, "Simpson Case Leaves a Trail of Shame," *Atlanta Constitution,* June 29, 1994, A15: "This is Willie Horton journalism at its worst."

12. Ibid.

13. In the end, R did end up working at the games. I met the senior citizen at a pre-Olympic boxing competition where in one breath he apologized to me, in the next denied he said it, and in the third said he would never say it again. This may serve as an extreme example of how deeply ingrained unconscious racism may be.

14. The social value of diversity in the sports setting is more difficult to assess than its value in the university or in broadcasting, which will be discussed below. But society and Mr. R would be better off with diversity in sports leadership than without.

15. See Jack Curry, "Yankees Put Faith in Howe as Closer," *New York Times,* October 15, 1994, 31.

16. See Mike Wise, "Strawberry Says He's Ready for New Start," *New York Times,* July 3, 1994, C7. After a season back in the National League with the Giants, Strawberry was once again kicked out of baseball, this time for a drug test failure. See Mike Lupica, "The Role Reversal of Darryl," *Sporting News,* February 20, 1995, 8.

17. See Jon Heyman, "New York Yankees," *Sporting News,* July 3, 1995, 27.

18. Mannie Jackson, owner, Harlem Globetrotters, interview with the author in New York, October 28, 1993.

19. See John Helyar, "Why Can't Athletes and Owners Learn to Play Nice Together?" *Wall Street Journal,* September 6, 1994, B1.

20. Ibid.

21. See "A $185 Million Deal," *Sports Industry News* (April 8, 1994): 128.

22. John B. Holway, "Baseball Blackout: How the Major Leagues Shut Out African-American Fans—and How to Win Them Back," *Washington Post,* April 4, 1993, C1.

23. See Shaun Powell, "Few Faces in Sports Crowds Are Black," *Miami Herald,* August 30, 1988, 4D.

24. Neil Lanctot, "Fair Dealing and Clean Playing: Ed Bolden and the Hilldale Club, 1910–1932," *Pennsylvania Magazine of History and Biography* 117 (January-April 1993): 3.

25. See Holway, "Baseball Blackout," C1.

26. Geoffrey C. Ward and Ken Burns, *Baseball: An Illustrated History* (New York: Alfred A. Knopf, 1994), 291.

27. See Holway, "Baseball Blackout," C1.

28. See Michael Santa Maria, "One Strike and You're Out!" *American Visions* (April 1990): 16, 20.

29. See Holway, "Baseball Blackout," C1.

30. Lawrence M. Kahn and Peter D. Sherer, "Racial Discrimination in the National Basketball Association," in *The Business of Professional Sports,* ed. Paul D. Staudohar and James A. Mangan (Chicago: University of Illinois Press, 1991), 72; emphasis added.

31. Jim Myers, "Do Whites Have a Reserved Spot?" *USA Today,* December 18, 1991, 4C.

32. See also Mike Wise, "Richmond Suddenly Brightest All-Star," *New York Times,* February 13, 1995, C10, citing Charles Barkley ending a news conference at the 1995 NBA All-Star Game by saying, "That's why I hate white people," in response to a query about the league's "groupies."

33. See the column "Jockclips," *Village Voice,* November 6–12, 1991, 166.

34. Ibid.

35. There is scholarly evidence that the racial composition of a team does not impact attendance. See, e.g., Paul T. Schollaert and Donald Hugh Smith, "Team Racial Composition and Sports Attendance," *Sociological Quarterly* 28 (1987): 71. Schollaert and Smith assert that it is advantageous to owners to promulgate this negative-impact-on-attendance theory in order to pay African-Americans less (84).

36. See Phillip M. Hoose, *Necessities: Racial Barriers in American Sports* (New York: Random House, 1989), 28.

37. See "Black Tennis Stars Winning Big Bucks but Snubbed for Commercials," *Jet,* July 20, 1987, 48.

38. See, e.g., Randall Lane, "The Forbes All-Stars," *Forbes,* December 19,

1994, 266, 267. In 1994, Jordan earned $30 million in endorsements, with Nicklaus's $14.5 million and Palmer's $13.5 million rounding out the top three.

39. See Rozelle, quoted in Rick Telander, "Shamefully Lily-White," *Sports Illustrated*, February 23, 1987, 80 (*supra*, Introduction, note 50 and accompanying text); and Bill Walsh, quoted in Claire Smith, "Too Few Changes Since Campanis," *New York Times*, August 16, 1992, sec. 8, 1 (see *infra*, Chapter 4, note 15 and accompanying text).

40. See, e.g., Timothy Bates, "Do Black-Owned Businesses Employ Minority Workers? New Evidence," *Review of Black Political Economy* (spring 1988): 51, 59: "Black-owned businesses in all major industry groups employ a predominantly minority work force. The evidence suggests, furthermore, that firm viability is not hampered by reliance upon minority workers." Bates's findings refute a conclusion by Lorenzo Brown that "discrimination, especially by black-owned businesses in favor of the black labor force, is costly" in terms of firm performance; see Lorenzo Brown, "Why Should Black-Owned Businesses Hire Predominantly Black Labor Forces?" *Review of Black Political Economy* (fall 1986): 119.

41. See, e.g., Peter Wright, Stephen P. Ferris, Janine S. Hiller, and Mark Knoll, "Competitiveness through Management of Diversity: Effects on Stock Price Valuation," *Academy of Management Journal* 38, 1 (1995): 272–87, a study concluding that diverse firms have a greater value in the marketplace than firms which are not.

42. See *supra*, note 18 and accompanying text.

43. See *infra*, note 47 and accompanying text.

44. For a history of the Negro Leagues and their formation as a result of national segregation policies see Robert Peterson, *Only the Ball Was White* (New York: Oxford University Press, 1970).

45. See Santa Maria, "One Strike and You're Out," 19.

46. Ibid.

47. Lanctot, "Fair Dealing and Clean Playing," 40, citing Peterson, *Only the Ball Was White*, 120.

48. Holway, "Baseball Blackout," C1.

49. Lanctot, "Fair Dealing and Clean Playing," 4.

50. See Bobby Clay, "Team Sold, He Seeks Deal," *Black Enterprise* (January 1993): 20.

51. See Gary Baines, "Bickerstaff Is Main Man for Nuggets," *Phoenix Gazette*, February 21, 1995, C1.

52. See Ken Picking, "NBA: Injuries, Contract Woes Alter Face of Champion Pistons," *USA Today*, October 25, 1990, 7C.

53. See "Sports People: Pro Basketball; Denver Accused of Bias," *New York Times*, September 26, 1990, A18.

54. See Hoose, *Necessities*, 41.

55. See Robert E. Suggs, "Racial Discrimination in Business Transactions," *Hastings Law Journal* 42 (1991): 1257. Suggs cites freedom-of-association issues as the primary reason for the lack of judicial intervention in private transactions:

> Unlike the statutory obligation in the public sector, that procurement can be accomplished with both competitive bidding and the acceptance of the lowest responsible bid, in the private sector customers often choose their suppliers for noneconomic reasons such as friendship, social, political, or ethnic ties, or feelings of animosity towards a competing bidder, or for economic reasons prohibited in public procurement, such as returning a business favor, or wanting to develop an alternative supplier. Prohibiting these bases of choice in the private sector would raise problems regarding freedom of association under the first amendment, or of due process infringement under the fifth or fourteenth amendments. (1284–85)

56. 497 U.S. 547 (1990).

57. *Metro Broadcasting, Inc. v. FCC*, 579.

58. 115 Sup. Ct. 2097 (1995).

59. *Adarand Constructors v. Pena*, 2112–14: "Requiring strict scrutiny is the best way to ensure that courts will consistently give racial classifications a detailed examination, as to both ends and means."

60. *Adarand Constructors v. Pena*, 2113.

61. *Adarand Constructors v. Pena*, 2127–28.

62. See *U.S. Code*, vol. 47, sec. 309(i)(3)(A)(1988).

63. See *Communications Act of 1934, U.S. Statutes at Large* 48: 1064, as amended, *U.S. Code*, vol. 47, secs. 151, 301, 303, 307, 309 (1982), in which Congress gives the Federal Communications Commission (FCC) exclusive authority to grant radio and television broadcast licenses. Internal Revenue Code Section 1071, which provided tax breaks for the sale of broadcast entities to designated minority-owned enterprises, was subsequently repealed in 1995. The FCC and the Court still maintain that promoting diversity is important. After the *Adarand* decision, FCC Chairman Reed Hundt said,

> The Supreme Court's decision in *Adarand v. Pena* . . . means that all of us who very much want to insure that the opportunities of the communications revolution are available to all Americans will have to work harder to demonstrate the compelling importance of creating opportunity for those historically excluded from communications businesses. (Harry A. Jessell, "Hundt: FCC Committed to Minority Ownership," *Broadcasting and Cable* [June 19, 1995]: 35)

Dissenting in *Adarand*, Justice Stevens stated, "I have always believed that . . . the FCC program . . . would have satisfied any of our various standards in affirmative action cases—including the one the majority fashions today" *Adarand*, 115 Sup. Ct., 2127.

64. The value of the sports industry is estimated at over $60 billion. See, e.g., Elizabeth Comte and Chuck Stogel, "Sports: A $63 Billion Industry," *Sporting News*, January 1, 1990, 60.

65. Congressional action has begun to erode some of this support. Tax breaks formerly awarded to those who sold broadcast licenses to minority buyers have been eliminated. See David Hess, "Affirmative-Action Fight Begins Heatedly in House," *Philadelphia Inquirer*, February 22, 1995, A1. See also *supra*, note 61 and accompanying text.

66. 438 U.S. 265 (1978); see also, e.g., *Hopwood v Texas*, 21 F3d 603 (5th Circ 1994). The University of California Regents' decision to end all affirmative action programs is reflective of a societal retreat on affirmative action. See Gale Holland and Maria Goodavage, "California to End College Entry, Hiring by Race," *USA Today*, July 22, 1995, A1.

67. *Regents of the University of California v. Bakke*, 313, 314. The sharing of ideas is in theory a good thing, but from personal experience I must admit that it does not happen as frequently in academia as one on the outside might imagine.

68. Another case amplifying the value of diversity in a university is *Hopwood v Texas*, *supra*, note 66, where an affirmative action admissions program was challenged.

69. *Regents of the University of California v. Bakke*, 313, 314.

70. The composition of the Court has changed substantially since *Bakke* was decided. The justices now are largely the appointees of administrations not supportive of affirmative action.

71. See Tom Povtak, "Cavs Play with Fire by Hiring Fratello," *Sporting News*, October 11, 1993, 71.

72. See Murray Chass, "Going, Going, Sold: Orioles Auctioned for $173 Million," *New York Times*, August 3, 1993, B9.

73. See Roy S. Johnson, "For Blacks, Locker Room Doesn't Lead to Board Room," *New York Times*, April 14, 1987, A1.

74. See also *Piazza v Major League Baseball*, 836 F Supp 269 (ED Pa. 1993), where the denial to purchase a sports franchise is challenged on antitrust grounds.

75. Although no cases are to this point, one can only assume that if a violation of the law did occur, the appropriate remedy would be some form of damages. For example, in the cases that follow in the text *infra*, the allegation of the plaintiffs is that their being denied sports-franchise ownership

violated antitrust laws; see *infra*, notes 76 to 82 and accompanying text. The remedy there probably would be treble damages, not an order for specific performance compelling the sale of the franchise to the plaintiff. Compelling the sale, a more equitable remedy, would be troublesome from a constitutional freedom-of-association standpoint. See, e.g., *New York State Club Association v. City of New York*, 487 U.S. 1, 18–20 (1988), O'Connor, J., concurring, stating that First Amendment rights to freely associate may shield private groups from antidiscrimination laws.

76. *Levin v NBA*, 385 F Supp 149 (SD N.Y. 1974).

77. *Levin v NBA*, 150.

78. 720 F2d 772 (3d Cir 1983).

79. See *infra*, note 81.

80. See *Mid-South Grizzlies v NFL*, 720 F2d 772; see also, *Seattle Totems v NHL*, 479 U.S. 932 (1986), and *Piazza v Major League Baseball, supra*, note 74 (this suit included antitrust issues as well as issues related to defamation of character; the principals settled out of court). See Ronald J. Sanchez, "MLB Owes Investors Apologies, $6 Million," *USA Today*, September 30, 1994, 11C.

81. Again, the freedom-of-association rights expressed in *New York State Club* (*supra*, note 75) are key here. A partnership is probably the closest approximation of the legal status of a sports league. Professor Gary Roberts has noted that confusion over the economic structure of sports leagues is caused by the mistaken equation of a sports league with the "service organization each league creates to perform certain functions that are better left to administrators than to the league's quasi-legislative governing body" ("Sports Leagues and the Sherman Act: The Use and Abuse of Section 1 to Regulate Restraints on Intraleague Rivalry," *UCLA Law Review* 32 [1984]: 219, 241n. 72). These administrative functions include "scheduling, resolving disputes among players and franchises, supervising officials, discipline and public relations" (*Los Angeles Memorial Coliseum Commission v Oakland Raiders, Ltd.*, 726 F2d 1381, 1389 [9th Cir 1984]). The interactions of the clubs are not necessarily analogous to the functions of the league office. A key element in this confusion is that the league office traditionally carries the name of the league itself, such as the National Football League and the National Basketball Association (Roberts, "Sports Leagues and the Sherman Act," 241). Commentators are quite correct when they state that the league does not precisely resemble any standard form of organization. Although the leagues have not been set up as partnerships, many view that form of association as the best approximation of the way in which the leagues operate. See, generally, Myron C. Grauer, "Recognition of the National Football League as a Single Entity under Section 1 of the Sherman Act: Implications of the Consumer Welfare Model," *Michigan Law Review* 82 (1983): 1. See also *Levin v NBA*, 152 (equating

joint venturers in the NBA with a partnership). But cf. Roberts, "Sports Leagues and the Sherman Act," 225 where he insists that a league resembles no other business entity, "including a partnership."

82. See *infra*, note 110.

83. *U.S. Code*, vol. 42, sec. 2000(e)(1) et seq (1988).

84. See, e.g., *Hishon v. King & Spalding*, 467 U.S. 69 (1984): "The contractual relationship of employment triggers the provisions of Title VII governing 'terms, conditions, or privileges of employment.' " And see Note, "Applicability of Federal Antidiscrimination Legislation to the Selection of a Law Partner," *Michigan Law Review* 76 (1977): 282: "The courts have interpreted [*U.S. Code*, vol. 42, secs. 2000e to (e)(i)(17)] as prohibiting only those discriminatory practices that occur within the context of an employment." (This source hereafter is referred to as "Discrimination in Law Partner Selection.") See *Hishon v. King & Spalding*, 467 U.S. 69. In *Hishon*, the petitioner alleged that she was denied partnership because of her sex. The Supreme Court reversed the U.S. Court of Appeals for the Eleventh Circuit, which had held that "Title VII was inapplicable to the selection of partners by a partnership." Although the Court did not answer this question, it held that because the underlying employment relationship is a contractual one, advancement to partnership is a benefit or privilege of employment but only when made explicit or implied as such. Here the petitioner alleged that such advancement had been used to induce her to work for the defendant. The Court held that the petitioner's allegation stated a claim under Title VII, because an explicit or implicit benefit or privilege of employment triggers the protection of Title VII inasmuch as it is "terms, conditions or privileges of employment." See *Hishon v. King & Spalding*, 74-75, 78-79.

85. *U.S. Code*, vol. 42, sec. 1981 (1988).

86. *U.S. Code*, vol. 42, sec. 1981 (1988); emphasis added.

87. "Discrimination in Law Partner Selection" (*supra*, note 84), 297.

88. See *Jones v. Alfred Mayer Co.*, 392 U.S. 409 (1968).

89. See "Discrimination in Law Partner Selection," (*supra*, note 84), 296.

90. But compare the following:

Whites had at the time when § 1981 was first enacted, and have, [with a few exceptions,] *no* right to make a contract with an unwilling private person, no matter what that person's motivation for refusing to contract. Indeed it is and always has been central to the very concept of a "contract" that there be "assent by the parties who form the contract to the terms thereof." *Restatement of Contracts* § 19(b) (1932). The right to make contracts, enjoyed by white citizens, was therefore always a right to enter into binding agreements only with willing second parties. Since the statute only gives Negroes the "same rights" to contract as is enjoyed by whites, the language of the statute confers no right on Negroes to enter into a contract with an unwilling person no matter what that person's motivation for refusing to contract. (*Runyon v. McCrary*, 427 U.S. 160, 193–94 [1976], White, J. and Rehnquist, J., dissenting)

91. Section 1981 protects both whites and nonwhites from racial discrimination in the making of contracts. See *McDonald v. Santa Fe Trail Transportation Co.*, 427 U.S. 273 (1976).

92. See *General Building Contractors Association v. Pennsylvania*, 458 U.S. 375 (1982)—disparate impact not encompassed by Section 1981.

93. *Setser v Novack Investment Co.*, 657 F2d 962, 966–67 (8th Cir) (en banc.), *cert. denied*, 454 U.S. 1064 (1981). A case where a race-conscious affirmative action plan to remedy past discrimination was approved.

94. See, e.g., *Blount v Xerox Corp.*, 405 F Supp 849, 853 (ND Ca. 1975) (footnote omitted): Section 1981 "cannot be construed to place an affirmative obligation on employers to adopt or to maintain affirmative action programs."

95. Johnny Clyde Parker, Note, "Civil Rights Legislation: Getting Black Executives Off First Base in Professional Team-Sports," *Columbia Business Law Review* (1986): 219, 227.

96. 420 F Supp 919 (SD N.Y. 1976), *aff'd mem.*, 559 F2d 1203 (2d Cir), *cert. denied*, 434 U.S. 920 (1977).

97. *EEOC v Kallir, Philips, Ross, Inc.*, 926.

98. See Parker, "Civil Rights Legislation," 225–30.

99. Ibid., 226.

100. See *supra*, note 75 and accompanying text.

101. 678 F2d 1022 (11th Cir 1982) rev'd 467 U.S. 69 (1984).

102. Ibid.

103. *Hishon v King & Spalding*, 1022, 1024.

104. See *Hishon v. King & Spalding*, 467 U.S. 69, 76–79 (1984).

105. *Hishon v King & Spalding*, 79.

106. *Hishon v King & Spalding*, 79.

107. *Hishon v King & Spalding*, 78.

108. See, generally, Paul J. Much and Alan Friedman, *Inside the Ownership of Professional Sports Teams* (Chicago: Team Marketing Report, 1995).

109. The distrust expressed in *Levin* is illustrative of this. See *supra*, note 76 and accompanying text.

110. See *supra* note 81 and accompanying text. In the gender discrimination case of *Hopkins v. Price Waterhouse*, however, the successful plaintiff received as part of her remedy from the District Court admission to a partnership. 737 F Supp 1202 (D.D.C. 1990), aff'd, 920 F2d 967 (D.C. Cir 1990). Even in doing so the court noted the distinction between elevating an employee to partnership

compared with granting the "retention of partnership or the regulation of the relationship among partners." *Hopkins* at 969.

111. See Howard Kohn, "Service with a Sneer," *New York Times Magazine,* November 6, 1994, 42.

112. Ibid., 47.

113. See ibid., 44.

114. See William C. Rhoden, "A Beacon of Light in Charlotte," *New York Times,* November 12, 1994, 31.

115. The United States Justice Department reached the conclusion that the Denny's matter was the largest case involving violations of the public accommodations section of the Civil Rights Act of 1964. See Kohn, "Service with a Sneer," 44.

116. Rhoden, "A Beacon of Light," 31.

117. Ibid.

118. See discussion *supra,* notes 71–82 and accompanying text.

119. Rhoden, "A Beacon of Light," 31.

120. As discussed in chapter 1, the racist comments of Cincinnati Reds owner Marge Schott and former Los Angeles Dodgers executive Al Campanis are well documented. See, e.g., Thomas Rogers, "Some Answers No One Expected," *New York Times,* April 8, 1987, B10 (regarding Al Campanis); and "Winking at Baseball's Racism," *New York Times,* February 5, 1993, A26 (regarding Marge Schott).

121. See Clay, "Team Sold," 20 (*supra,* note 50 and accompanying text).

122. See Lapchick and Benedict *1994 Racial Report Card,* appendix 3.

123. See *Report of Equal Opportunity Committee* (New York: Major League Baseball, 1994).

124. See discussion *supra,* notes 111 to 119 and accompanying text.

125. See Harvey Araton, "Player's Man in the Owner's Boardroom," *New York Times,* October 24, 1994, C1.

126. See "Ownership Ranks Remain Limited," *USA Today,* August 3, 1994, 7C.

127. See "SportsPeople: Johnson Buys Stake in Dream in Lakers," *New York Times,* June 28, 1994, B12.

128. See *Washington Capitols Basketball Club, Inc. v Barry,* 419 F2d 472, 474 (9th Cir 1969).

129. See *supra,* notes 30 to 38 and accompanying text.

130. See, e.g., John C. Coffee, Jr., "Unstable Coalitions: Corporate Governance as a Multi-Player Game," *Georgetown Law Journal* 78 (1990): 1495.

131. See ibid., 1523.

132. See "Rival Baseball League Offers Franchise Stake, Profit-Sharing," *Sports Industry News* (November 4, 1994): 422.

133. In contrast to pilots, athletes have far shorter careers, averaging four

years in the major sports leagues, and thus may not have as long a view of the needs for a business to succeed. In the current structure of sports leagues there is rarely an ownership interest held by athletes. With an equity interest, however, athletes' long-term desire for a more diverse business may develop.

134. One need only examine the annual list in *Black Enterprise* magazine of the one hundred largest black businesses; see, e.g., Alfred Edmond, Jr., "The Black Enterprise 100 22nd Annual Report on Black Business," *Black Enterprise* (June 1994): 75. Adequate finances among African-American individuals and groups are available.

135. See discussion *supra,* notes 7 to 14 and accompanying text.

136. See *supra,* notes 76–77 and 100–110 and accompanying text.

137. See Lapchick and Benedict, *1994 Racial Report Card,* appendix 3.

138. Jackson, interview with the author (*supra,* note 18).

139. See *supra,* notes 55 to 65 and accompanying text.

140. See *Regents of the University of California v. Bakke,* 438 U.S. 265 (1978). See also *Hopwood v Texas,* 21 F3d 603 (5th Circ 1994).

141. See *Metro Broadcasting, Inc. v. FCC,* 497 U.S. 547 (1990), where Justice Kennedy wrote in a dissenting opinion, "I cannot agree with the Court that the Constitution permits the Government to discriminate among its citizens on the basis of race in order to serve interests so trivial as 'broadcast diversity.' "

142. This is particularly true in light of the transition to a more conservative Court that has taken place since the rulings in *Metro,* which has certainly resulted in a court less receptive to the value of diversity.

143. Lanctot, "Fair Dealing and Clean Playing," 21, citing the *Baltimore Afro-American,* April 11, 1925. In 1922, Bolden was the only black member elected to the Board of Governors of the Philadelphia Baseball Association, a white-dominated organization of sixty-five teams.

Chapter Three

1. See, e.g., *Local No. 93, International Association of Firefighters v. City of Cleveland,* 478 U.S. 501, 533 (1986), White, J., dissenting.

2. See, e.g., *Johnson v. Transportation Agency,* 480 U.S. 616, 637 (1987).

3. For a collection of essays on both sides, see Nicolaus Mills, ed., *Debating Affirmative Action: Race, Gender, Ethnicity, and the Politics of Inclusion* (New York: Delta Books, 1994).

4. This basic concept was amplified by the Supreme Court in *Adarand Constructors, Inc. v. Pena,* 115 Sup. Ct. 2097 (1995). There the Court aligned the previously more relaxed "intermediate" standard for federal affirmative action programs to the same level of strict scrutiny as exercised by state and local governments. Any reviews of private affirmative action programs may be pushed to higher levels of scrutiny as well.

5. See *Wygant v. Jackson Board of Education,* 476 U.S. 267, 273 (1986), citing *Fullilove v. Klutznick,* 448 U.S. 448, 491 (1980).

6. *Fullilove v. Klutznick,* 448 U.S. 448, 537 (1980), Stevens, J., dissenting.

7. See Michael Sovern, "Legal Restraints on Racial Discrimination in Employment" (New York: Twentieth Century Fund, 1966): 7–8; cited by Derrick Bell, *Race, Racism, and American Law* (Boston: Little, Brown, 1992), 814.

8. Ibid.

9. Owen Fiss, "A Theory of Fair Employment Laws," *University of Chicago Law Review* 38 (1971): 235.

10. *U.S. Code,* vol. 42, sec. 2000(e) et seq.; and *U.S. Code,* vol. 42, sec. 1981.

11. *McDonnell Douglas Corp. v. Green,* 411 U.S. 792, 802 (1973).

12. *McDonnell Douglas Corp. v. Green,* 802.

13. For a discussion of the rule and the Uniform Guidelines on Employee Selection Procedures, see Mark A. Rothstein, *Employment Law* (St. Paul, Minn.: West Publishing, 1994), 131–32, sec. 3.18.

14. See, e.g., *Griggs v. Duke Power Co.,* 401 U.S. 424 (1971).

15. See *Wards Cove Packing Co. v. Atonio,* 490 U.S. 642, 656–68 (1989). *Wards Cove* addressed the disparate-impact theory of discrimination citing the rule as first presented in *Griggs v. Duke Power Co.,* 401 U.S. 424 (1971): a "disparate impact case is one in which the plaintiff alleges that a facially neutral test or employment criterion disqualifies a protected class from employment, promotion, or other opportunity that is not job-related." See Johnny C. Parker, "Civil Rights Legislation: Getting Black Executives Off First Base in Professional Team Sports," *Columbia Business Law Review* 1 (1986): 219, 224n. 26. *Griggs* (at 431) held that employment practices having a disparate impact on blacks were unlawful unless the employer could show that the policies were job-related and justified by a business necessity.

16. 401 U.S. 424 (1971).

17. Newton Jackson, consultant, NAACP, telephone interview with the author, January 15, 1995.

18. See, e.g., Kingsley R. Browne, "Statistical Proof of Discrimination: Beyond 'Damned Lies'," *Washington Law Review* 68 (1993): 477.

19. *U.S. Code,* vol. 42, sec. 2000(e)-2a(2)(1994).

20. See *supra,* note 11 and accompanying text.

21. See "Parcells Denies Racism," *New York Times,* May 31, 1992, sec. 8, 3. New York Giants head coach Bill Parcells denied that race was a factor in the hiring decision on Lance Hamilton as assistant coach. Parcells stated that Hamilton was not qualified.

22. See "Ex-Linebacker Loses Again in Giants Case," *New York Times,* November 3, 1993, B16.

23. Ibid.

24. See *Congressional Record*, 102d Cong., 1st sess. 137, 155 (October 25, 1991): 5152–34.

25. 490 U.S. 642 (1989).

26. *Wards Cove Packing Co. v. Atonio*, 490 U.S. at 650, citing *International Brotherhood of Teamsters v. United States*, 431 U.S. 324, 339 (1977), and *Hazelwood School District v. United States*, 433 U.S. 299, 307–8 (1977).

27. *U.S. Code*, vol. 42, secs. 1981, 1981a, 2000e.

28. See Parker, "Civil Rights Legislation," 219, 224n. 26.

29. See, e.g., *Johnson v University of Pittsburgh*, 435 F Supp 1328, 1371 (WD Pa. 1977); *Cussler v University of Maryland*, 430 F Supp 602, 605–6 (D Md. 1977).

30. See *Crouch v NASCAR*, 845 F2d 397 (2nd Cir 1988).

31. See generally, Kenneth L. Shropshire, "New Concepts of Contract Liabilities in College Sports: Member Institutions v. the National Collegiate Athletic Association," *Hastings Communications and Entertainment Law Journal* 11 (1988): 1–33.

32. See *Wards Cove Packing Co. v. Atonio*, 656–68.

33. *Wards Cove Packing Co. v. Atonio*, 650.

34. For discussions on unconscious racism see Charles R. Lawrence III, "The Id, the Ego and Equal Protection: Reckoning with Unconscious Racism," *Stanford Law Review* 39 (1987): 317.

35. *International Brotherhood of Teamsters v. United States*, 431 U.S. 324, 339 (1977).

36. See the interpretive memorandum of Senators Joseph Clark and Clifford Case, in *Congressional Record*, 88th Cong., 2d sess. 110 (April 8, 1964): 7213.

37. Section 703(j) of the act provides,

> Nothing in this subchapter shall be interpreted to require any employer . . . to grant preferential treatment to any individual or to any group . . . on account of an imbalance which may exist with respect to the total number or percentage of persons of any [protected class] in comparison with the total number or percentage of persons of such [protected class] in . . . the available work force. (*U.S. Code*, vol. 42, sec. 2000e-2[j])

38. Kingsley R. Browne, "The Civil Rights Act of 1991: A 'Quota Bill,' a Codification of *Griggs*, a Partial Return to *Ward's Cove*, or All of the Above?" *Case Western Reserve Law Review* 43 (1993): 287, 320.

39. 443 U.S. 193 (1979).

40. *United Steel Workers v. Weber*, 208.

41. *United Steel Workers v. Weber*, 208.

42. *United Steel Workers v. Weber*, 208.

43. 480 U.S. 616 (1987). See also *United States v. Paradise*, 480 U.S. 149 (1987).

44. *Johnson v. Transportation Agency*, 616.

45. *Johnson v. Transportation Agency*, 616.

46. A concurring opinion in *Adarand*, however, maintains that there is no distinction between types of discrimination. According to Justice Clarence Thomas, "In my mind, government-sponsored racial discrimination based on benign prejudice is just as noxious as discrimination inspired by malicious prejudice. In each instance, it is racial discrimination, plain and simple" (*Adarand Constructors v. Pena*, 115 Sup. Ct. 2097, 2119 [1995] [footnote omitted]).

47. Larry Alexander, "What Makes Wrongful Discrimination Wrong? Biases, Preferences, Stereotypes, and Proxies," *University of Pennsylvania Law Review* 141 (1992): 149, 217–18. Alexander listed five reasons backing his position:

> The moral case for voluntary affirmative action is not as certain as its legality. Voluntary affirmative action is rarely the product of bias. Working in favor of voluntary affirmative action is its potential to counteract the negative social effects of disparate group impact. . . . Factors working against voluntary affirmative action plans, however, include various negative social effects it may itself engender, particularly when sponsored by major private institutions. Ultimately, the moral case for or against voluntary affirmative action plans is an empirical one that cannot be settled from the armchair. Nonetheless, some potential negative effects of affirmative action that bear on its morality are worth mentioning. First, when major private institutions award jobs based on race, they tend to produce or exacerbate racial balkanization and racial politics. Racial groups will fight over their allocations of jobs. Some subgroups will demand their own allocation, while others will wish to be included within larger groupings.
>
> Second, individuals will attend less to improving their own productivity and more to racial politics if racial group membership is an alternative to productivity as a means of advancement. Third, more productive groups will feel great resentment at being discriminated against because of their race. Civil strife born of resentment will replace the civil strife born of unequal group status. Fourth, negative biases toward and negative stereotypes regarding the beneficiaries will as likely be reinforced or increased in number as eliminated.
>
> Fifth, the beneficiaries themselves may feel stigmatized, suffer self-doubt, and in order to protect their self-esteem adopt what Chris Wonnell calls the "affirmative action ideology," the claim that meritocratic

values are racist or sexist. Indeed, affirmative action beneficiaries will be more likely to adopt this ideology when the values behind the ordinary preferences that affirmative action trumps are deeply held by the affirmative action beneficiaries and others.

Finally, affirmative action raises the costs to the employer and thus to the consumer of satisfying ordinary preferences. Productivity is reduced in the sense that priorities are shifted from producing ordinary goods and services to producing more equality of groups.

48. 488 U.S. 469 (1989).

49. *City of Richmond v. J. A. Croson Co.*, 528.

50. *City of Richmond v. J. A. Croson Co.*, 561.

51. *Adarand Constructors v. Pena*, 115 Sup. Ct. 2097 (1995).

52. Civil Rights Act of 1991, sec. 116.

53. See William B. Gould, *Agenda for Reform: The Future of Employment Relationships and the Law* (Cambridge, Mass.: MIT Press, 1993), 254.

54. Ibid. For an analysis of the legislation's validation of affirmative action, see Alfred W. Blumrosen, "Society in Transition IV: Affirmation of Affirmative Action under the Civil Rights Act of 1991," *Rutgers Law Review* 45 (1993): 903.

55. Civil Rights Act of 1991, sec. 2000 (e)-b.

56. See Janet L. Fix, "Reno to Banks: Push Services in Minority Area," *USA Today*, August 23, 1994, B1.

57. See *Chronicle of Higher Education*, September 21, 1994, A13.

58. *Burton v. Wilmington Parking Authority*, 365 U.S. 715, 722 (1961).

59. See also *Herkl v City of Pontiac*, 470 F Supp 603 (ED Mich. 1979).

60. See *Ludtke and Time, Inc. v Kuhn*, 461 F Supp 86 (SD N.Y. 1978).

61. However, the Department of Labor currently is investigating some top colleges.

62. *City of Richmond v. J. A. Croson Co.*, 498–99.

63. The major sports legislation that did pass in the 1960s relates to league mergers and television. The other major piece of federal sports legislation was the Amateur Sports Act (*U.S. Code*, vol. 36, sec. 380 [1978]), which regulates the Olympic movement in this country. Numerous topics have been debated, however, from sports-agent regulation to sports-franchise relocation regulation.

64. See William B. Gould IV, "Time for Affirmative Action," *San Francisco Examiner*, July 6, 1986, C8.

65. Arguably as a consequence of recent Supreme Court rulings the presence of such plans could decline. For a discussion of reductions in affirmative action in contracting see Paul M. Barrett, "Pentagon Move to Hurt Minority Builders," *Wall Street Journal*, October 25, 1995, B2.

Chapter Four

1. For biographical information on Edwards, see Robert Lipsyte, "An Outsider Joins the Team," *New York Times,* May 22, 1988, 34.

2. This was the primary concern expressed by the members of the Baseball Network.

3. "Edwards Hires Campanis to Assist Baseball Job," *Jet,* 48 September 14, 1987, 148.

4. It is important to recognize from the outset of any analysis of hiring in sports that not all athletes are interested in that progression as a logical career change. Baseball Hall of Famer Joe Morgan has said,

> You have to realize, when you're a professional athlete, one of the problems with a professional athlete is that you think that your career is going to go on forever. And a lot of people do not start to think about what they're going to do after the game. And when you have the players making the amount of money they are making today, they are not really concerned with having a job in baseball after it's done. And I think therein lies part of our problem. (on "Both Sides with Jesse Jackson," Cable News Network [CNN] transcript 73 of broadcast, May 29, 1993)

5. See Charles Grantham, "NBA: A Land of Unequal Opportunity," *Chicago Sun-Times,* September 27, 1992, 30. See *supra,* Introduction, notes 14 to 17.

6. See "Royals' Brett Ready to Go Out in Style," *USA Today,* September 27, 1993, 3C.

7. The appointment of Isiah Thomas as general manager by the Toronto Raptors of the NBA, noted in chapter 2, is certainly an exception.

8. Hank Aaron on ABC's *Nightline,* "Blacks in Baseball's Front Office," transcript of broadcast, June 5, 1991.

9. Dave Anderson, "When the Dodgers Ignored Robinson," *New York Times,* April 15, 1987, B7.

10. Ibid.

11. See "Managerial Facts in Black and White," *USA Today,* April 23, 1987, 3C.

12. Ibid.

13. See Lou Ransom, "Black Named NFL Head Coach after Seven Decades," *Jet,* October 23, 1989, 48–50.

14. See Bill Lyon, "The Confident New Coach Makes a Good Impression," *Philadelphia Inquirer,* February 4, 1995, 1.

15. Claire Smith, "Too Few Changes since Campanis," *New York Times,* August 16, 1992, sec. 8, 1.

16. "Race in the Workplace," *Business Week,* July 8, 1991, 50, 52.

17. See Grantham, "NBA: A Land of Unequal Opportunity," 30.
18. Ibid., 30.
19. See discussion *supra,* Chapter 2.
20. Anshel also found that

> a second area of discomfort for the subjects was the coach's pregame behaviors. They understood the coach's need to behave in a highly aggressive and excitable manner prior to the contest, although they personally did not respond favorably to it. However, less constructive was the tendency of white coaches to criticize selective black athletes for their apparent "lack of enthusiasm" as determined purely from observations. Although the team's single black assistant coach, a former college football athlete, understood the preferences of black athletes in their pregame mental preparation, white coaches wrongly confused the players' virtual absence of verbal assertiveness with low motivation and a "don't care" attitude about the team. Black players resented the coach's demands to conform to his expectations which were more the norm for white than for black players. Several of the players echoed the following sentiment: "I respond more to a challenge; white players respond more to intimidation." (Mark H. Anshel, "Perceptions of Black Intercollegiate Football Players: Implications for the Sport Psychology Consultant," *Sport Psychologist* 4 [1990]: 235, 242)

21. See Alan Wertheimer, "Jobs, Qualifications, and Preferences," *Ethics* 94 (October 1983): 99–112.
22. Regarding guidelines for bona fide occupational qualifications, see, e.g., *Wilson v Southwest Airlines Co.,* 517 F Supp 292 (ND Tex. 1981).
23. Wertheimer, "Jobs, Qualifications, and Preferences," 100–101. Wertheimer further cites as examples

> (1) An elementary school principal must choose S or T to teach first grade. S has superior pedagogical skills but has a thick foreign accent which six-year-olds find odd and difficult to understand. The children will actually learn more from T. (2) A high school principal must choose U or V to teach a ninth-grade class with serious discipline problems. Whereas U is better trained, he is short and has a high-pitched voice. V is tall, muscular, and has a deep authoritative voice. For this reason, V will have fewer discipline problems and will elicit more learning. . . . (3) An advertising agency must choose Y or Z to model swimwear. Although Y's posing technique is superior, Z has the physical attributes (tall, thin, small bustline) which make this swimwear appear more attractive. (4) A university health service must choose M (male) or F (female) as staff gynecologist. M is a superior diagnostician, but many

female students feel more at ease with a female gynecologist, will respond better to a female's advice, and will not seek needed medical care from a male physician. There will, therefore, be fewer medical problems if F is chosen. . . . (6) An appliance store owner must choose H or L as a salesman. H has superior knowledge of appliances but has an aggressive hard-sell personality. L is low-key, and customers in this region (although not in all regions) will buy more from low-key salesmen. (7) A baseball manager must choose R (right-handed) or L (left-handed) to pitch a crucial game. R is faster and has better control, but because the opposition has mostly left-handed batters who have trouble hitting left-handed pitches, L is more likely to win.

24. Ibid., 100.

25. See Gwen Knapp, "His Quiet Demeanor Isn't Biggest Hurdle Dungy Must Face," *Philadelphia Inquirer,* January 1, 1995, C10.

26. Wertheimer, "Jobs, Qualifications, and Preferences," 107.

27. Ibid.

28. S. A. Paolantonio, "Coach Feels Race Important, but Not Everything," *Philadelphia Inquirer,* December 11, 1994, C10.

29. S. A. Paolantonio, "Good Cops, Bad Cops on a Hot Day at Camp," *Philadelphia Inquirer,* July 23, 1995, C2.

30. Mary Davis, vice president of human resources, National Basketball Association's Washington Bullets, telephone interview with the author, March 23, 1995.

31. Confidential interview with the author.

32. See Rick Wartzman, "Clinton Is Still Struggling to Get Message Across to 'Angry White Males' Who Have Tuned Out," *Wall Street Journal,* January 24, 1995, A24. As with any poll some of the animosity shown in the results may be due to the phrasing of the question. According to pollster Louis Harris, "Affirmative action, which most Americans favor, and preferential treatment, which most oppose, are conflicting ideas. To destroy affirmative action for women and minority groups, Republicans want to create confusion so that the two ideas are perceived as synonymous." See Louis Harris, "Affirmative Action and the Voter," *New York Times,* July 31, 1995, A13.

33. See James Ledvinka and Vida G. Scarpello, *Federal Regulation of Personnel and Human Resource Management* (New York: Van Nostrand, Reinhold, 1991), 166–67.

34. One of the earliest uses of the term *affirmative action* was in the Wagner Labor Relations Act of 1935. That usage, however, had no relation to race. The term was probably popularized by President Lyndon B. Johnson in Executive Orders 11246 and 11375, which sought to increase minority and female contractors. Prior to this, President John F. Kennedy issued Executive Order

10925, which required employers to recruit minorities into their applicant pools. Lance Liebman ("Justice White and Affirmative Action," *University of Colorado Law Review* 58 [1987]: 471, 472n. 8) cites Kennedy as the source of the term in his executive order which states "The contractor will take affirmative action to ensure . . ."

35. Randall Kennedy, "Persuasion and Distrust: A Comment on the Affirmative Action Debate," *Harvard Law Review* 99 (1986): 1327, 1332.

36. In much of the critical race theory literature on affirmative action, the focus is on merit and the invalidity of many of the standards established in the workplace. There has been a particular focus on the standards used for hiring law professors. See, e.g., Daniel A. Farber, "The Outmoded Debate over Affirmative Action," *California Law Review* 82 (1994): 893.

37. See John R. Dorfman and Udayan Gupta, "Choice Positions for Four Blacks Mask Problems," *Wall Street Journal*, February 3, 1995, B1.

38. See Steven A. Holmes, "Programs Based on Sex and Race Are Under Attack," *New York Times*, March 16, 1995, 1.

39. Ted Leland, director of athletics, Stanford University, telephone interview with the author, April 10, 1995.

40. Harold Henderson, executive vice president, National Football League, telephone interview with the author, April 10, 1995.

41. Ralph Stringer, president, Ralph Stringer and Associates, telephone interview with the author, March 4, 1995.

42. See, e.g., Karen Paul and Steven D. Lydenberg, "Applications of Corporate Social Monitoring Systems: Types, Dimensions and Goals," *Journal of Business Ethics* 11 (1992): 1–10.

43. Ibid.

44. Brent Benner, President, Brent Benner and Associates, telephone interview with the author, May 17, 1995.

45. Jimmy Lee Solomon, Director of minor league operations, Major League Baseball, interview with the author, April 25, 1995.

46. Walter E. Williams, "Affirmative Action Symposium: The False Civil Rights Vision," *Georgia Law Review* 21 (1987): 1119, 1128.

47. *Watson v. Fort Worth Bank and Trust*, 487 U.S. 977 (1988), O'Connor, J., concurring.

48. Ibid.; emphasis added.

49. See William B. Gould, *Agenda for Reform: The Future of Employment Relationships and the Law* (Cambridge, Mass.: MIT Press, 1993).

50. See *United Steel Workers v. Weber, supra,* chapter 3, note 39 and accompanying text.

51. Indicative of this mood is a California initiative to eliminate all affirmative action programs in the state. See Kevin Johnson, "Affirmative Action Next Target in Calif.," *USA Today*, January 11, 1995, A1.

52. Cornel West, *Race Matters* (Boston: Beacon Press, 1993), 52. West went on to write, "Black conservative claims about self-respect should not obscure this fact, nor should they be regarded as different from the normal self-doubts and insecurities of new arrivals in the American middle class. It is worth noting that most of the new black conservatives are first-generation middle-class persons, who offer themselves as examples of how well the system works for those willing to sacrifice and work hard. Yet, in familiar American fashion, genuine white peer acceptance still preoccupies—and often escapes—them. In this regard, they are still affected by white racism" (53).

53. Jesse Helms's senatorial reelection television advertisement, 1990.

54. Martin Luther King, Jr., *Why We Can't Wait* (New York: Harper and Row, 1964), 134.

55. See, generally, Charles R. Lawrence III, "The Id, the Ego and Equal Protection: Reckoning with Unconscious Racism," *Stanford Law Review* 39 (1987): 317.

56. Patricia J. Williams, *The Alchemy of Race and Rights* (Cambridge, Mass.: Harvard University Press, 1991), 60 (footnote omitted).

57. *Fullilove v. Klutznick*, 448 U.S. 448, 530n. 12 (1980).

58. Thomas Ross, "Innocence and Affirmative Action," *Vanderbilt Law Review* 43 (1990): 297, 304n. 17.

59. Gunnar Myrdal, *An American Dilemma: The Negro and Modern Democracy* (New York: Harper & Brothers, 1944), 69–70.

60. See, generally, Kenneth L. Shropshire, *The Sports Franchise Game: Cities in Pursuit of Franchises, Events, Stadiums and Arenas* (Philadelphia: University of Pennsylvania Press, 1995).

61. "He Was Caught in the Middle," *Sporting News*, June 7, 1993, 9.

62. The 1995 California initiative seeking to eliminate all affirmative action programs is indicative of this. See Johnson, "Affirmative Action Next Target in Calif.," 1.

63. Harvard professor Nathan Glazer has been credited with coining the term *reverse discrimination*. See, e.g., Ruben Navarrette, Jr., "If You Hadn't Been Mexican," in Mills, *Debating Affirmative Action: Race, Gender, Ethnicity and the Politics of Inclusion* (New York: Delta Books, 1994), 129, esp. 131. Navarrette's interpretation of Glazer's analysis is that

> once a society has liberated its employment and educational opportunities and fully met the burden of its democratic principles . . . any further tampering with the laws of appropriation through race-preference programs constitutes impermissible "reverse discrimination."

64. Stanley Fish, "Reverse Racism or How the Pot Got to Call the Kettle Black," *Atlantic Monthly*, November 1993, 128, 130.

65. T. Alexander Aleinikoff, "A Case for Race-Consciousness," *Columbia Law Review* 91 (1990): 1060, esp. 1068–69, citing Goldberg, "MAP Does More Harm than Good," *Res Gestae*, February 8, 1989, 3.

66. 438 U.S. 265 (1978).

67. See Shelby Steele, "A Negative Vote on Affirmative Action," in Mills, ed., *Debating Affirmative Action*, 37, 41.

68. See Peter Applebome, "Duke Learns of Pitfalls in Promise of Hiring More Black Professors," *New York Times*, September 19, 1993, 1.

69. Ibid. During the five-year period, twenty-five black faculty members were hired but seventeen departed. That represents a departure rate of 68 percent.

70. Critical race legal theorists have been particularly negative toward the standards of merit for hiring in academia. See, e.g., Richard Delgado, "Brewer's Plea: Critical Thoughts in Common Cause," *Vanderbilt Law Review* 44 (1991): 12n. 58; Derrick Bell, *Faces at the Bottom of the Well: The Permanence of Racism* (New York: HarperCollins/Basic Books, 1992), 5; Derrick Bell, "Xerxes and the Affirmative Action Mystique," *George Washington Law Review* 57 (1989): 1595–96.

71. See "The Kids Club," *Sporting News*, October 24, 1994, 36.

72. See, e.g., "The Lunch Club," *American Lawyer* (March 1994): 70; "See No Evil," *American Lawyer*, (September 1994): 60; and "Numbers That Count," *American Lawyer*, (October 1993): 14.

73. See Mark T. Gould, "In Whose 'Best Interests'? The Narrowing Role of Baseball's Commissioner," *Entertainment and Sports Lawyer* 12 (1994): 1; and Matthew B. Pachman, "Limits on the Discretionary Powers of Sports Commissioners: A Historical and Legal Analysis of Issues Raised by the Pete Rose Controversy," *Virginia Law Review* 76 (1990): 1409.

74. See National Football League Constitution, art. 8 and bylaws.

75. See, generally, Paul C. Weiler and Gary R. Roberts, *Cases, Materials, and Problems on Sports and the Law* (St. Paul, Minn.: West Publishing, 1993), 1–63.

76. This is probably best exemplified by the deal Peter Ueberroth struck after his success with the 1984 Olympics. See Daniel Okrent, "On the Money," *Sports Illustrated*, April 10, 1989, 41.

77. Ellis Cose, *The Rage of a Privileged Class* (New York: HarperCollins, 1994), 163.

78. See "Blacks' Spending Power Outpaces U.S. as a Whole," *Wall Street Journal*, August 4, 1994, B4. The study found that African-American buying power would increase to $399 billion by 1995, an increase of 33.9 percent. The gain in black buying power was attributable to overall rising incomes coupled with a growing black population.

79. But see Grantham, "NBA: A Land of Unequal Opportunity," 30, an

opinion article by the then executive director of the NBA Players Association condemning the hiring of twenty-five consecutive white head coaches by NBA teams (see *supra,* notes 17 to 18 and accompanying text).

80. Of course, there appears to be a correlation between the sports people participate in and the ones they attend. This is evidenced by African-American communities' declining interest in in baseball and nearly nonexistent interest in hockey.

Chapter Five

1. William Oscar Johnson, "How Far Have We Come?" *Sports Illustrated,* August 5, 1991, 38, 39.

2. For an extensive discussion of racism in college athletics, see Timothy Davis, "The Myth of the Superspade: The Persistence of Racism in College Athletics," *Fordham Urban Law Journal* 22 (1995): 202.

3. See "New Initial-Eligibility Standards Recommended," *NCAA News* (June 15, 1994): 1. The article notes a committee's recommendation to delay the implementation date to August 1996, as well as revisions to the proposed changes.

4. See Franz Lidz and Christian Stone, eds., Scorecard, "Indecent Proposal," *Sports Illustrated,* July 17, 1995, 11. The article notes further, "Within 10 years, the NCAA assured its critics, this trend would reverse itself." The NCAA reported the stability of black freshman enrollment in "Participation of Blacks at pre-Prop 48 Level," *NCAA News* (Feb. 1, 1995): 1. The article projects a return to pre-Proposition 48 rates by studying statistical samples.

5. See William C. Rhoden, "Blacks No Longer Face Physical Fences, but Barriers Still Exist," *New York Times,* August 28, 1994, 9.

6. Out of a total of 9,063 Division I athletes (ibid.).

7. Ibid.

8. See Harry Blauvelt and Steve Wieberg, "Black Caucus Hears Case of Coaches," *USA Today,* October 20, 1993, 1C.

9. See "Sidelines," *Chronicle of Higher Education,* September 21, 1994, A43.

10. Ibid.

11. Ibid.

12. See Howard J. Savage, *American College Athletics* (New York: Carnegie Foundation for the Advancement of Teaching, 1929), vi.

13. See Knight Foundation Commission on Intercollegiate Athletics, *Keeping Faith with the Student Athlete: A New Model for Intercollegiate Athletics,* (March 1991).

14. See Paul Lawrence, *Unsportsmanlike Conduct* (New York: Praeger, 1987), 22–23.

15. See Kenneth L. Shropshire, *Agents of Opportunity: Sports Agents and*

Corruption in Collegiate Sports (Philadelphia: University of Pennsylvania Press, 1990), 59.

16. See Lawrence, *Unsportsmanlike Conduct,* 41.

17. Ibid., 43.

18. Ibid.

19. See Paul C. Weiler and Gary R. Roberts, *Cases, Materials and Problems on Sports and the Law* (St. Paul, Minn.: West Publishing, 1993), 532, describing NCAA Bylaw 4–6–(b)-(1). (Hereafter cited as *Sports and the Law.*)

20. Ibid.

21. See, e.g., *Parrish v NCAA,* 361 F Supp 1220 (WD La. 1973).

22. See Weiler and Roberts, *Sports and the Law,* 537.

23. One of the earliest critics of the racial impact of initial eligibility requirements was University of Wisconsin law professor Linda Greene. See Linda S. Greene, "The New NCAA Rules of the Game: Academic Integrity or Racism?" *Saint Louis University Law Journal* 28 (1984): 101.

24. See Table 7.

25. Ibid.

26. See Murray Sperber, *College Sports Inc.: The Athletic Department versus the University* (New York: Henry Holt, 1990), 218.

27. See Greene, "New NCAA Rules," 112.

28. See Greene, "New NCAA Rules," 104, citing a letter from Derek C. Bok, president of Harvard University and chairman of the ad hoc committee, and J. W. Peltason, president of the Academic Council on Education, to NCAA Division I members (undated).

29. Prior to the implementation of Proposition 48, students were required to have an overall high school grade point average of 2.0 in order to be eligible to participate in college athletics as freshmen. (See Table 7.) The eligibility requirement allows a student-athlete to not only participate in sports for four years but also to receive financial aid from the NCAA member institution. See discussion in text accompanying note 4, *supra,* regarding the decline in black freshman scholarships.

30. See Table 7.

31. Quoted in Johnson, "How Far Have We Come?" 38, 51.

32. This was, in fact, the harshest element of an earlier version of the proposition, which initially banned all forms of financial aid to the partial qualifier.

33. Quoted in Wiley, "Hardaway: A Daunting Proposition," *Sports Illustrated,* August 12, 1991, 26.

34. See Othello Harris, "African-American Predominance in Collegiate Sport," in *Racism in Collegiate Athletics: The African-American Athlete's Experience,* ed. Dana Brooks and Ronald Althouse (Morgantown, W. Va.: Fitness Information Technology, 1993), 51–74.

35. The counterargument is, of course, that the same numbers of African-Americans may participate, but they will be those who do meet the higher academic standards. Their success will compel those who come after them to excel academically.

36. See, e.g., Richard Lapchick and John Slaughter, eds., *The Rules of the Game: Ethics in College Sports* (New York: Macmillan, 1989), 18.

37. For a thorough examination of the legal issues in testing, see Mark Kelman, "Concepts of Discrimination in 'General Ability' Job Testing," *Harvard Law Review* 104 (1991): 1158.

38. See *1995–96 NCAA Manual* (March 1995), 235, Bylaw 17.1.5.1.

39. Pamela Zappardino, speech to the Rainbow Coalition for Fairness in Athletics, June 23, 1995, Washington, D.C.

40. For a thorough examination of the SAT as predictor of future academic performance, see James Crouse and Dale Trusheim, *The Case against the SAT* (Chicago: University of Chicago Press, 1989).

41. See Liz Robbins, "Prep Athletes vs. Standardized Tests," *St. Petersburg Times*, March 30, 1993, 1C.

42. See, e.g., Stanley Fish, "Reverse Racism or How the Pot Got to Call the Kettle Black," *Atlantic Monthly*, November 1993, 128, 132–35.

43. Ibid.

44. See, e.g., Ellis Cose, *The Rage of a Privileged Class: Why Are Middle-Class Blacks Angry? Why Should America Care?* (New York: HarperCollins, 1993), 162.

45. See Fish, "Reverse Racism," 135.

46. See ibid.

47. See ibid., 128, 132–35.

48. The last two options are not so objectionable, but should the opportunity to attend a major research institution be taken away based on a single test score?

49. See Davis, "The Myth of the Superspade," 201, esp. 252n. 266.

50. See Steve Wieberg, "Congresswoman: NCAA Panel 'Tainted'," *USA Today*, December 14, 1993, C1.

51. See "NCAA Uses Bad Statistics Group Says," *New York Times*, September 23, 1994, B13.

52. See "New Initial-Eligibility Standards Recommended," 1.

53. The data in Table 8 reflect the SAT scores prior to "recentering." The scoring on the exam was readjusted in 1995 so that the raw scores would be more reflective of where they fell on the 1600 scale with 800 serving as the center. See "Score of 820 Established as Minimum Standard," *NCAA News*, March 15, 1995, 1.

54. 709 F Supp 345 (SD N.Y. 1989). See Marcia Thurmond, "The FairTest Case: Nothing Special, Just Equality," *Civil Liberties: The National Newsletter of the ACLU*, 380 (spring 1994): 17.

55. See Thurmond, "The FairTest Case," 17.

56. See ibid.

57. See Greene, "New NCAA Rules," 150.

58. See *National Collegiate Athletic Association v. Tarkanian,* 488 U.S. 179 (1988).

59. 776 F Supp 1518 (MD Al. 1991).

60. Title VI of the Civil Rights Act of 1964, as amended, *U.S. Code,* vol. 42, secs. 2000(a) through 2000(d).

61. *Groves v Alabama State Board of Education,* 1518, 1520.

62. *Groves v Alabama State Board of Education,* 1521.

63. *Groves v Alabama State Board of Education,* 1521.

64. *Groves v Alabama State Board of Education,* 1522 (footnote omitted).

65. *U.S. Code,* vol. 42, sec. 2000(d) (1994).

66. See *Franklin v Gwinnett County Public Schools,* 911 F2d 617, 620 (11th Cir 1990), *cert. granted,* 501 U.S. 1204, 115 L. Ed. 2d 969, 111 Sup. Ct. 2795; *Castaneda v Pickard,* 781 F2d 456, 465n. 11 (5th Cir 1986).

67. *Georgia State Conference of Branches of NAACP v Georgia,* 775 F2d 1403, 1417 (11th Cir 1985), quoting *Alexander v. Choate,* 469 U.S. 287, 293 (1985).

68. See *Georgia State Conference of Branches of NAACP v Georgia,* 1417.

69. *Groves v Alabama State Board of Education,* 1524.

70. *Groves v Alabama State Board of Education,* 1518, 1526 (citations omitted).

71. *Groves v Alabama State Board of Education,* 1532.

72. See Jack L. Copeland, "Division 1 to Implement Prop 16 Scale in '96," *NCAA News* (January 11, 1995): 1.

73. See 1995 NCAA Convention Official Notice, no. 36, 38.

74. In Lapchick and Slaughter, eds., *The Rules of the Game,* 22.

75. Gregory R. Anrig, president, Educational Testing Service, letter to Richard Schultz, executive director, National Collegiate Athletic Association, January 18, 1989 (photocopy on file with author).

76. See Crouse and Trusheim, *Case against the SAT.*

77. See, e.g., Blauvelt and Wieberg, "Black Caucus Hears Case of Coaches," 1C.

78. The argument is largely financial at all levels, as most freshman and junior varsity teams have been eliminated.

79. University of Wisconsin law professor Linda Greene proposed five alternative solutions to the initial eligibility problem in a *Saint Louis University Law Review* article when Proposition 48 was introduced in 1984:

(1) Permitting the entering freshmen to demonstrate academic potential by presenting either a minimum test score or a minimum grade point average; (2) dropping the use of standardized test scores from the formula altogether; (3) providing a special exemption to the rule for black

colleges and universities [at the time one major concern was the impact the rule would have on historically black colleges and universities, particularly as these schools were not represented on the committee that proposed the rules]; (4) lowering the minimum test score required for freshman athletic eligibility; and (5) replacing the new initial eligibility rules with the NCAA old 1.6 rule, which used a combination of factors to predict a student's chances for success. (Greene, "New NCAA Rules," 146)

80. See Crouse and Trusheim, *Case against the SAT,* 151–54.

81. See Paul Schaffner, "Competitive Admissions Practices when the SAT Is Optional," *Journal of Higher Education* 56 (1985): 55–72.

82. Robbins, "Prep Athletes vs. Standardized Tests," 1C, quoting Donald Stewart, president of the College Board, speaking to his colleagues in 1989.

83. The RCFA annually publishes the racial composition of the athletic departments of the teams in the NCAA Final Four. See *Rainbow* 2, 13 (March 31, 1994).

84. George Raveling, speech to the Rainbow Coalition for Fairness in Athletics, June 23, 1995, Washington, D.C.

85. See Dean Anderson, "Cultural Diversity on Campus: A Look at Intercollegiate Football Coaches," *Journal of Sport and Social Issues* (April 1993): 61–66, esp. 63.

86. Ted Leland, athletic director, Stanford University telephone interview with the author, April 10, 1995.

87. Cited in Phil Taylor and Shelley Smith, "Southern Cal: Exploitation or Opportunity? USC Debates Whether It's Committed to Helping Blacks Succeed Academically," *Sports Illustrated,* August 12, 1991, 46.

88. Ibid.

89. See Earl Gustkey and Matt White, "Jury Awards $2.1 Million to Cobb in USC Bias Suit," *Los Angeles Times,* June 7, 1994, C1.

90. Marvin Cobb, interview with the author in Washington, D.C., June 23, 1995.

91. Ibid.

92. Ibid.

93. Rudy Washington, speech to the Rainbow Coalition for Fairness in Athletics, June 23, 1995, Washington, D.C.

94. Leland, telephone interview with the author, April 10, 1995.

95. See Knight Foundation Commission on Intercollegiate Athletics, *Keeping Faith with the Student-Athlete.*

96. Leland, telephone interview with the author, April 10, 1995.

97. See, generally, Note, "Judicial Control of Actions of Private Associations," *Harvard Law Review* 76 (1963): 983. For a thorough discussion of this

area of the law as it relates to the NCAA, see Kenneth J. Philpot and John R. Mackall, Note, "Judicial Review of Disputes between Athletes and the National Collegiate Athletic Association," *Stanford Law Review* 24 (1972): 903. Philpot and Mackall define a private association as "any group of individuals who have joined together in some type of formalized structure for the attainment of common purposes" (909).

98. For a more extensive discussion of the state-action requirements of the Fourteenth Amendment, see chapter 3.

99. See *National Collegiate Athletic Association v. Tarkanian*, 488 U.S. 179 (1988).

100. See, generally, Timothy Davis, "Examining Educational Malpractice Jurisprudence: Should a Cause of Action Be Created for Student-Athletes?" *Denver University Law Review* 69, 1 (1992): 57.

101. 957 F2d 410 (7th Cir 1992).

102. *Ross v. Creighton University*, 740 F Supp 1319 (ND Il. 1990).

103. I was prepared when I reentered in 1995. I discovered that year that the primary culprits for the lack of both ethnic and gender diversity were the Division I-A schools.

Chapter Six

1. For discussions of race consciousness and its conflict with notions of color blindness in American law, see, e.g., T. Alexander Aleinikoff, "A Case for Race-Consciousness," *Columbia Law Review* 91 (1990): 1060; and Gary Peller, "Race Consciousness," *Duke Law Journal* (1990): 758.

2. See discussion *infra*, notes 16 to 28 and accompanying text. The Rainbow Coalition for Fairness in Athletics called a meeting of black agents to discuss the rule in Washington, D.C., on November 17, 1985. Although sports is often called a microcosm of society, the sports-agent business is unique. Certainly, some issues raised here regarding the hiring of professionals and the role race should play in that process may be applicable to society at large.

3. See, e.g., Earl Ofari Hutchinson, "Fighting the Wrong Enemy," *The Nation*, November 4, 1994, 554.

4. Ibid. See also Lucie Cheng and Yen Espiritu, "Korean Businesses in Black and Hispanic Neighborhoods: A Study of Intergroup Relations," *Sociological Perspectives* 32 (1989): 521.

5. See, e.g., Barry Cooper, "Black Sports Agents Beat Odds with Top Clients," *New Pittsburgh Courier*, July 13, 1994, A10, where the same story is recounted by the national director of the Rainbow Coalition for Fairness in Sports. While the myth of some sort of white intellectual superiority permeates the African-American community, there is also the myth of white athletic inferiority. *White Men Can't Jump* is not just a movie title but a belief. I recall

my high school experience at the all-black inner-city Dorsey High School in Los Angeles when we went to play North Hollywood High School in football in 1973. A banner held by the Dorsey student rooting section set forth the ominous words in white on a black background: "A Black Day for North Hollywood." We would beat them with our superior speed, we all believed. I remember two years later having to run a timed forty-yard dash against a member of that North Hollywood team when we both arrived at Stanford. He beat me handily. The shock injected a needed dose of reality into my own thinking. See also Miki Turner, "White Girls Can't Jump," *Women's Sports and Fitness* 14 (1992): 62.

6. Neil Lanctot, "Fair Dealing and Clean Playing: Ed Bolden and the Hilldale Club, 1910–1932," *The Pennsylvania Magazine of History and Biography* 117 (January–April 1993): 43.

7. Calvin Sims, The Nation, " 'Buying Black' Approach Paying Off in Los Angeles," *New York Times,* May 23, 1993, sec. 4, 5.

8. Ibid.

9. William Grimes, "Should Only Blacks Make Movies about Blacks?" *New York Times,* March 28, 1994, C11. Filmmaker Spike Lee was selected over Ken Burns to produce and direct a motion picture on Jackie Robinson. Rachel Robinson, Jackie's widow, said, "I wanted the very best product I could get. And I really felt, and I still feel, that a black man can understand another black man and all the nuances of his life better than anyone else can. I would feel that way about a woman. Not that white writers cannot write about blacks. There have been white writers who have written about black people and done a good job. I just think you have an edge when you come out of the same experience." See William C. Rhoden, "Jackie Robinson, Warrior Hero, through Spike Lee's Lens," *New York Times,* October 30, 1994, sec. 8, 11.

10. For a discussion of the role of the sports agent, see, generally, Kenneth Shropshire, *Agents of Opportunity: Sports Agents and Corruption in Collegiate Sports* (Philadelphia: University of Pennsylvania Press, 1990); Robert P. Garbarino, "So You Want to Be a Sports Lawyer, or Is It a Player Agent, Player Representative, Sports Agent, Contract Advisor, Family Advisor or Contract Representative?" *Villanova Sports and Entertainment Law Forum* 1 (1994): 11.

11. Ibid. Most could not make a living otherwise.

12. See Shropshire, *Agents of Opportunity,* 6, for an overview of the business; for a summary of the statutory framework, see Appendix 3 therein.

13. See Bobby Clay, "Black Agents Compete for Blue Chip Athletes," *Black Enterprise* (July 1992): 48.

14. See Mickey Spagnola, "Dallas Cowboys," *Sporting News,* September 27, 1993, 43.

15. See, e.g., Randall Lane, "The Forty Top-Earning Athletes," *Forbes,* December 19, 1994, 266. For example, of Michael Jordan's $30.01 million in earn-

ings in 1993, $30.0 million came from endorsements. (The remaining $10,000 came from his minor league baseball contract.) For Shaquille O'Neal, of $16.7 million, $12.5 million came from endorsements. For golfer Jack Nicklaus, of $14.8 million in earnings, $14.5 million came from endorsement fees.

16. If an athlete desires to get out of a contract with an agent, the fees must still be paid, but an order of specific performance compelling the two to work together will probably not be granted due to the personal nature of the relationship. See, generally, John D. Calamari and Joseph M. Perillo, *Contracts,* 3d ed. (St. Paul, Minn.: West Publishing, 1987) at 666. See also *Lumley v. Wagner,* 42 Eng. Rep. 687, Lord Chancellor's Court (1852).

17. Barry Cooper, "Black Sports Agents Are Working Hard to Even the Score," *Orlando Sentinel,* June 26, 1994, D14.

18. Ibid.

19. As compiled by the author. Note that in 1992 and 1993, African-American agent Len Elmore represented two athletes in the first round; in 1993, African-American agent Bill Strickland represented three first-round picks; and in 1994, African-American agent Fred Slaughter represented two first-round draft picks.

20. See Carolyn White, "Agents See More Racial Diversity," *USA Today,* May 7, 1993, 9C.

21. See Robert Ruxin, *An Athlete's Guide to Agents* (Lexington, Mass.: Stephen Greene, 1989), 30.

22. See Steve Wieberg, "Study Faults Colleges on Minority Hiring," *USA Today,* August 18, 1994, 1C.

23. On the subject of the selection of head coaches, see Claire Smith, "Too Few Changes Since Campanis," *New York Times,* August 16, 1992, sec. 8, 1, and Hall of Fame football coach Bill Walsh's statement (quoted *supra,* chapter 4, note 15 and accompanying text).

24. See discussion *infra,* notes 42 to 55 and accompanying text.

25. Clay, "Black Agents Compete," 7.

26. See Cooper, "Black Sports Agents Are Working Hard," D14.

27. C. Lamont Smith, address at the Wharton School, University of Pennsylvania, December 9, 1994.

28. Quoted in Phillip M. Hoose, *Necessities: Racial Barriers in American Sports* (New York: Random House, 1989), 29.

29. See Cooper, "Black Sports Agents Beat Odds," A10.

30. Ibid.

31. Ibid.

32. Clay, "Black Agents Compete," 7.

33. Kellen Winslow, interview with the author in Philadelphia, January 5, 1995.

34. See *supra,* chapter 5, notes 5 to 7 and accompanying text.

35. C. Lamont Smith, address at the Wharton School, December 9, 1994.

36. Ibid.

37. See Juan Williams, *Eyes on the Prize: America's Civil Rights Years, 1954–1965* (New York: Viking Press, 1987), 20.

38. Ibid.

39. See Yvonne S. Lamb, "Doll Play and a Child's Self Image," *Washington Post,* September 9, 1991, 135.

40. "Williams Today Would Hire Minority," *USA Today,* February 9, 1993, 4C.

41. Ibid.

42. See discussion *supra,* chapter 4, notes 21 to 24 and accompanying text, with analysis by Alan Wertheimer.

43. See, e.g., Mark H. Anshel, "Perceptions of Black Intercollegiate Football Players: Implications for the Sport Psychology Consultant," *Sport Psychologist* 4 (1990): 235–48, esp. 242.

44. See Arthur Ashe and Arnold Rampersad, *Days of Grace* (New York: Alfred A. Knopf, 1993), 1.

45. There are agents, however, who have taken the idea of being able to relate to African-American athletes too far. When two African-Americans student athletes encountered one agent, "I thought he was black, having spoken to him on the phone. . . . His actions were black. . . . Like, he walked with a slight limp. You know, how a lot of blacks walk, kind of cool. A strut." See Ruxin, *An Athlete's Guide to Agents,* 29.

46. There is a strong argument that if an athlete is accustomed to a white male as an authoritarian figure and that is the type of role he desires his agent to play, then the agent's "whiteness" may constitute a positive factor.

47. See Alan Wertheimer, "Jobs, Qualifications, and Preferences," *Ethics,* 94 (October 1983): 106.

48. In fact, one sports agent told me that a different level of success would be achieved when African-American agents commonly represented white as well as black athletes.

49. See, e.g., Paul Farli, "Parting Company at ProServ," *Washington Post,* April 6, 1992, F1, discussing the departure of the few African-Americans and women from ProServ.

50. See, e.g., Ruxin, *Athlete's Guide to Agents,* 27, citing the commissioner of the Central Intercollegiate Athletic Association as saying, "A lot of black athletes are misled by black legmen to think that they will be represented by a black firm." After a protracted negotiation with one major sports management firm, over a dozen years into the sports law business, I realized that my primary perceived value to them was as a black recruiter. One notable exception to this limited role is William Strickland, the African-American president of International Management Group's basketball division.

51. See Grimes, "Should Only Blacks Make Movies about Blacks?" 11.

52. Analogous decisions have been made in the sports industry regarding league partners in the ownership scenario. See, e.g., *Levin v NBA,* 385 F Supp 149 (SD N.Y. 1974) and *Mid-South Grizzlies v NFL,* 720 F2d 772 (3d Cir 1983). (See *supra,* chapter 2, notes 74 to 79 and accompanying text.)

53. See discussion *supra,* chapter 2, notes 83 to 92 and accompanying text.

54. *U.S. Code,* vol. 42, sec. 2000e et seq.

55. See, e.g., *Hishon v. King & Spalding,* 104 Sup. Ct. 2229, 2233 (1984), cited *supra,* chapter 2, in note 84. See also Note, "Applicability of Federal Antidiscrimination Legislation to the Selection of a Law Partner" (hereafter referred to as "Discrimination in Law Partner Selection"), *Michigan Law Review* 76 (1977): 282, also cited *supra,* chapter 2 in note 84.

56. *Civil Rights Act, U.S. Code,* vol. 42, sec. 1981 (1976).

57. See *supra,* chapter 2, notes 85–93.

58. But see *Runyon v. McCrary,* 427 U.S. 160, 193–94 (1976), White, J., and Rehnquist, J., dissenting (cited *supra,* chapter 2, note 90).

59. See *General Building Contractors Association v. Pennsylvania,* 458 U.S. 375 (1982) (disparate impact not encompassed by Section 1981).

60. See *Taylor v Jones,* 495 F Supp 1285, 1295 (ED Ark. 1980).

61. See, e.g., *Blount v Xerox Corporation,* 405 F Supp 849, 853 (ND Calif. 1975) (footnote omitted): Section 1981 "cannot be construed to place an affirmative obligation on employers to adopt or to maintain affirmative action programs."

62. 678 F2d 1022 (11th Cir 1982).

63. See *supra,* note 55, *Hishon v. King & Spalding,* 104 Sup. Ct. 2235.

64. Winslow, interview with the author, January 5, 1995.

65. A recent trend has been noted in the number of African-American athletes choosing to attend historically black colleges and universities. See, e.g., Suzanne Alexander, "Black Athletes in Switch, Pick Black Colleges," *Wall Street Journal,* June 28, 1993, B1.

Chapter Seven

1. John Hope Franklin, *The Color Line: Legacy for the Twenty-first Century* (Columbia: University of Missouri Press, 1993), 45.

2. See, e.g., *City of Richmond v. J. A. Croson Co.,* 109 Sup. Ct. at 726, 727: "There are numerous explanations for [the] dearth of minority participation [in the construction industry] including past societal discrimination in education and economic opportunities as well as both black and white career and entrepreneurial choices."

3. I use the term *multiculturalism* with some hesitation. Cornel West has pointed out that all people of color could be removed from this country and

the United States would still be multicultural (speech by Cornel West, Starrett at Spring Creek Conference, New York, March 10, 1995).

4. See *supra*, Introduction, note 50 and accompanying text, Rick Telander, "Shamefully Lily-White," *Sports Illustrated*, February 23, 1987, 80.

5. See Jay Reeves, "Blaze Guts School Tense over Its Prom," *Philadelphia Inquirer*, August 7, 1994, A6. The prom ended up being held, and protesters held an alternative event. The Randolph County High School was subsequently burned down, and arson was suspected in the racially divided community.

6. Franklin, *The Color Line*, 72.

7. Cheryl Nauman, director of human resources, National Basketball Association's Phoenix Suns, telephone interview with the author, March 22, 1995.

8. See United Steelworkers v. Weber, 443 U.S. 193, 208 (1979).

9. Alex M. Johnson, Jr., "*Bid Whist, Tonk, and United States v. Fordice:* Why Integrationism Fails African-Americans Again," *California Law Review* 81 (1993): 1401, 1457–58 (footnotes omitted).

10. William Oscar Johnson, "How Far Have We Come?" *Sports Illustrated*, August 5, 1991, 41.

11. See "Sen. Moseley Braun's Bill Seeks $6 Million to Aid Youth Basketball League," *Jet*, June 14, 1993, 8.

12. See, e.g., Don Terry, "Basketball at Midnight: 'Hope' on a Summer Eve," *New York Times*, August 19, 1994, A18.

13. See *Wygant v. Jackson Board of Education*, 476 U.S. 267 (1986).

14. As a student-athlete at Stanford in the early 1970s, I was one of a few African-Americans on a football team with no African-American coaches. Most of us had been recruited by an African-American assistant, who left before I arrived on campus.

A strike of any sort by us would have been useless, much like African-Americans boycotting a hockey match—we did not make up a major part of the team. But a few of us did play an important role—two or three of the African-Americans (not myself) filled a few of the key skill positions. That was the case at Stanford as well as at other institutions at the time. It was unthinkable as well to ask the two or three key players to take any political actions or risks individually.

The other area where we had some clout was in the recruitment of high school athletes to play at Stanford. African-American Stanford student-athletes were used to recruit more African-American high school student-athletes. Without any formal strategy, we told one of the first recruits of the year to ask in his private meeting with the coaching staff, "How many black assistant coaches do you have?" We then followed up by telling the coaching staff that it looked as if the recruit wanted to come to Stanford, but not with the present composition of the coaching staff. That recruit, a kid from inner-city Los Angeles, Floyd "Bull" Perry, had no problem asking the question and was sincere in his concern. With the other recruits, some asked directly; otherwise we feigned, as though it were a big issue for them. With a number of the recruits, the word from the coaching staff was "Tell them we're going to hire somebody." Stanford soon hired an African-American assistant coach. The next year Denny Green was hired as an assistant coach, and years later he became Stanford's head coach and then the head coach of the NFL's Minnesota Vikings. (Maybe we did not realize what we were doing but we also did not have multimillion dollar salaries or endorsement deals at stake.)

15. "Pirates' Barry Bonds Suggests Racism in Baseball Pay Scales," *Jet*, October 28, 1991, 46.

16. Confidential interview on file with author.

17. Howard Fineman, "An Older, Grimmer Jesse," *Newsweek*, January 10, 1994, 24.

18. Brent Benner, president, Brent Benner and Associates, telephone interview with the author, May 17, 1995.

19. John Ed Bradley, "Justice Prevails," *Sports Illustrated*, June 6, 1994, 66, 70–71.

20. Ibid.

21. See interview with the Reverend Arthur Williams, "Episcopalian Pastoral Letter Condemns Racism," transcript 1071–12 of National Public Radio's *Weekend Edition:* May 14, 1994.

22. See Charlie Nobles, "Dolphin Suing NFL over Civil Rights," *New York Times*, July 27, 1994, B11.

23. Johnson, "How Far Have We Come?" 41.

24. Harold Henderson, executive vice-president, National Football League, telephone interview with the author, April 10, 1995.

25. See Frank Litsky, "The Pieces Are in Place for Affirmative Action," *New York Times*, July 5, 1987, sec. 5, 3.

26. See, e.g., Daniel A. Farber, "The Outmoded Debate over Affirmative Action," *California Law Review* 82 (1994): 893, esp. 913.

27. Drew S. Days III, "Fullilove," *Yale Law Journal* 96 (1987): 453, 458.

28. Lal Hennigan, NFL Management Council, interview with the author, April 12, 1995.

29. Charlie Sifford, with James Gould, *Just Let Me Play: The Story of Charlie Sifford, the First Black PGA Golfer* (New York: British American Publishing, 1992), 98.

30. See "Newswire," *Los Angeles Times*, June 2, 1994, C8.

31. Ibid.

32. See "High Fives and Low Lights," *Sporting News*, December 12, 1994, 6.

33. Mark Asher, "Jackson Plans Summit on Minority Concerns," *Washington Post*, April 19, 1995, B2.

34. See Geoffrey C. Ward and Ken Burns, *Baseball: An Illustrated History* (New York: Alfred A. Knopf, 1994), 338.

35. David Margolick, "Boston Case Revives Past and Passions," *New York Times*, March 23, 1986, sec. 5, 1.

36. See "Suit against Red Sox," *New York Times*, February 1, 1986, 22; and "Baseball," *Washington Post*, January 31, 1986, C2.

37. "Sports People: Charges Denied," *New York Times*, February 14, 1986, A26.

38. See "Panel Said to Support Harper," *New York Times*, July 3, 1986, 28.

39. See Bob Cohn, "Peso Bill's Bailout," *Newsweek*, February 13, 1995, 24.

40. See Peter Hadekel, "Legislative Action Is Certainly Not the Way to Settle Baseball Strike," *Montreal Gazette*, February 10, 1995, D1.

41. See Michael Gee, "Prez Pitches to Congress," *Boston Herald*, February 8, 1995, 76.

42. See Kenneth L. Shropshire, *The Sports Franchise Game: Cities in Pursuit of Franchises, Events, Stadiums and Arenas* (Philadelphia: University of Pennsylvania Press, 1995), 61.

43. See Stephen Labaton, "Denny's Restaurants to Pay $54 Million in Race Bias Suits," *New York Times*, May 25, 1994, A1.

44. See *Talbert v City of Richmond*, 648 F2d 925 (4th Cir 1981).

45. Nauman, telephone interview with the author, March 22, 1995.

46. Leslie Alexander, owner, National Basketball Association's Houston Rockets, telephone interview with the author, March 15, 1995.

47. Rob Moor, president, National Basketball Association's Minnesota Timberwolves, interview with the author, April 25, 1995.

48. See Kenny Moore, "A Courageous Stand," *Sports Illustrated*, August 5, 1991, 61, 77. See also Jack Scott, "Black Power at Mexico City," in *The Athletic Revolution*, ed. Jack Scott (New York: Free Press, 1971), 86–88.

49. In contrast, when the Black Coaches Association called for a boycott of collegiate basketball games in 1993 to attack discrimination at the collegiate level, one of the issues was whether African-American students would stand up with them. A member of the Rhode Island University team, coached by African-American Al Skinner, said, "It would have been a tough decision, but I probably would have played, even though I support Coach Skinner. You can only do so much when you are just one person. I didn't want to walk off if it was going to be just by myself. But if I knew there was more support with other players out there, maybe I would do it" ("The Controversy Aside, Owls Come Up Winners," *New York Times*, January 16, 1994, 6).

50. Shelby Steele, *The Content of Our Character: A New Vision of Race in America* (New York: St. Martin's Press, 1990), 172–73.

51. Kimberlé Crenshaw, "Race, Reform, and Retrenchment: Transformation and Legitimation in Antidiscrimination Law," *Harvard Law Review* 101 (1988):

1331, 1346. See also Derrick Bell, *Race, Racism, and American Law* (Boston: Little, Brown, and Company, 1992), 819: "The very presence of anti-discrimination laws on the books is viewed by much of the society as a complete and final remedy for the racial discrimination blacks have suffered throughout history."

52. For an expanded discussion on the difficulties of removal of formal race barriers compared with those of changing the racial hierarchy, see Bell, *Race, Racism,* 816–19.

53. Cited in Bob Herbert, "After Brown, What?" *New York Times,* May 18, 1994, A23.